OHIO
WINE COUNTRY
EXCURSIONS

PATRICIA LATIMER

emmis
books

1700 Madison Road, Cincinnati, Ohio 45206

Library of Congress Cataloging-in-Publication Data

Latimer, Patricia.
Ohio wine country excursions
by Patricia Latimer ; foreword by Arnie Esterer.
p. cm.
Includes index.
ISBN 1-57860-237-8
1. Wine and wine making--Ohio--Guidebooks.
2. Wineries--Ohio--Guidebooks. 3. Ohio--Wine--Guidebooks. I. Title.
TP557.L366 2005
641.2'2'09771--dc22

2005008486

Cover designed by Carie Reeves
Interior designed by Stephen Sullivan
Edited by Jessica Yerega
Cover photo of Flint Ridge Vineyard by Carl Jahnes

PRINTED IN OHIO

Dedication

This book is dedicated to the men and women in my family who over three generations sought adventure and opportunity as they journeyed across the United States. It is a story of chance and choice from Connecticut to Ohio and on across the plains and mountains to their destination, California. They passionately pursued their dreams, and were challenged by the lure of California to live them, but ultimately were called home to Ohio to replenish them.

The record of this historic adventure began in Harrisburg, Iowa, March 2, 1850, as seven men and my great-grandfather, Leonard Straight, started west by horse and wagon, traveling for more than one hundred days through hardship and struggle to give reality to their dream of finding gold in the Sierra Nevada. Returning to Ohio with pockets of plenty, my great-grandfather purchased a farm, to serve both his avocation and vocation, in northern Ohio for his wife and eight children.

But the dream did not die. In the early twentieth century, my grandmother, Lenore Straight Latimer, the youngest daughter of Leonard Straight, headed west, and she and her physician husband settled in Pomona, California, in 1918. During the height of the Spanish flu pandemic, while trying to save his patients, the young doctor became ill and suddenly died. This time California offered no gold. The young wife was left a widow with a son of ten. Her anguished letters are witness to her decision to return to Ohio, where a large family would help her.

Her son, Vernon Straight Latimer, grew up in Cleveland and attended Case Western Reserve and then Harvard Business School, yet he remembered his California childhood amongst the orange groves and olive orchards. Stories of the 1920s inspired me, Vernon's youngest daughter, to make a mid-twentieth-century trip to California after college. For several decades I remained in San Francisco, where I became a writer and author on California wine, then later an entrepreneur, representing the wineries of Napa, Sonoma, and Mendocino, each with its own thrilling story.

By the late 1990s, my life took a dramatic turn when my father became ill. I found myself traveling back and forth between California and Ohio. In Ohio I reacquainted myself with my family's heritage and my own interest in viticulture. I brought with me the gift of inquiry, interviewing people and penning Ohio's untold wine story.

Thus, three generations later, influenced by my extraordinary California wine experience, there is new hope in the Buckeye State to share the vision of Ohio families, past and present, who believe in an Ohio wine empire. This book is dedicated to those in my family who came before and encouraged me to pursue my dreams in my two favorite places.

Table of Contents

Lake Erie and Wine Islands Tour West

Lake Erie and Grand River Tour East

Canal and Lock Tour

Appalachian Country Tour

Mountains to the Plains Tour

Ohio River Valley Tour

Foreword

by Arnie Esterer

WELCOME TO OHIO, WITH ALL ITS wines and the people who make them.

Historically, Ohio ranks as a great wine state, and this book covers both the wonderful early story and the amazing rebirth by the current generation.

You will enjoy details that cover the Buckeye State's two major winegrowing regions, Lake Erie and the Ohio River Valley, and interesting people and wineries in between. Like the world wine business, the Ohio industry grows from family interests and their long-term views. As winery owners happily pour their vintages, they share their personal winemaking philosophies and cultural heritage. By touring Ohio with this book, you will discover the wine heartland and the colorful families and members who built it.

Today, I believe wine to be a food, both healthy and nutritious, the beverage of moderation, to be consumed with meals but not to be misused. This tradition goes back ages to when bread and wine were staples used as offerings, and later became sacraments.

"Americans should drink the best wines!" Dr. Konstantin Frank said, and he demonstrated how to grow wine grapes to make the most of each vintage in the Finger Lakes region in upstate New York. Winegrowing at Markko Vineyard, in Conneaut, adapted his practice to Ohio's Lake Erie. Now his influence shows that wines from Lake Erie grapes can complement the daily meals we share at home and when dining out as well as any.

Remember, every wine differs by vintage, winery, and bottling. No two wines are the same. Each wine has its own personality, just like people, and changes occur with age—some better than others.

Let this book be your guide as you find, meet, and follow these Ohio wines each year. As you buy, drink, and then grow to understand and appreciate each wine, you can share your feelings. Your feedback gives growers and winemakers important guidance on which direction to take. And by doing this, you shape Ohio wines; it becomes your own region.

What an exciting experience! Just enjoy the fun of discovering the beauty of these heartland wines and the human hands that make them.

Gladden your heart. Cheers to the wines, the dreams, and the memories!

Phil Masturzo

Arnie Esterer pruning vines at Markko Vineyard

Introduction

THE DIVERSITY OF OHIO'S LANDSCAPE invites guests, visitors, residents, and tourists to explore its beautiful grape vineyards, appellation by appellation and viticultural district by viticultural district.

As you drive along the south shore of Lake Erie, the lake serves as a spectacular backdrop for acres of gently rolling green vineyards. Its cerulean-blue waters share 262 miles of northern Ohio's border, all the way from the port at Conneaut past Cleveland and Sandusky Bay to Toledo and the Maumee estuary.

The Lake Erie Plains, a fertile swath of land, are part of the Great Lakes Plains, which sweep southward from Lake Erie into Ohio. Farther inland, the fertile farmlands of the dramatic, rolling Central Plains and the sweeping corn belt are intermittently dotted with lush vineyards. The Allegheny Plateau to the east, which merges with the hills and valleys of the Appalachian Mountains, is planted to vines and descends to the Bluegrass along the winding waters of the Ohio River Valley, home to more breathtaking vineyards.

Whenever you visit the Ohio wine country, there is a chance to observe the cycle of life in the vineyards. In the spring, the sleeping vines burst with buds; in the summer, the vines form branches of leafy green; in the fall, the celadon and purple clusters glisten amid the burgundy and gold vineyards; and in the winter, the dormant, darkened, earthy vines rest. Then the cycle repeats itself.

Early on, the Ohio River Valley attracted the paleo-Indians: the Archaic, the Woodland, and the Hopewell. Although they were followed later by the Shawnee, the Miami, the Wyandot, and others, it was the arrival in 1788 of early settlers who had fought in the Revolutionary War and were given land for their service that stimulated the rush to settle Ohio and promote its agriculture.

Traveling by flatboat down the Ohio River, or by horse and wagon over the Appalachian Mountains, these eager young pioneers were determined to build settlements. This led to their planting small crops—fruits, vegetables, orchards, and vineyards. The determination and experimentation by one Nicholas Longworth, a

An antique basket press at the former Old Mill Winery in Geneva, Ohio

Phil Masturzo

prominent lawyer and horticulturist, in 1813 in and around Cincinnati laid the foundation for experimental grape trials, resulting in the making of champagne and still wine from the Catawba grape.

During the heyday of wine in Ohio during the 1850s, Cincinnati and its environs were the center of American wine production. By the late 1860s, powdery mildew and black rot devastated the vineyards. The wine industry moved from the Ohio River Valley in the south to the shores of Lake Erie around Sandusky and the Erie Islands.

This region gained prominence in 1869, and it became Ohio's new grape-growing and wine-producing capital. By the early 1900s, the largest wineries in the Lake Erie Island region were situated there. The eastern grape belt, of which this was a part, started by migrations of Germans, French, Italians, Czechs, Hungarians, Slovenians, and Shakers, extended from Sandusky to Conneaut and

into Pennsylvania and western New York. From 1920 to 1933, Prohibition closed many wineries and vineyards. Wineries that produced sacramental wines and vineyards making nonalcoholic grape-based products were the exception. The sixties wine revolution in California inspired viticulturists to experiment with vinifera, labrusca, and hybrids and vintners to practice better winemaking in Ohio.

Today, the ribbon of towns, villages, and cities that crisscrosses the Buckeye State has defined its wine country. Just off of I-90 along Lake Erie, there are wineries and vineyards that appeal to wine aficionados, families, friends, and neighbors from around the globe. They range across the Lake Erie Plains around Bryan, Toledo, Sandusky, Port Clinton, Kelleys Island, Put-in-Bay, Oregon, Avon Lake, Cleveland, Madison, Geneva, Ashtabula, and to Conneaut. These communities generate a lifestyle-workstyle

Phil Masturzo

Courtesy of The Ashtabula County
Convention & Visitors Bureau

for their citizenry and provide their patrons with lodging, fine dining, wine tasting, recreation, and relaxation.

As wine lovers travel any of the three north-south corridors, I-75, I-71, or I-77, they pass through some of the most gorgeous farm country in America, the heart of Amish Country, where horse and buggies are de rigueur and huge barns, tall silos, well-manicured crops, and herds of cattle catch the imagination. Here the wineries and vineyards are tucked among hills and valleys or grace the flat plains in towns like Versailles, Dover, Newcomerstown, Coshocton, Aurora, Valley City, West Lafayette, Wooster, Kent, Navarre, and Norton. Farther to the southwest, wine towns include Manchester, Ripley, Bethel, Cincinnati, Morrow, and Silverton.

Proprietors of these wineries encourage the public to stop by and experience the Ohio wine country. Some sixty-plus wineries—sometimes occupying elegant chateaus, old castles, threshing barns, bank barns, modern wonders, or humble cottages—are located on hilltops or in valleys alongside lakes, rivers, and streams. The public can taste and compare some of the most eclectic wines in the world, whether from estate-grown vineyards or farm wineries. Ohio is on the rise as a major player in the American wine industry!

Everywhere, there are restaurants, bistros, and delis for romantic picnics or family outings. Clubs, resorts, hotels, lodges, and bed and breakfasts make for inviting accommodations. Throughout this book, a quick guide included with each winery profile details contact information, owners, directions, hours, tours, events, winemaking procedures, best wines, and nearby places to visit. To all who explore the pages of this wine book, here is an invitation to join us in an Ohio wine country adventure!

Depiction of one of Nicholas Longworth's vineyards along the beautiful Ohio River

First of the Ohio River Valley Visionaries

WHAT WE KNOW AS OHIO WAS ONCE a vast unexplored region. Prior to the 1780s, except for traveling Indian tribes, Ohio was a wilderness of forests, rivers, fertile deltas, grasslands, rolling hills, and beautiful valleys.

In 1787, the United States Congress passed the Northwest Ordinance, which encouraged the settlement of the lands between the Allegheny Mountains and the Mississippi River. By 1788, John Cleves Symmes had been granted a charter to develop the Miami Purchase, a tract between the Great Miami and Little Miami rivers. In November of that year, Benjamin Stites and a party of twenty-six settled Columbia, just west of the Little Miami River's mouth. By December, Colonel Robert Patterson, along with eleven families and twenty-four men, colonized the 747-acre site called Losantiville opposite the Licking River. But it was Arthur St. Clair, the first governor of the Northwest Territory, who renamed it Cincinnati.

Ohio's penetration by larger numbers of settlers increased when participants of the Revolutionary War were given land as payment for their services. Rivers provided cheap and relatively easy means of transportation. Cincinnati grew rapidly, settled by people who arrived by flatboat or overland by horse and cart.

The southern hillsides along the Ohio River were used for experimental vineyards and grape trials. Swiss-born Jean Jacques Defour, a viticulturist, had read about the possibilities of grape growing in the United States given its geography, climate, soil, and native varieties. Upon his arrival in America, he embarked on a campaign to educate Americans about the benefits of viticulture. In 1799, Defour established the Kentucky Wine Company, which at first failed due to vineyard disease and reduced yields.

When Defour visited Washington, D.C., he made a proclamation to the United States Congress that one day the Ohio River would rival the Rhine River for growing outstanding vines. Many representatives were dubious. In 1802, Defour's luck changed, and he successfully planted grapes on a land grant along the Ohio River.

In 1804, the dashing Nicholas Longworth departed Newark, New Jersey, and arrived in Cincinnati, the shining hillside city, where the realization of one's dreams often led to great fortune. Though a gifted lawyer, he preferred horticulture, especially grape growing, which led to his wealth and ability to support his passion.

From 1813 onward, Longworth tested the best varietals suitable for the Ohio River Valley. The cumulative effect of the fertile limestone soils, the modified continental climate, and the gently rolling topography were ideal for quality grapes and intensely flavored wines. He just had to find the right match. A four-acre vineyard planted to Cape and Alexander resulted in the production of a good white wine. Longworth's cellar yielded a Madeira copycat, which he fortified with brandy and sugar to make it more palatable. He planted European varieties by type, variety, and species for the next three decades. He persevered until the late 1840s, ever hopeful that his vitis vinifera would one day thrive in the Ohio River Valley.

Vintage after vintage, Longworth cultivated new native American varieties, shipped by friendly viticulturists from across the states. But it wasn't until 1825 that John Adlum, a wine patriarch, gave Longworth a gift of Catawba grape cuttings. Mistakenly identified as Hungarian Tokay, the Catawba, which grew wild near

Nicholas Longworth

Asheville, was named for the Catawba River, which flows from the mountains of the Carolinas. Adlum gained national fame for his discovery that the native Catawba made good wine, which he simultaneously publicized in his *Memoir on the Cultivation of the Vine in America and the Best Mode of Making Wine.*

Longworth wrote in the *Horticulturist*, "Major Adlum had a proper appreciation of the value of the Catawba grape. In a letter to me he remarked: 'In bringing this grape into public notice, I have rendered my country a greater service than I would have done, had I paid off the national debt.' I concur in this opinion."

Classified as vitis labrusca, the Catawba reflected nuances of classic vitis vinifera. A coveted 150-year-old eastern variety, the grape had bold-textured, dark-green foliage with flowers that self-fertilized. Its purplish-red medium-sized berries produced a clean, austere wine with an aroma of spice and a distinctive flavor. This fast-growing climber survived both heat and cold and loved the sun. Grown throughout the United States, the Catawba flourished best along the Ohio River, southern Lake Erie, and in the Finger Lakes. It was originally used for making sparkling wine, still wine, and grape juice.

Longworth mapped out a business plan for the establishment of Longworth's Wine House and Vineyards. He planted the best native American varieties, from which he produced a substantial dry table wine. His investments placed Cincinnati and the Ohio River Valley as the center of the American wine industry. Skilled German immigrants who produced his Rhine-style wines added taste and cachet to the mix.

Beginning in the 1830s Cincinnati and the agricultural lands along the Ohio River became famous as the home of America's first commercial vineyards. The viticultural district was later dubbed "Rhineland of America." During this time, Longworth was a reputable 3,000-gallon premium producer, winning prizes for his Catawba. The Ohio wine boom took place after 1842, when Longworth accidentally produced a terrific sparkling Catawba. Convinced of the potential of this style of wine, he hired a French champagne-maker in the late 1840s to produce pure, natural sparkling Catawba in quantity to market outside of Cincinnati.

By 1848, Longworth had designed a 60,000-bottle cellar for the production of classic methode champenoise sparkling Catawba. After completion of the first fermentation, a dose of sugar was added to the wine. A second fermentation was completed in the bottle; the sediment was cleared by riddling, the process of turning the bottles stored in racks by hand. In 1851, Longworth built a second 75,000-bottle cellar and hired a second French

champagne-maker from Rheims. Sparkling Catawba became a rising star on the national wine scene, and Longworth's Wine House and Vineyards prospered.

A promoter, Longworth curried favor with the press by sending a letter and a wine sample. He also entered his Catawba in state, national, and international competitions. Longworth presented wine to Henry Wadsworth Longfellow, America's most noted nineteenth-century poet, and in return he received a poem, "Ode to Catawba Wine."

Nineteenth-century poster for Nicholas Longworth's sparkling Catawba, Isabella, and other fine wines

While Longworth was revered as an American wine industry leader and Cincinnati wine entrepreneur, other commercial growers quickly followed in his footsteps. Prominent names included Robert Buchanan, C. W. Elliott, A. H. Ernest, John Motier, Stephen Mosher, Louis Rehfuss, William Resor, and John A. Warder. Other Catawba vineyards flourished in Hamilton, Brown, and Clermont counties, as did vineyards along the Ohio

Ode to Catawba Wine

by Henry Wadsworth Longfellow

This song of mine
Is a song of the vine,
To be sung by the glowing embers
Of wayside inns,
When rain begins
To darken the drear Novembers.

It is not a song
Of the Scuppernong,
From warm Carolinian valleys,
Nor the Isabel
And the Muscadel
That bask in our garden alleys.

Nor the red Mustang,
Whose clusters hang
O'er the waves of the Colorado,
And the fiery flood
Of whose purple blood
Has a dash of Spanish bravado.

For richest and best
Is the wine of the West,
That grows by the Beautiful River,
Whose sweet perfume
Fills all the room
With a benison on the giver.

And as hollow as trees
Are the haunts of the bees,
Forever going and coming,
So the crystal hive
Is all alive
With a swarming and buzzing and humming.

Very good in its way
Is the Verzenay
Or the Sillery soft and creamy;
But Catawba wine
Has a taste more divine,
More dulcet, delicious and dreamy.

There grows no vine
By the haunted Rhine,
By Danube or Guadalquivir,
Nor on island or cape,
That bears such a grape
As grows by the Beautiful River.

Drugged is their juice
For foreign use,
When shipped o'er the reeling Atlantic,
To rack our brains
With fever pains,
That have driven the Old World Frantic.

To the sewers and sinks
With all such drinks,
And after them tumble the mixer,
For poison malign
Is such Borgia wine,
Or at best but a Devil's elixir.

While pure as spring
Is the wine I sing,
And to praise it, one needs but name it;
For Catawba wine
Has need of no sign,
No tavern-bush to proclaim it.

And this Song of the Vine,
This greeting of mine,
The winds and the birds shall deliver
To the Queen of the West,
In her garlands dressed,
On the banks of the Beautiful River.

River in Kentucky and Indiana. Soon, there were some three hundred established vineyards in southwest Ohio.

As had Longworth, the proprietors of Cincinnati's wine houses employed German workers. Though for each vintage they cult-ivated the grapes and made the wine, there was no consistent standard for quality. The national demand for Catawba coerced large owners to upgrade production, distribution, and storage. Smaller wine operations fell by the wayside. Advocates of natural wine typically harvested and sorted the grapes by hand. The clusters were destemmed, crushed, and fermented naturally without sugar. If the sugar level was acceptable, the fermentation was completed. Early on, if the sugar level was unacceptable, vintners were permitted to add sugar to complete the fermentation.

The 1850s were the heyday of Ohio wine. One of the first organizations of its kind, the American Wine Growers Association of Cincinnati published viticultural information and promoted natural wine. As America's leading wine center, Cincinnati produced 245,000 bottles of sparkling wine (at $1.50 a piece) and 205,000 bottles of still wine (at 40 cents a piece), valued at around $400,000.

Courtesy of of Meier's Wine Cellars

John Michael Meier

The Ohio River Valley growers and vintners were buoyed by the prospect of healthy vineyards and huge profits. John Michael Meier came from the vine-yards of Bavaria in 1856 and established a 164-acre homestead and vineyard in Kenwood, which he plant-ed to German rootstock that failed. His son John Conrad Meier sought advice from Nicholas Longworth and replaced their German varietals with Catawba. This decision influenced winegrowing and wine-making at Meier's Wine Cellars for more than 140 years.

The greater Cincinnati wine community became alarmed, however, by the rise and fall of black rot (reddish-brown circular to angular spots) and powdery mildew (small grayish-white patches) which attacked the vine and the fruit. Black rot was often mistakenly attributed to soil, climate, cultivation, or other factors. The native American powdery mildew, on the other hand, had ravaged vineyards in Europe before it wiped out ones in Ohio, so growers recognized the problem. These intruders reduced vine growth, yield, fruit, quality, and winter hardiness. At the end of the 1860s, grape growing had diminished in the Ohio River Valley, and the Catawba no longer reigned as king.

Aerial view of world-famous North Bass Island, one of the premiere winegrowing districts for pedigree wine grapes

Viticulture of Sandusky and the Erie Islands

Courtesy of the Ohio Wine Producers Association

AFTER THE CIVIL WAR, OHIO GRAPE growing moved from the Ohio River Valley in southern Ohio to the shores and islands of Lake Erie and to other areas of the state. The southern rim of Lake Erie became home to German immigrants. In 1830, Clevelander H. C. Coit made a prediction that one day Lake Erie would become a world-famous viticultural district. Growers and vintners organized the Lake Shore Grape and Wine Growers' Association (later renamed the Ohio Grape Growers Association to quiet the prohibitionists) and showcased their best wines at the fashionable Paris Exhibition and other international festivals. The growers promoted the Catawba vineyards, which were later dominated by the Concord vineyards east of Cleveland. Popular wineries included Dover Bay Grape Wine Company, Lake View Wine Farm, and Louis Harris Winery.

The most distinctive winegrowing area was the region centered in the Lake Erie Islands, which dot the lake's western basin. The region consists of North Bass, Middle Bass, and South Bass islands, Catawba Island, Kelleys Island, Danbury Township on the Marblehead Peninsula, and the city of Sandusky.

Harlan Hatcher writes in *Lake Erie*, "The Lake Erie Islands, though often visited, were settled relatively late. The discovery that they were uniquely adaptable to grape culture attracted settlers in numbers around the middle nineteenth century."

From 1865 up to the advent of Prohibition in 1920, Ottawa and Erie Counties dominated wine production in Ohio, accounting for two-thirds or more of the state's production. Wines from the Lake Erie Islands were distributed in overseas markets and domestic markets in the South, Midwest, and along the East Coast. Lake Erie Island wines won medals and commendations in competitions in the United States and abroad.

The Erie Islands, also called the Wine Islands, distinguished themselves for having the longest growing season in the northeastern United States. The islands' growing season averaged 190 days, while inland Ohio's growing season averaged 178 days or less. Island wine grapes are typically harvested up to six weeks later than mainland grapes. Lake Erie absorbs heat four times more slowly than the land and, conversely, retains heat four times longer than the land. Subsequently, the air over the lake reflects the water's more moderate temperature. In the Lake Erie Appellation of Origin, the regional autumn temperatures are warmer than Ohio's interior districts. The first harsh frost of fall is delayed by the warmer temperatures. Catawba and other late-ripening grapes thrived in these conditions.

In spring, the air around Lake Erie causes the shoots and buds to develop slowly, after the spring frosts. The fog and dew-free air over the islands eliminates any conditions for fungus, rot, and mildew during the growing season. The air over the islands is in constant motion because of the differences in temperatures between the land and water. The low rainfall compares favorably with Germany's winegrowing region along the Rhine River.

Datus Kelley planted Isabella cuttings on Kelleys Island in 1842 and founded the winegrowing industry in the Lake Erie Islands. His son-in-law, Charles Carpenter, developed the first commercial vineyard in 1845 and pressed the district's first wine in 1850. Kelleys Island wine was taken to Cincinnati, where it was judged to be of comparable quality to wine that was produced in the Ohio River Valley.

Datus Kelley

Carpenter built the first wine cellar on Kelleys Island in 1854.

The Erie Islands proved to be one of the better viticultural districts to cultivate some eighty varieties of grapes. The loamy topsoil with its porous underpan of cracked limestone was ideal because it absorbed Lake Erie water in the hot summer to moisten the roots. John Adlum's remarkable discovery of the Catawba's potential for good wine awakened a new spirit, and jump-started the economy.

From the 1840s until after World War II, Ohio winegrowers planted native American labrusca grapes, such as Catawba, Delaware, and Concord. French-American hybrids were introduced, such as Baco Noir, Chlois, and Seyval Blanc. More recently, European vitis vinifera varietals have thrived, including Chardonnay and Johannisberg Riesling. Traditionally, the best wines produced on the islands were Catawba, Delaware, Niagara, Baco Noir, and Johannisberg Riesling.

The region held the greatest appeal to hordes of German newcomers, who believed the climate and soil matched that of their native Germany. They gambled everything to purchase land and plant grapes. The prosperity of the grape culture spread from Kelleys Island to the nearby Bass Islands to the Marblehead Peninsula between Lake Erie and Sandusky Bay and the outskirts of Sandusky. During the 1860s and 1870s, speculative grape growing started at $50 an acre and rose to a high of $1,500 an acre.

Gradually, as the black rot and powdery mildew destroyed the vineyards in Cincinnati and its environs, the Lake Erie Island region became the new center of Ohio grape growing. Cincinnati wine merchants established new business patterns: purchasing grapes or finished wine from the island region, or building wineries there themselves. John G. Dorn founded a winery in Sandusky in 1869, outfitting it with ancient oak casks from Longworth's wine cellar. Queen City wine wholesalers the Rheinstrom Brothers started a Sandusky winery. Vintner Alsatian Michael Werk invested in a Middle Bass winery. Joseph R. Peebles, a grocer and wine merchant, developed vineyards on North Bass Island. Nicholas Longworth, who is often remembered as the father of winegrowing on South Bass Island, is said to have given Philip Vroman, also a friendly grower, grape stock from his Cincinnati vineyards. Vroman planted them on South Bass Island, getting $400 for the first vintage and $3,000 for the second vintage.

In the excitement, small American wineries took root, and winemaking traditions originated in the Lake Erie Islands. Growers harvested and aged their wine in press houses on their farms or in the cellars of their homes. Across the United States and Europe, different generations have emulated this practice, from the home industries in Cleveland to the boutique wineries in Napa Valley to the garagistes in Bordeaux.

In 1866, the Kelleys Island growers founded the Kelley's Island Wine Company, a cooperative that allowed them to control

Duroy and Haines Wine Company, a prominent name in Ohio wine in the nineteenth century

their grape prices. Located in a stone castle with twin turrets, the 350,000-gallon winery was the largest on the island. Growers on North Bass, Middle Bass, and South Bass also started cooperatives, bridging the relationship between the small producer and the large producer. Several wineries rose to great heights—William Mills, Diamond Wine Company, M. Hommel Wine Company, Sweet Valley Wine Company, Thaddeus Lorch, Conrad Ernest, Duroy & Haines Wine Company, and John Andrews. Others included Steuk Wine Company, Engles & Krudwig, Lenk Wine Company, Golden Eagle Winery, Lonz Wine Company, and Gustav Heineman.

In the early twentieth century, Kurt Boker wrote that professor W. B. Alwood, head of the United States Bureau of Chemistry, had studied the content of Lake Erie grapes and discovered that the most superb Delaware grapes in the world were grown in the Lake Erie Islands. He rated the Catawbas as second. Alwood continued that the overall growing conditions, soil, and climate favored the Erie Islands to produce some of the best basics for wine, surpassing the most famous winegrowing regions of Europe.

Arnold F. Elfers, a poet, author, and longtime Kelleys Islander until his death, always felt that "Earth hath no fairer spot than this!" In tribute, he wrote several poems, such as this one:

> *The rose may bloom in England,*
> *The lily for France unfold;*

> *Ireland may honor the Shamrock,*
> *And Scotland her thistle bold;*
> *But the shield of Kelleys Island*
> *Shall be with Grapes inscrolled.*

The popular Lonz Winery on Middle Bass Island has been a landmark since the 1800s. Launched during the Civil War as the Golden Eagle Winery, it became a 500,000-gallon wine and juice producer, one of the largest in America, by 1875. In 1884, Peter Lonz produced wines on Middle Bass Island, and then his son George Lonz designed the magnificent Gothic castle and vineyard estate that became Lonz Winery. It was visited by no fewer than five United States presidents and countless dignitaries. They were captivated by the winery's huge fireplace made from island stone and its hand-painted ceiling murals with poetry about the fruit of the vine. President Theodore Roosevelt once enjoyed a game of billiards in the tower room, which was also an observatory. In the mid-1970s, the late wine statesman Robert S. Gottesman, president of Cleveland's Paramount Distillers, Inc., purchased the Lonz Winery and several Erie Island vineyards. The facility remained open until July 2000, when tragically one afternoon a side terrace of the castle caved to the ground. One person was killed, and seventy people were injured.

In 2003, John Kronberg, a real estate developer, and Claudio Salvador, a respected winemaker, formed a holding company that they called Lonz Winery, Inc. It bought the Lonz name and other wine and vineyard properties from Paramount Distilleries, Inc. Though wine is no longer produced on the island, the current owners maintain Concord and Catawba vineyard contracts and send the wine grapes to the mainland for processing.

In 2004, Ohio Governor Bob Taft acquired 87 percent of 677-acre North Bass for $17.4 million in state and federal funds from the island's longtime owner, Meier's Wine Cellars, Inc. (a division of Paramount Distilleries, Inc.) The purchase price was well below market value and reflected Gottesman's desire to preserve the island's grape heritage, undeveloped shoreline, natural coastal wetlands, geologic features, and habitats for endangered species and spawning grounds for the benefit of all Ohioans. In addition, the purchase protected North Bass Island as the last undeveloped island of its size in Lake Erie. Wine grape production has been a major part of the island's heritage and will continue on eighty-seven acres remaining under lease to Firelands Winery in Sandusky.

In northwest Ohio, the Lenk Wine Company was one of Toledo's most distinguished institutions. Brothers Peter and Carl

Antique Engles and Krudwig Winery poster featuring the commuter airline between Sandusky and the Lake Erie Islands

Lenk started a nursery with F. C. Hansen. It was modeled after nurseries in Bavaria, where Peter had learned to grow grapes and make fine German wines. In 1862, the brothers harvested fruit from their vines and purchased Catawba from Put-in-Bay.

In 1868, Lenk & Company built the first wine cellar in Toledo and produced 15,000 gallons of wine. By 1887 the winery with the arched cellars covered two acres, processed 3,000 tons of grapes, and made 700,000 gallons of wine annually. Fruit was sourced from the Lake Erie Islands and the south shore of Lake Erie. The cellar consisted of four hundred casks, holding from 1,000 to 36,000 gallons. Its largest cask was also the largest one in existence, built by Mueller Brothers, Toledo coopers.

By the early 1900s, the largest wineries in the Lake Erie Island region were situated around Sandusky. While the winery proprietors were dependent on the island vineyards for grapes, they were lured by the city's extensive railroads and lake shipping, which provided easy, affordable access to out-of-state markets. On the eve of Prohibition, Sandusky was billed as the third-largest winegrowing center in America.

Winegrowing East of Cleveland

THE EXPANSION OF COMMERCIAL winegrowing east of Cleveland, home to vineyards as early as the 1830s, played a significant but lesser known role in developing Ohio's wine and grape industry. The Lake Erie viticultural district stretched west to Sandusky and east to Conneaut and into Pennsylvania and eastern New York. Identified as the eastern grape belt, the growing area has a history of being the largest in the United States outside of California. While western Sandusky and the Erie Islands became known for Catawba, eastern Geneva and Ashtabula became known for Concord.

The 1840s and 1850s were experimental growth years. Although the early 1860s were stifled by the Civil War, by the late 1860s wine entrepreneurs were passionate about winegrowing. Cleveland developed as a burgeoning city center with vineyards displaced by neighborhoods and industry. A significant number of varietal plantings and wineries were built to the east.

"In the mid-nineteenth century, like the rest of East Cleveland's Township, the area that became Cleveland Heights was farmland, quarries, and vineyards, owned by men and women of northern and western European descent who had come from New England, Ohio, and neighboring states and had acquired substantial property," Mary J. Morton wrote in *Cleveland Heights, The Making of an Urban Suburb*. "In 1864, John Peter Preyer bought 75 acres of farmland, moved his family into a spacious home built in the 1820s of local sandstone, and planted vineyards for his Lake View Wine Farm."

Other successful grape growers were the Shakers, members of a religious community influenced by the Quakers. Two Shaker communities existed in Ohio: Union Village in Lebanon, 1805, and North Union in Shaker, 1822. They designed their lives to bring heaven to earth, expressed through their creativity and industry. The Shaker Vineyards Land Company was one such example.

In 1892, Joseph Shingleland, head elder of the Western Shakers, settled in Wickliffe when raising grapes along Lake Erie had become profitable business. In one Shaker Historical Society letter, a Wickliffe resident

Officers of the Jewish Farmers Association that organized the Geneva farmers, some ninety families, who at one time produced sixty percent of the district's grape crop

wrote, "Elder Shingleland was not imbued with the Shaker simplicity, but had been bitten by a 'get rich quick' desire … He was building a handsome dwelling and administrative building at Union Village and needed ready money." Shingleland bought some 1,000 acres of vineyards and two packing houses. "It takes three years for a vine to mature, and the first crop was harvested in 1897, when four carloads of grapes went out daily," the letter continues. "Here the work went on night and day in season."

Shingleland later converted the packing houses into wineries, where he installed presses and wooden vats. He hired an expert winemaker and for a time made money, but this was contrary to Shaker beliefs. A frost destroyed many of the vineyards, and the death of the chief overseer caused Shingleland to sell the property.

For more than forty years, the Geneva Jewish farmers flourished in agriculture. During the 1900s, the Geneva farmers, also recognized as the Lake Erie Jewish Community, comprised ninety families who had departed Cleveland for a better life. Wealthy European financier Baron Maurice de Hirsch, a humanitarian, was concerned about the welfare of Russian Jews after the assassination of Czar Alexander the II. In 1881, de Hirsch gave $2.4 million to fund farm colonies; the

Joseph Golomb atop his tractor

1927

The farmhouse of Joseph and Rachael Golomb

Geneva farmers were one such group. They constructed homes surrounded by grape vineyards and fruit orchards. During the week, the men were employed in the Cleveland garment and needle trades, and on the weekends they commuted to their farms, where they grew Concord in Lake and Ashtabula counties. At one time, this enterprising community produced 60 percent of the area's grape crop.

Cleveland families such as that of Judith Orkin Rosenthal were among the first Jewish farmers to settle in Unionville in 1902. Rosenthal's maternal grandparents, Joseph and Rachael Golomb, came to Cleveland from the Ukraine in 1910. They established a two-hundred-acre farm in Cork, just outside of Geneva, where they cleared the woods for a Concord vineyard

and pastured horses and cows. It was an example of a model vineyard, used by the Ohio State University Department of Agriculture. Golomb and his friend Morris Brody headed the wine cooperative so they could monitor grape prices. During depressed years, a bushel of grapes sold for two cents. After a late frost when grapes were scarce, they went for $100 a ton.

Also notable in Geneva was the Cohodas Brothers Produce Company, founded by Morris and Bessie Cohodas. They raised grapes, corn, strawberries, tomatoes, peas, potatoes, and other crops. Later, their son Norman Cohodas purchased Highland Farms from Rosenthal's paternal grandparents, and his brother Alvin became an agricultural consultant with a keen interest in grapes and wine.

The Lake Erie shoreline at Geneva-on-the-Lake, home to high-quality vineyards, wineries, and prestigious wines

At the turn of the twentieth century, Morris and Anne Brody established the 118-acre Brody's Fruit Farm on South River Road in Geneva. Brody was a leader in the affairs of the Jewish farm community and one of the most prominent fruit growers in eastern Ohio. The Ohio State Experimental Station used his orchards for tests to manage insects and diseases.

The community prospered until the Depression, when small farms failed and people moved into the city for work. After World War II, the community's farming activities ceased because the younger generation went on to college under the G.I. Bill. After observing how hard their parents had worked to live on a farm, the younger generation was never committed to perpetuating their dreams.

As northeast Ohio shifted from "truck farming" to "grape growing," people of all nationalities and cultures settled there. Far from home, these immigrants shared their treasured traditions, customs, rituals, and lore—specifically as they related to wine and food—with each other. They included the English, the Italians, the French, the Germans, the Austrians, the Hungarians, the Slovenians, the Czechoslovakians, and the Scandinavians. Families such as the Ferrantes, the Virants, the Debevcs, and the Grubers loved the land; they planted orchards and vineyards and built farmhouses and barns for horses, cattle, sheep, chickens. As wine pioneers, these families blazed the trail for grape growing and winemaking to produce bulk wines and, later, private-label wines.

In the early 1960s, Joseph Gruber Sr., a pioneering Geneva grape grower, read about the tradition of grape festivals in other wine states. Joseph and his brother Ray presented the idea for a similar event in 1963 to the Tri-County Grape Growers Association and the Geneva Area Chamber of Commerce. What resulted was the now-historic Jamboree Grape Festival, a two-day celebration of the grape harvest first started in 1964, held the last weekend of September. People and grapes are featured in parades, contests, exhibits, arts and craft fairs, and a farmer's market.

Vineyards at dawn in Wooster

Vintner's Challenge

IN 1806, EDWARD PHELPS AND HIS family moved from Windsor, Connecticut, to five hundred fertile acres of farmland along Alum Creek in the frontier town of Westerville, Ohio. Ten years later, they were joined by the Westervelt brothers from New York, and by the late 1840s there was a sizeable settlement. In 1858, the town was officially incorporated and a year later legally banned "the sale, barter, or gift of wine, fermented cider, beer, and spirituous liquors." That controversial decision was to affect the history of Westerville and the United States for more than a century.

Henry and Phyloxena Corbin, proprietors of a new saloon on Westerville's Main Street, vehemently challenged the law. In the Westerville Whiskey War of 1875, the citizenry demonstrated and blew out the saloon's windows and roof with gunpowder. For four years, this act stopped the war until 1879, when it was refought. Afterward, Westerville became a dry town, and no fermented spirits have been sold there since.

Over time, grape growing and winemaking gradually declined in the Buckeye State. By the mid-1870s, inexpensive California wine was shipped to the Midwest and East. In the 1880s, Henry Howe, a historian, wrote how the adulteration of wine and the California competition had dramatically affected Ohio's standing in the world. The Erie Island producers, Ohio's premiere viticulturists, could no longer be compared favorably to France. In addition, older grape growers in the most productive regions were faced with aging vineyards, where quality and yields were threatened. Crop failures due to unexpected plagues hit the island growers at random over many decades.

From the late 1880s to the late 1890s, Ohio growers and vintners witnessed the increase of viticulture and vinification in Michigan, Pennsylvania, and New York. Ohio entrepreneurs were troubled by the competition's low pricing. As a strategy to win back their clientele, Ohio vintners lowered the price of their wine, which was made from the same amount of juice, but added alcohol, water, sugar, and berries.

In 1893, a national temperance movement was founded in Oberlin, Ohio. Later headquartered in Washington, D.C., the Anti-Saloon League of America vowed to close the country's saloons and promote abstinence by agitation, legislation, and enforcement. The league and the town joined forces when Westerville offered a permanent location for establishing the league's publishing center for anti-alcohol publications, booklets, and posters. Westerville was chosen because it was a viewed as a socially clean and morally upright community.

This partnership, dubbed the noble experiment, and Prohibition, in effect from 1920 to 1933, contributed to the Ohio wine industry's decline. During the early 1920s, the Erie Island winegrowers benefited from Prohibition because grape prices for Catawba peaked at around $100 a ton as demand for nonalcoholic grape juice replaced wine sales. People converted grape juice into homemade wine. But by the late 1920s, commercial winegrowers were confronted with a surplus of grapes. Soon, vineyards around the Erie Islands region and the state were abandoned.

Interestingly, several Ohio and California bulk wineries were permitted by law to produce wine for the sacrament or medicine. Cleveland's Hammer Company, an importer and distributor of wine from around the world, was founded in 1914 by Alfred Joseph Hammer. "With Prohibition in 1920, my grandfather realized he would be out of a job; his older brother, a priest in the Cleveland Diocese, suggested that he sell sacramental wines to churches. So, he bought muscatel, port, tokay, Chablis, and burgundy from Beaulieu Vineyard in the Napa Valley and other wineries," says A. J. Hammer, former president of the company,

now owned by Glazer Distributors, Inc.

The repeal of Prohibition in 1933 brought hope to a handful of Ohio wineries, who applied for licenses and planted new vineyards. But the demand for grapes never materialized, and the commercial winegrowers left the industry in droves. World War II brought a renewed interest in grapes and an upturn in wine sales, but it was the tumultuous sixties that brought dramatic change to the Ohio wine industry. The U.S. government spearheaded a campaign to reach new and existing winegrowers. Wine legend Dr. Garth A. Cahoon, professor emeritus at Ohio State University, led the charge and spent ten years, from 1953 to 1963, at University of California, Riverside, conducting research on citrus physiology before coming to Ohio. Plant nutrition was his research emphasis throughout his career.

> I began my work in Ohio with grapes in 1963 and retired in 1992. I did extensive work with several hundred hybrids at many locations around the state during this period of time. I consider my venture back into the southern part of this state, where the industry originally began, to be the start of the revival of the grape and wine industry in Ohio. The number of wineries grew rapidly during this period … To further test the value of the hybrids I established a series of plots with growers, in 15 counties

adjoining the Ohio River, which I called 'Research Demonstration Vineyards' …

I don't anticipate that the acreage of new vineyards will increase in any major way under the present industry environment but hope that I am wrong. Vinifera wines now seem to receive the major emphasis and have the best sales appeal. Looking back at where we started in the sixties current Ohio wines are now light years ahead.

An enologist of high merit, Dr. James F. Gallander, professor emeritus at Ohio State University for thirty-five years, is the winner of awards from the American Wine Society and the Eastern Section of Enologists and Viticulturists. He writes, "Much of our early research, mid-1960s, dealt with the evaluation of French hybrids, selections from eastern institutions, and a few vinifera varieties for their table wine quality. Attention was given to those grapes which yielded high-quality wines without the characteristic flavors and aromas of American species. Some of the most successful grapes included: Seyval, Vidal, Riesling, Chardonnay, Foch, and De Chaunac."

Dr. Gallander stated his vision for Ohio for the twenty-first century. "Continue the

Glasses set up for comparative wine tasting in Wooster

growth of small boutique wineries and strive to produce superior table wines, particularly white wines that are distinguishable from other regions. An emerging challenge to the Ohio wine industry will be the discovery of a premium red variety."

The Ohio State University Viticulture and Enology research program provides the commercial grape and wine industry and its citizens practical research in viticulture and enology to enhance quality Ohio wine. Viticulture trials research crop levels, training systems, clones, rootstock, and cold hardiness. Enology trials show how these viticultural practices enhance quality by evaluating yeast strains, malolactic fermentation, and pressing treatments. The annual Ohio Grape-Wine Short Course founded by Cahoon and Gallander serves as a major avenue of distribution of these findings.

Commercial experiments are conducted in viticulture and enology at Ohio's research centers in Kingsville, Ripley, and Wooster, all different climates and growing conditions. The research plots consist of two American hybrid, six French-American hybrid, and eight vitis vinifera vineyards. To ensure quality Ohio premium wine, the Ohio Grape Industries Committee and Ohio Agriculture Research and Development Center (OARDC) have partnered in offering wine analysis and trouble-shooting free to the Ohio wine industry. The Ohio Wine Competition, part of the OARDC Enology program, provides Gold, Silver, or Bronze Medal winners a complete wine analysis in the interest of education and excellence. Ohio is once again reclaiming its rightful reputation for improved standards.

Arnie Esterer and Tim Hubbard, founders of Markko Vineyard in Conneaut, planted the first all-vitis vinifera vineyard in 1968. During the seventies, new commercial grape growing commenced in southern Ohio, where viticulture had begun in the early 1800s. In 1970, Wistar and Ursula Marting, pioneers of several new and experimental vineyards, founded the Tarula Farm Winery near Clarksville. The Martings had an interest in French hybrids, then later vitis vinifera. They shared an association with Ken Schuchter Sr., owner of Valley Vineyards, twelve miles west in Morrow, and the two families actively planted grapes and made wine. Nearby, Meier's Wine Cellars in Silverton developed a 125-acre vineyard of an experimental French hybrid.

Encouraged by the results, others followed their lead until large tracts of considerable size were under cultivation in the Ohio River Valley. The grapes produced wines on a caliber of classic European vitis vinifera varietals. The rebirth of the Ohio wine industry in the south caused a shift in the north on the Erie Islands and around Sandusky, where new French-American hybrid and vitis vinifera vineyards were developed.

The Ohio Wine Producers Association (OWPA), an eclectic group of growers and vintners, was organized in 1975 supported by leadership from researchers at the Ohio

State University Research and Development Center. Its early founders included Ray Gruber, Arnie Esterer, Tony Debevc, Ken Schuchter, Sr., Ken and Mary Rush, Estel Cloud, Louis Heineman, Dr. James Gallander, and Dr. Garth A. Cahoon. The association aims to produce quality grapes and wines, build a positive public awareness of Ohio wines, encourage unity within the industry, ensure a climate that sustains its long-term viability, and coordinate other member services.

Donniella Winchell, executive director of the Ohio Wine Producers Association, assesses the future of Ohio wines: "Our industry faces several major tasks in the coming decades: We must continue to identify appropriate clonal selections of world-class varietals and to locate more amenable growing sites for that fruit. We must find a way to protect those unique vineyard plots against urban encroachment. In the cellar, we must improve winemaking techniques to attract the most sophisticated palates and find more ways to attract visitors to 'wine country.' We must establish additional off-site tasting opportunities at restaurants, seminars, and festivals."

In the 1980s the Ohio General Assembly passed legislation that created the Ohio Grape Industries Program, a vehicle for vintners and viticulturists to access marketing and research programs. In the 1990s Governor George Voinovich established programs to increase grape acreage such as tax credits, planting grants, and the addition of a state viticulturist. Ohio wines have regained name recognition and good-will at local, state, national, and international festivals and competitions.

The establishment of Ohio Appellations of Origin specifies the precise geographic location or origin of grapes used to produce a specific wine type. The appellations reflect the *terroir*, or the sum of the characteristics of the place that include the vineyard site and its history, geography, climate, soil, and grape variety. In Ohio, there are five distinct viticultural districts. The Lake Erie Appellation of Origin, the first, consists of grapes grown along or near the shores of Ohio, Pennsylvania, and New York. Its two sub-appellations are the Isle St. George, the second, and Grand River Valley, the third. The Ohio River Valley Appellation, the fourth, parallels the Ohio River from Wheeling, West Virginia, to Evansville, Indiana. The Loramie Creek Appellation, the fifth, in Shelby County is bordered by Loramie and Tuttle creeks on State Route 47 but has no vineyard or winery within its parameters.

The Lake Erie Quality Wine Alliance (LEQWA) was formed in 1993 to represent farm wineries in Ohio, Pennsylvania, and western New York. The association espouses standards and practices in viticulture and the production of grape-based products. "Creating elegant wines through the reflections of our unique *terroir*, The Lake Erie Quality Wine Alliance expresses international excellence through regional character," LEQWA President Ken Tarsitano says.

Ohio Vineyard Lands

THE OHIO WINE COUNTRY PROVIDES unique advantages for winegrowing. The Lake Erie Plains expand in a rolling band along the banks of the lake and then widen into fertile lowlands some fifty miles west in the Maumee Valley. The Ohio shoreline parallels Lake Erie from Conneaut in the east, where there are high clay bluffs, to Toledo farther west, where there are sandy clay beaches, a total of 262 miles. One of America's most fertile farming districts, the Till Plains in western Ohio are sporadically planted with grapes in what is called the corn belt. The Appalachian or Allegheny Plateau comprises the half of Ohio to the south of the Lake Erie Plains. The ruggedly beautiful, mineral-rich plateau has thin, depleted soils contrasted with its northern hills and valleys and its much steeper southern hills and deeper valleys. A small triangular section of the Bluegrass Region, which spills north from Kentucky, includes the thin soils that make up that part of southern Ohio.

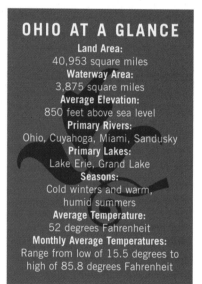

OHIO AT A GLANCE

Land Area:
40,953 square miles
Waterway Area:
3,875 square miles
Average Elevation:
850 feet above sea level
Primary Rivers:
Ohio, Cuyahoga, Miami, Sandusky
Primary Lakes:
Lake Erie, Grand Lake
Seasons:
Cold winters and warm, humid summers
Average Temperature:
52 degrees Fahrenheit
Monthly Average Temperatures:
Range from low of 15.5 degrees to high of 85.8 degrees Fahrenheit

Dedicated Ohio winegrowers, vintners, and scientists have collaborated to discover which types of grapes grow best in which districts. In 1983, American wines were formally identified with specificity by the distinct regions of the United States where the grapes were cultivated. These winegrowing regions were defined by the political subdivision by county and state, or by a viticultural district named for its particular climate, soil, topography, and history. These elements precisely mirror the personality and character of the locales where the grapes were cultivated.

Climate is the challenge with winegrowing in Ohio. Noble varieties such as Chardonnay, Riesling, Cabernet Sauvignon, and Pinot Noir are hard to grow in the cold climes of northern Ohio. Though the hardier, winter-resistant grapes like Catawba and Delaware produce quaffable Ohio table wine, a large percentage of consumers prefer the gentler bouquet and taste of California and European wines. A native vitis labrusca varietal, an acidic Concord (used in jams, jellies, and juices), thrives in Ohio and is softened by the addition of sugar and water so it is drinkable.

Vintners have even gone so far as to blend native Ohio grapes with California wines. Wine expert and vitis vinifera advocate Dr. Konstantin Frank made history planting the noble varieties in the Finger Lakes in protected environments near large bodies of water. Through the decades his pioneering work has changed the thinking of serious Ohio winegrowers, and classical varietals are constantly changing the landscape of wines offered.

Following the phylloxera epidemic of the twentieth century, French wine growers grafted the delicate classic vines onto sturdy, disease-resistant American rootstocks. The grape species retained their original traits and did not acquire negative aspects. Further, the French crossed true grape species that resulted in vines that adapted to different growing conditions, the fruits of which would make good wine. The grapes are called French hybrids in the United States and Canada and American hybrids in France.

With its present 2,200 acres of grapes and five Appellations of Origin, Ohio has produced some outstanding dry table wines from vitis vinifera grapes for more than thirty-five years. Specific to Ohio is its historic production of sweet table and dessert wines produced from vitis labrusca grapes and hardy French hybrids.

Lake Erie has the greatest annual temperature variation of any of the Great Lakes, resulting in a longer growing season. The history of major bodies of water located near top-quality vineyards is known throughout the world. The Guadalquivir in Spain's Sherry district; Jerez de la Frontera, Germany's Rhine; Mosel, France's Loire; Rhone and Gironde Estuary, California's Napa River and Russian River; and New York's Finger Lakes have established unique appellations with regional climates. The larger the body of water, the greater its influence on the district's climate, weather, and vineyards. It is said that Lake Erie provides the foundation to produce wines of excellence. Weather variations continuously challenge the vintner, resulting in a marked difference in the style and variety of wine from vintage to vintage. Such variation is typical of the Lake Erie viticultural district, a cool climate region, but the nature of the wines there is awesome.

Today, Lake Erie is noted for its vitis viniferas and its French-American hybrids. The European varietals produce higher yields per acre than French-American hybrid varietals and a superior taste with more bottle aging. The white viniferas include Chardonnay, Riesling, Gewürztraminer, and Pinot Gris. The red viniferas are Cabernet Sauvignon, Pinot Noir, and Cabernet Franc. The French-American hybrid varietals were developed for winter hardiness and resistance to dis-

An aerial view of lush vineyards and a holding pond in Harpersfield with the winding Grand River in the background

ease, enhanced by a complexity of flavors. The white hybrids highlighted are Vidal Vignoles, Seyval Blanc, and Cayuga. The red hybrid most featured is Chambourcin. The region's other noted hybrid varieties are Baco Noir, Chancellor, Chelois, Concord, De Chaunac, Ives Noir, and Marechal Foch.

The Grand River Valley Appellation of

Origin, situated in Lake, Geauga, and Ashtabula counties, is a sub-appellation. Again, Lake Erie's moderating effect on climate and the growing season is the dominant geographical feature. The Grand River Valley viticultural district is confined to the portion of the Lake Erie viticultural district that is within two miles in any direction of the river. It consists of all the land west of Ohio State Route 45 in any direction of the river and within fourteen miles of the shore of Lake Erie. The climate is the river valley's most distinguishing feature. The Grand River Valley's excellent air drainage supercedes that of the Lake Erie area. And the isobars, the exact place where the pressure of air is the same, for the 170-day and 180-day growing seasons pass directly through the Grand River Valley Appellation.

A second sub-appellation, Isle St. George is a small viticultural area in the western part of Lake Erie in Ottawa County. This appellation is the northernmost of the Bass Islands. It's one-and-one-half miles wide and slightly less that in length, and is eighteen miles from Port Clinton on the mainland. The first grapes were planted on the island in 1853 by Peter and Simon Fox. Catawba and other grapes have flourished here for more than 117 years. At its conception as an appellation, half of the island was devoted to vineyards. At the turn of the twentieth century, there were only two wineries that processed these grapes: one North Bass Island winery and Cincinnati's Meier's Wine Cellars. All the grapes on the island are sent by boat to the Ohio mainland for processing as no wineries currently exist on the island.

Isle St. George has distinctive topography, soils, and climate from other identified regions for the cultivation of grapes. It is basically flat; no point is more than fourteen feet above the surface of Lake Erie. The soil comprises shallow sandy loam and silt loam with limestone bedrock twenty to thirty inches deep in some places. The lake-influenced climate allows for a frost-free period of 206 days, longer than any other place in Ohio, and annual precipitation is less than the adjacent areas. Isle St. George has 26.7 inches, while Kelleys Island has 31.7 inches and Sandusky has 32.1 inches.

The Ohio River Valley Appellation of Origin was established as a 26,000-square-mile viticultural area in Ohio, Indiana, West Virginia, and Kentucky. At the onset, there were 570 acres of vines, grown by 463 grape growers and eighteen wineries. The Ohio River Valley viticultural region is known for its rare pattern of rainfall, the "Ohio type," in which water accumulates in excess of 2.3 inches within twenty-four hours. Robert De Courcy Ward in *The Climates of the United States* explains that this phenomenon, which occurs monthly except in October, could result in severe flooding but for two features. Gray-Brown Podzolic, the dominant soil type only to this area, has slow to moderate permeability, and the Ohio River Valley landscape drains rapidly. Within a few miles of the river, there is a more moderate climate that has fewer extremes during the growing season and is tempered by winds.

Ohio Wineries at a Glance

1   Al-Bi Winery
2   Biscotti Family Winery & Pasta
3   Breitenbach Wine Cellars
4   Buccia Vineyard
5   Candlelight Winery
6   Chalet Debonné Vineyards
7   Cicero's Winery
8   Coffee Cake Winery
9   Farinacci Winery, Ltd.
10 Ferrante Winery & Ristorante
11 Firelands Winery
12 Flint Ridge Vineyard & Winery
13 Georgetown Vineyards
14 Grande Wine Cellars
15 Harmony Hill Vineyards
16 Harpersfield Vineyard
17 Heartland Vineyards
18 Heineman Winery
19 Henke Winery
20 It's Your Winery
21 Jilbert Winery
22 Johlin Century Winery
23 John Christ Winery
24 Kelley's Island Wine Company
25 Kinkead Ridge Estate Winery
26 Klingshirn Winery
27 The Lakehouse Inn Winery
28 Laleure Vineyards
29 Laurello Vineyards
30 Maize Valley Winery
31 Maple Ridge Vineyard
32 Markko Vineyard

33 Meier's Wine Cellars
34 Metrillo Wine Cellars
35 Mon Ami Restaurant
    & Historic Winery
36 Moyer Vineyards, Winery
    & Restaurant
37 Old Firehouse Winery
38 Perennial Vineyards
39 Rainbow Hills Vineyards
40 Ravenhurst Champagne Cellars
41 Raven's Glenn Winery
42 Sand Hill Vineyard and Winery
43 Sarah's Vineyard
44 Shamrock Vineyard
45 Shawnee Springs Winery
46 Single Tree Winery
47 Slate Run Vineyard
48 South River Vineyard
49 St. Joseph Vineyard
50 Stoney Ridge Winery
51 Swiss Heritage Winery
52 Tarsitano Winery
53 Terra Cotta Vineyards
54 Troutman Vineyards
55 Valley Vineyards
56 Viking Vineyards and Winery
57 Vinoklet Winery
58 Virant Family Winery, Inc.
59 The Winery at Versailles
60 The Winery at Wolf Creek
61 Woodstone Creek Winery

Lake Erie and Wine
Islands Tour West

Lake Erie and Grand
River Tour East

Canal and Lock
Tour

Appalachian Country
Tour

Mountains to the
Plains Tour

Ohio River Valley
Tour

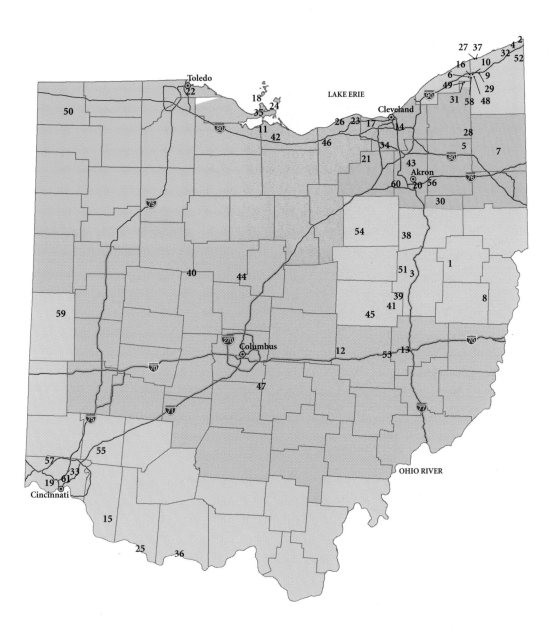

Toledo

LAKE ERIE

Cleveland

50

18
24
35
11
42
26 23
17
46
14
34
21
43
Akron
60 20 56
54
38
30
40
44
51 3
1
59
39
41
8
45
Columbus
12
53 13
47
57
55
33
19 61
Cincinnati
15
25
36

27 37
16
10
6
49
31 58 48
28
5
7
29

OHIO RIVER

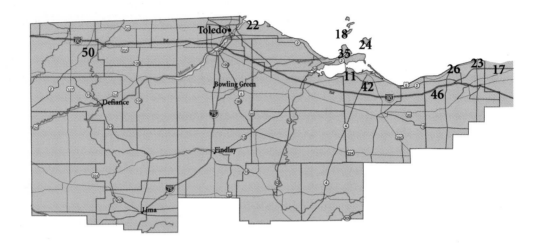

Lake Erie and Wine Islands Tour West

The cellar of the Mon Ami Restaurant & Historic Winery

Firelands Winery

917 Bardshar Road
Sandusky, OH 44870
Tel: (419)625-5474 or (800)548-WINE
Fax: (419)625-4887
E-mail: Info@firelandswinery.com
Web site: www.firelandswinery.com
Owners Lonz Winery, Inc., includes John Kronberg and Claudio Salvador
Winemaker Claudio Salvador
Founded 1880

Between 1776 and 1783, Connecticut citizens whose domiciles were ravaged by the British during the Revolutionary War migrated to the Firelands region of north-central Ohio, where they were granted homesteads as compensation. These proud but practical New Englanders brought a tradition of growing grapes and making wine to the Midwest. One such gentleman, Edward Mantey, was enticed by the thriving wine industry along Lake Erie's south shore. He learned that this viticultural district, now the Lake Erie Appellation of Origin, had a promising reputation for its climate, soil, grapes, and wines.

In 1880, Mantey, a German settler, built a fruit farm that became Mantey Winery. Highly coveted, the Mantey wines, especially the Catawbas, were sold both locally and as far east as Pittsburgh and as far west as Chicago. Mantey and his two ambitious sons, Sylvester and Aloysius, expanded the winery's production to 50,000 gallons.

With the advent of Prohibition in 1920, Mantey Winery ceased to operate. The wine barrels and aging casks were destroyed, but the vineyards and orchards were maintained. Grapes were sold for fruit or juice. With the repeal of Prohibition in 1933, Sylvester rebuilt Mantey Winery. Demand soared for labeled wines packaged in glass bottles. Customers no longer filled their jugs with wine or purchased wine by the barrel.

By 1945, Paul and Norman Mantey, the grandsons of founder Edward, assumed leadership. They established a reputation for fine wines and loyal patrons. "Three generations of Manteys worked here for one hundred years," current vice president and winemaker Claudio Salvador says. In 1980, after the Manteys retired, they sold the jointly owned Mantey Winery and Mon Ami Restaurant & Historic Winery (of which Norman was the sole owner) to the late Robert Gottesman, founder of Cleveland's Paramount Distillers, Inc.

"Overnight, Gottesman transformed the place," Salvador says. "He named the venture

Summer concerts on the lawn at Firelands Winery

Firelands, planted some of the region's early vitis vinifera wines, and retained the Mantey line of native American wines."

When Ohio vintners began to challenge themselves to grow new grape types, Gottesman, a wine pioneer in his own right, was quick to respond. He replaced fifty acres of Catawba and Concord at Firelands' vineyards on North Bass Island (once known as the Isle of St. George) with vitis vinifera. Gottesman planted and replanted a test vitis vinifera vineyard until he achieved the right mix of grapes. It featured twenty-five acres of Riesling; five acres of Gewürztraminer; five acres of Chardonnay; five acres of Pinot Noir; five acres of Cabernet Sauvignon; and five acres of Petit Verdot, Alicante, Pommard, and other varieties.

"1984 was the first vintage of vinifera grapes that I processed in Ohio," says Salvador, who is originally from Italy. "It took me a couple of years to understand the growing season in this part of the world. We introduced a revolutionary and different style of Firelands wines. They were characterized as young, lighter, fruitier, drinkable, and affordable—whites such as Pinot Grigio and Riesling and good hearty reds such as Cabernet Sauvignon and Merlot."

Time and again, Salvador has changed his style of winemaking to meet the demands of the market. The late eighties were a period of experimentation and expansion. "I made a fruity Chardonnay, but consumers said they preferred a Chardonnay that was chewy with oak aging. So, that is the kind of Chardonnay I produced. Sales went up, and we began to win medals," he says.

In 2003, Salvador and John Kronberg, a real estate developer, formed Lonz Winery, Inc., a holding company that purchased Firelands Winery and Mon Ami Restaurant & Historic Winery from Paramount Distillers, Inc. "Our emphasis consists of creating quality wine products," Salvador says. "We make wine in the vineyard, but because of the Ohio weather, we must be prepared to help the wine in the cellar."

The Firelands wine-production center is equipped with the newest equipment and the latest technology. It is both a boutique winery and a juice processor for Firelands, Mon Ami, and Cincinnati's Meier's Wine Cellars, owned by Paramount Distillers, Inc.

Firelands Winery

Directions Take I-90 to Ohio 2 west. Exit at U.S. Route 6 toward Fremont/Sandusky. Turn left onto Fremont Avenue/U.S. 6, then right on Bardshar Road to the winery.

Hours June–September, Monday–Saturday 9 a.m.–5 p.m., Sunday 1–5 p.m.; October–December, Monday–Saturday 9 a.m.–5 p.m.; January–May, 10 a.m.–4 p.m. daily

Tours Self-guided tours; deluxe group tours for 20 or more cost $2.50 per person, which includes four wines, juices, cheese and crackers, and a souvenir glass

Tastings Daily when open

Gifts Wine and wine-related artifacts

Picnics Picnics are welcome in the gazebo overlooking the vineyard

Highlights at Winery Lovely outdoor picnic facilities; lively tasting room with lots of good wines; excellent winery video presentation

Events Christmas Open House, February Wine and Chocolate

Prices $4.79–$29.99; 10 percent case discount on wine; UPS shipping in Ohio

Brand Names Firelands, Mantey

Type of Production Traditional

Method of Harvesting Mechanical

Pressing and Winemaking Pressurized screw press for volume juice; bladder press for vinifera; traditional winemaking

Aging and Cooperage Stainless steel and oak cooperage

County Erie

Appellation Lake Erie

Acreage 50

Waterway Lake Erie

Climate Moderating lake effect; 200-day frost-free growing season

Soil Clay loam

Varieties Vinifera, French-Amercian hybrids, labrusca

Wines Cabernet Sauvignon, Merlot, Cabernet Franc, Chardonnay, Chardonnay Select, Pinot Grigio, Pinot Noir, Country Estate Red, Country Estate White, Gewürztraminer, Riesling, Walleye White, Country Estate Blush, Ice White, Vin Rose, Delaware, Niagara, Blue Face, Pink Catawba, Fifty-Fifty, Haut Sauterne, Crème Catawba, Mellow Concord, Blackberry, Cream Sherry, Firelands Champagne Brut, Firelands Champagne Brut Rose, Firelands Riesling Champagne

Best Reds Merlot and Cabernet Sauvignon

Best White Pinot Grigio

Best Other Wine Gewürztraminer

Nearby Places to Visit Picturesque Sandusky; Historic Port Clinton

Heartland Vineyards

24945 Detroit Road
Westlake, OH 44145
Tel: (440)871-0700
E-mail: heartlandwines@aol.com
Web site: www.heartlandvineyards.com
Owner/Winemaker Jerome Welliver
Founded 1934

At one time, Dover Vineyards, located in a chalet on Detroit Road in Westlake, was one of Cleveland's largest wineries. In 1934, its founder, Zoltan Wolfovitz, a dashing Hungarian, established this winery and seafood restaurant. His customers arrived from Romania, Lithuania, Slovenia, Hungary, and Czechoslovakia with an appreciation for the culinary arts. Wolfovitz provided these patrons with the crafts for making wine and brewing beer at home.

Clevelander Jerome Welliver, of Czech descent, grew up in the same Westlake neighborhood as the winery. He and his own family live in the original Welliver residence with a tiny vineyard, just off of Clague Road. In 1971, he made his first Concord wine on these premises, a tradition he has continued to this day. During the eighties, Welliver's career with a national restaurant chain segued into studies in power and physics at Omaha Community College, followed by employment there. A chance to head a major wine venture called Welliver back to Cleveland. In 1997, he purchased Dover Vineyards and renamed it J. W. Dover, Inc. It became the city's top purveyor of ingredients and equipment for making beer and wine. At the same site, in 1998, the motivated Welliver created the 4,000-gallon Heartland Vineyards, producers of table wines, mead (honey wine), and melomel (fruit and honey wines). "My avocation developed into my vocation," he says.

On Saturdays during harvest, it isn't unusual for groups of foreign-speaking customers to be lined up outside J. W. Dover's bright red door. "Our philosophy—just quality," Welliver says, and his clients affirm that reputation.

The busy retail store buzzes with beverage enthusiasts. They cruise the aisles in search of the ultimate wine or beer primer. *The Art of Wine Making* and *The Complete Joy of Home Brewing* often catch their interest. Oenophiles check out the wine kits and the varietal juices shipped from California or Ohio, along with filters, presses, racks, and barrels. Brewers buy yeasts, grains, malts, hops, keg equipment, and gadgets. People love the pickles, honeys, jams, and jellies in currant, blackberry, and blueberry.

The white banquet room with its mahogany mirrored bar is decorated with Ohio wine posters, antique bottles, corkscrews, labels, awards, ribbons, sepia photographs, and presses. Clevelanders dine on swordfish, clams, steak, or pizza, or enjoy a Heartland Vineyards Chenin Blanc or Red Zinfandel.

In the J. W. Dover Wine and Beer School, Welliver certifies novices and experts who become discriminating brewers, winemakers, and tasters. Seven-student classes are held in the test kitchen, where they work on a stainless steel table using scales, instruments, presses, kegs, and jugs. Vintage olive oil cans and historic beer and wine bottles fill the rafters.

"We have found our own niche market," Welliver says. "We have the right climate, the right grapes, and the right wines. I go with what I can do well, and others follow."

Welliver has interested home winemakers by bringing in juice from coveted single vineyards. In California, he finds Old Vines Zinfandel in Modesto and Cabernet Sauvignon, Chardonnay, and Riesling in the Russian River. Pinot Noir comes from Oregon.

Heartland Vineyards' cellars are spotless and reflect Welliver's organization and detail. "Wine production is both natural and traditional," he says. He uses older basket presses and hydraulic basket presses. "We make minimal adjustments." The wines are fermented in stainless steel tanks or American white oak barrels. They are racked, pumped over, and held in stainless steel, glass, and oak.

Variety and simplicity give Heartland Vineyards' wines their personality. Some examples are its Ohio bird series: Pink Splendor (a pink flamingo), Celiege (pileated woodpecker), Pinot Noir (a great horned owl), Syrah (a scarlet tanager), and Riesling (a finch). Its grape series includes Fredonia, Red Cabernet, Steuben, Autumn Crest, and Catabara, and its Melomel series includes Blueberry Melomel, Cherry Melomel, Raspberry Melomels, and Mead.

"The wine dictates," Welliver says. "We have to see where the wine is going and prevent any difficulties. My role is to guide the wine—no guessing here!"

Directions Take I-90 west. Take the Columbia Road Exit and go south. At Detroit Road continue left and east to the winery, on the south side near Mahle's Restaurant.

Hours Tuesday 10 a.m.–8 p.m.; Wednesday–Thursday 10 a.m.–6 p.m.; Friday–Saturday 10 a.m.–10 p.m.

Tours Daily 20-minute guided informational tours before 5 p.m.

Tastings Fifty cents per taste

Highlights at Winery Mead and melomel wines; beer and winemaking classes; formal tastings; emphasis on education by doing

Events Heartland Vineyards Cuisine Program; Huron Chamber of Commerce Wine Artisans' Festival; Make-a-Wish Foundation

Prices $5.75–$15; 10 percent case discount

Brand Name Heartland Vineyards

Type of Production Traditional

Method of Harvesting Hand-harvested

Pressing and Winemaking Basket press and hydraulic basket press. Wine dictates.

Aging and Cooperage American white oak barrels, glass demi-johns, stainless steel tanks

County Cuyahoga

Appellation Lake Erie

Acreage 1/4 planted; 2 available

Waterway Lake Erie

Climate Cool region moderated by Lake Erie

Soil Mineral base with clay and sandy loams

Varieties St. Pepin

Wines Red Zinfandel, Caberent Sauvignon, Chardonnay Syrah, Ruby Cabernet, Catabara, Chenin Blanc, Autumn Crest, Pink Splendor, Fredonia, Steuben, Pink Catawba, Mead Cherry Melomel, Blueberry Melomel, Peach Melomel, Raspberry Melomel, Pinot Noir, Riesling, Celiege, Apple Wine

Best Red Syrah

Best White Chenin Blanc

Other Best Wine Fredonia

Nearby Places to Visit Rock and Roll Hall of Fame; Huntington Beach

Lake Erie
Pinot Grigio

12.0% Alc./Vol.
PRODUCED AND BOTTLED BY HEINEMAN WINERY
PUT-IN-BAY, OHIO 43456, BW#112

Heineman Winery

978 Catawba Avenue, Box 300

Put-in-Bay, OH 43456

Tel: (419)285-2811

Fax: (419)285-3412

Owner Louis V. Heineman

Winemaker Edward Heineman

Founded 1888

The blue-and-white ferry boat from Catawba plied the choppy, white-capped waters and gusty winds at the western end of Lake Erie on its run to Put-in-Bay, the only town on South Bass Island. It was from the harbor called Put-in-Bay that Oliver Hazard Perry sailed to defeat the British fleet under Robert H. Barclay during the War of 1812. This gray morning, the skies accentuated the limestone cliffs as the ferry

boat tooted its horn and pulled into the dock. A gentleman of distinction, Louis V. Heineman, third-generation owner of the family-owned and -operated Heineman Winery, awaited on shore, delighted to share tales of one of Ohio's most revered viticultural treasures.

Grape growing and winemaking commenced on this small, two-by-four-mile island in the early 1850s. Real estate mogul Joseph de Rivera, a Spanish merchant, purchased South Bass Island and its sister islands for $44,000, dividing the land into ten-acre parcels. As South Bass Island's reputation grew as a fashionable resort, tourists from Canada and the Great Lakes came by steamship to stay at the popular Victory Hotel.

In 1880, Gustav Heineman, Louis's grandfather, left Freiburgim-Breisgau, a prized grape-growing district along the Rhine, and headed for America. With other German immigrants from that country's grape-growing district, he journeyed inland to Ohio. "Gustav worked at Golden Eagle Winery, later Lonz Winery, on Middle Bass Island, then visited Germany in 1882," Louis says. "Upon his return, the Erie Islands were prospering and valued by growers and producers as a highly recognized viticultural district. Simultaneously, Stephanie (Fanny) Zeller, a beauty from Baden-Baden, won Gustav's heart, and the newly married Heinemans relocated to the island."

The Heinemans found the legendary

Lake Erie Islands, with their clay limestone soils and temperate climate, ideal for a vineyard. "The island temperatures are five degrees Fahrenheit warmer—more like Detroit and Toledo—than the east side of Cleveland," Louis says. His grandfather planted labrusca grapes, such as Concord, Niagara, Delaware, and Catawba, and then, in 1888, started the winery. By 1900, there were seventeen wineries on Put-in-Bay, close to eight varieties, and four hundred acres planted to vines. "Put-in-Bay had a street car line that transported tourists to the Heineman Winery," Louis says. "My father, Norman, who inherited the winery from Gustav, used to sell wine to visitors outside the winery."

With the advent of Prohibition in 1920, Norman focused his production on grape juice, offered in five- to fifty-gallon lots with a little bootlegged wine thrown in on the side. Stocks departed on the ferry boat from Put-in-Bay to arrive in Sandusky, then were shipped east by rail.

Tourists flocked to Crystal Cave on the Heineman property, which houses one of the world's largest known geodes (hollow rocks lined with crystals), some thirty feet in diameter. Samples of these crystals are on display at the Smithsonian Natural History Museum in Washington, D.C.

After Prohibition, Norman applied for a grower's permit to make wine. Louis outlines his entry into the business: "At nine in 1935, I cleared tables; after World War II, at twenty-two in 1948, I ran the bar." By 1953, his brother Harry Heineman bought the Port Clinton-headquartered Heineman Distributing Company from Otto Heineman, his cousin, and Heineman Trucking, a beverage wholesaler serving six counties. Today Louis runs the winery with his son Edward, the winemaker, and his daughter Angie, the retail shop manager.

At 50,000 gallons, Heineman Winery considers itself a "small producer," selling 90 percent of its stocks—70 percent labrusca and 30 percent vinifera and French hybrid—at the winery at retail. "I grew up drinking labrusca wines, which are fruity and grapey. I aspire to make wines so they taste like the grape," says Edward, who graduated in enology and food technology from Ohio State University in 1980.

Heineman Winery produces a wide variety of wines from grapes grown on the island, with Sauterne being Louis's favorite blend of native grapes. Recently the Heineman Winery won the Director's Choice Award, the highest commendation in Ohio (given by the director of agriculture) for its White Riesling and its Put-in-Bay Ice Wine. "I love living on the island, where I was born and raised," Edward says. "I like making wine taste good and pleasing the people." That's exactly what his father, Louis, said, too: "It's all about the people!"

Heineman Winery

Directions Take I-80 to U.S. Route 250 north to U.S. Route 2 west to 53 north to ferry dock: 20-minute, $6 ferry ride by Miller Boat Line from Point Catawba or Port Jet Express from downtown Port Clinton; two cruise lines from Sandusky: Goodtime and City of Sandusky from Marblehead to Put-in-Bay.

Hours May–October, 10 a.m.–7 p.m. daily

Tours Combined tours of winery and Crystal Cave May–September, 11 a.m.–5 p.m. daily

Tastings May–September part of wine tour

Gifts Variety of mineral and fossil specimens and wine-oriented gifts

Picnics None

Highlights at Winery Beautiful "wine garden"; Crystal Cave featuring largest deposit of celestite crystals in world; wood carvings by artist Bruno Weber

Restaurant Light fare: cheese and wine

Prices $8–$20; 10 percent case discount

Brand Names Heineman's Winery

Type of Production Vitis vinifera, French-American hybrids, vitis labrusca, and grape juice

Method of Harvesting Hand and machine

Pressing and Winemaking German membrane press

Aging and Cooperage Stainless steel tanks and oak barrels

Vineyards Founded 1900

County Ottawa

Appellation Lake Erie

Acreage 25

Waterway Lake Erie

Climate Moderated by Lake Erie

Soil Clay limestone, Put-in-Bay Dolomite

Varieties Vitis vinifera, vitis labrusca, French-American hybrids

Wines Sweet Belle, Sweet Catawba, Sweet Concord, Pink Catawba, Rose, Burgundy, Sauterne, Delaware, Dry Catawba, Niagara, Cabernet Sauvignon, White Riesling, Chardonnay, Pinot Grigio, Island Chablis, Island Blush, Vidal Blanc, Cedar Woods Red, Champagne: Heineman's and Admiral's Select, Put-in-Bay Ice; Non-Alcoholic Grape Juice: Concord, Catawba

Best Red Burgundy

Best White White Riesling

Other Best Wine Pink Catawba

Quote "We make wine the Old World way." —Louis V. Heineman

Nearby Places to Visit Perry's Victory and International Peace Memorial; Crystal Cave

Johlin Century Winery

3935 Corduroy Road
Oregon, OH 43616
Tel: (419)693-6288
Fax: (419)693-6429
Owners Richard and Lovie Johlin
Winemaker Richard Johlin
Founded 1870

The Johlin Century Winery, housed in the land-mark Johlin family farm on the outskirts of Toledo, sits squarely at the crossroads of a time and place in Ohio's history when agriculture was king and these industrious Midwesterners shipped their fruits and vegetables across the United States.

As a child, Jacob Johlin grew up in Freiburgim-Breisgau, the largest city by the Rhine River on the edge of the Black Forest, silhouetted against the snow-peaked Alps. The sophisticated city had a reputation for fine wines, art museums, gothic cathedrals, winter sports, and extensive timber. In the 1860s, at nineteen, the daring solo adventurer left his German family and set sail for New York. He ended up in the Ohio Grape Belt, at one time one of the most productive viticultural regions in the United States.

"My great-grandfather [Jacob] purchased three hundred acres of marshland, rich with ash, elm, and hickory, which he cleared for grapes, fruits, corn, hay, and livestock. He got things done, returned to Germany, and brought the entire family to America," says Richard Johlin, today's patriarch and proprietor. Jacob willed the Johlin Century Winery to his son Edward. Later Richard and his wife, Lovie, purchased the winery from his Uncle Edward's estate. Richard and Lovie have merged their talent with their grandsons, Bolan and Jarrod, and together they are breathing new life into an established tradition.

"Our plans are to make quality wines at affordable prices," say Bolan and Jarrod, who got their start in Cleveland's restaurant business.

Located just off of Corduroy Road in Oregon, Johlin Century Winery is approached via a long driveway laid by hand in 1944 with red brick pavers from the Hocking Valley Brick Company. It passes the 1870s red brick Victorian Johlin home, an architectural treasure situated among tall pines that was constructed at the height of the Ohio brick industry and reflects the taste and style of the period.

Vineyards were planted in the silty clay loams inland from Lake Erie in the late 1800s. The long, hot days and the cool nights that characterized the Ohio Grape Belt climate were ideal for growing Delaware, Catawba, Niagara, and Concord. "Eventually, the family replaced the vineyards with a reduced 150 acres of corn, soy, and hay," Richard says.

The two-story winery dates to 1939. Its upper level consists of a sales room and a work room. The lower level, made from concrete, features a stainless steel production center and aging cellars. "Our production fluctuates between 2,000 gallons and 5,000 gallons," Jarrod says. Under Jacob Johlin's reign, the winery had a 15,000-gallon capacity.

"We have three kinds of customers: everyday locals, occasional locals, or tourists from Maumee Bay State Park," Richard says. The Johlin Century Winery produces an array of appealing wines from vitis vinifera, vitis labrusca, and French-American hybrid grapes.

Johlin Century Winery

Directions Take I-280 north to the first Oregon exit, Navarre Avenue. Go east and right on Navarre Avenue for 1.25 miles to North Coy Road. Turn left on North Coy Road, which dead-ends at Corduroy Road. Proceed right and west on Corduroy Road for 1/2 mile to the winery, on the left.
Hours Monday–Saturday 11 a.m.–6 p.m.
Tours None
Gifts Wine only
Highlights at Winery Historic Toledo perspective on agriculture and commerce; display of antique farm winery equipment and tools
Prices $5.25–$14.00
Brand Name Johlin Century Winery
Type of Production Vitis labrusca, vitis vinifera, French-American hybrids
Method of Harvesting Selected from Ohio and Pennsylvania grape growers
Pressing and Winemaking Select juice and follow traditional methods
Aging and Cooperage Stainless steel tanks
Appellation Lake Erie and American
Varieties Niagara, Catawba, Merlot, Concord, fruits, berries, honey
Wines Vin Rose, Haut Sauterne, Catawba, Concord, Raspberry, Blackberry, Strawberry, Sour Cherry, Merlot, Maumee White, Crème Niagara, Autumn Spice, Mead (honey wine)
Best Red Wine Vin Rose
Best White Wine Crème Niagara
Other Best Wine Catawba
Nearby Places to Visit Toledo Museum of Art; Maumee Bay State Park

John Christ Winery

32421 Walker Road
Avon Lake, OH 44012
Tel: (440)933-9672
Web site: www.ohiowines.org
Winemaker Mac McLelland
Founded 1946

The site of the original twenty-three-acre Horwittel Concord and Niagara Vineyard on Walker Road in Avon Lake dates from the 1930s. These prime vineyards were part of the Lake Erie Grape Belt, which extended as far west as Michigan and as far east as western New York. Even with the repeal of Prohibition in 1933, the sale of table grapes did not prove profitable for Horwittel. Native Macedonians Toda and John Christ breathed new life into the property when they purchased the vineyard and established the John Christ Winery in 1946.

The Christs built a simple but elegant Swiss chalet with scalloped trim. The foyer leads to a magnificent great room with a curved tasting bar, beamed ceilings, and hand-painted grapes covering the walls. The room has a warm and open welcoming atmosphere reminiscent of old Europe. A bright red pot-bellied stove with a hearth heats the room during the winter months. Banks of windows look to the vineyards and the lawn for summer picnics. Just off the foyer, the John Christ wines are artistically displayed in a green sales room. Another door leads to the wine-production center with its lab, bottling line, tiers of Italian stainless steel tanks, and aging cellar. Informal tours are available if the staff is free.

The Christs, along with Alex, their son, Zora, his spouse, and Andy, their godson, built a quality reputation as producers of labrusca and French-American hybrid wines until 1999. After fifty-three years of continuous family ownership, the Christs sold their wine estate to a local developer. The Legacy Pointe/Sweetbriar Golf Community replaced most of the vineyards. The remaining five-acre agricultural preserve includes a farmhouse, the John Christ Winery, and a vineyard framed by tall pine trees. "The winery was intended for the community," says Mac McLelland,

now manager and winemaker. "Almost 100 percent of our sales are retail."

McLelland began making wine at home during the nineties while he completed his business administration degree at Alabama's Auburn University. "I made a native, floral Muscadine wine. It wasn't too bad—even okay. I knew I wanted a career I enjoyed," he says. So, he looked for work in the Ohio and Georgia wine industry. McLelland apprenticed with the Christ family. "I was taught old-fashioned winemaking using labrusca grapes." After the winery sold, McLelland was retained by the new owner, and he ushered in a new era of winemaking at the John Christ Winery. "I experimented and introduced some of our first vitis vinifera wines."

The 5,000-case John Christ Winery has a reputation for its production of hand-crafted wines. McLelland's enthusiasm speaks to his philosophy that "a winemaker's best tool is his glass." This time-consuming approach to winemaking reflects the Christs' care and McLelland's innovation.

The Lake Erie Appellation of Origin is the locale of all the grapes the winery owns or purchases. At harvest, the grapes are pressed, crushed, and fermented, then held in easy-to-clean, variable-capacity, minimal-oxidation, Italian stainless steel tanks or American white oak barrels. "My style of winemaking is to let the wines settle out through racking," McLelland says. "I don't touch the wines unless something needs my attention, as it did this year. It was a cool summer, and the grapes came in under-ripe. After fermentation, I do filtering just before bottling to polish the white wines. I do a very loose pre-bottle filtration with the red wines."

John Christ Winery produces award-winning Gold and Silver Medal wines. They include Chardonnay, Johannisberg Riesling, Gewürztraminer, Cabernet Sauvignon, Merlot, Claret, Labrusca, Natural Peach, Vignoles, Cayuga, Vidal Blanc, Niagara, Vin Gris Rose, Pink Catawba, Raspberry, Blackberry, Late Harvest Concord, Special Blend, and Vidal Blanc Ice Wine. These John Christ wines—a mixture of vinifera, hybrids, and labrusca—reflect the historic struggle of Ohio winemakers to find their way and establish the region's true wine identity once and for all.

John Christ Winery

Directions Take I-90 west to State Route 83 north in Avon Lake for two miles. Turn right on Walker Road for 1/2 mile to the winery.

Hours Monday–Wednesday 10 a.m.–6 p.m.; Thursday–Saturday 10 a.m.–12 p.m.; Sunday 1–6 p.m. (seasonal)

Tours No formal tours

Tastings Daily when open

Gifts Wine-related

Picnics Lovely garden and lawn with picnic tables

Highlights at winery Premium winemakers; great location for people to gather for fun on weekends

Events Steak fry in June; barbeques in July; pig roasts in August; clambakes in September and October

Wine Bar Light fare and appetizers

Prices $6–$27; 10 percent case discount, UPS shipping in Ohio available

Brand Names John Christ

Type of Production Hand-crafted wines

Method of Harvesting Hand-harvesting

Pressing and Winemaking Bladder press and non-intrusive winemaking

Aging and Cooperage Oak barrels and stainless steel tanks

Vineyards Founded Planted in late thirties; established in 1946

County Lorain

Appellation Lake Erie

Acreage 5

Waterway Lake Erie

Climate Long, cool growing season

Soil Clay and lime

Varieties Vinifera, French-American hybrids, labrusca

Wines John Christ Chardonnay, Gewürztraminer, Johannisberg Riesling, Cabernet Sauvignon, Merlot Claret, Labrusca, Raspberry, Blackberry, Late Harvest Concord, Special Blend, Vidal Blanc Ice Wine, Natural Peach, Vignoles, Cayuga, Vidal Blanc, Niagara, Vin Gris Rose, Pink Catawba

Best Red Merlot

Best White Riesling

Other Best Wine Vidal Blanc Ice Wine

Quote "A winemaker's best tool is his glass." —Mac McLelland

Nearby Places to Visit Avon Lake's Sweetbriar Golf Course; Vermilion's Mill Hollow Park

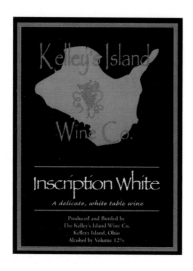

Kelley's Island Wine Company

418 Woodford Road
Kelleys Island, OH 43438
Tel: (419)746-2678
Fax: (419)746-2678
E-mail: kiwineco@aol.com
Web site: www.kelleysislandwine.com
Owners Kirt and Robby Zettler
Winemaker Kirt Zettler
Founded 1983

The family-owned and -operated Kelley's Island Wine Company, now the region's only wine producer, lies on the southernmost side of Kelleys Island, the largest and easternmost of Ohio's Lake Erie Islands. Brothers Datus and Irad Kelley bought the 2,888-acre island in the 1830s, and with other settlers prospered from fishing, quarrying, lumbering, and grape growing. Charles Carpenter, Datus Kelley's son-in-law, started the first commercial vineyard there in 1845, planting forty-six Isabella and forty Catawba vines. In 1850, Carpenter had an acre of grapes and pressed 100 gallons. By 1854, he had established the first wine cellar north of Cincinnati.

Around that time, a migration of German immigrants from that country's wine district settled on Kelleys Island, and they established the island as a leading winegrowing center from the late 1800s through the early 1900s, with many firms and more than one thousand acres of grapes. On the eve of Prohibition, there were but five wineries in operation; upon repeal only one reopened, and grape growing declined.

When Kirt and Robby Zettler arrived on the island in the seventies, there were a handful of growers and one winery, Sweet Valley Wine Company. Kirt had studied viticulture and enology at the University of Australia while his parents were on assignment there for the U.S. Department of State, and had continued his studies at Ohio State University upon his return. In 1979, the Zettler family purchased twenty acres of island farmland on Woodford Road for commercial vineyards. "We planted Chardonnay, Riesling, Cabernet Sauvignon, and Pinot Noir, which we thought ideal in this unique temperate microclimate," Kirt says. "We were motivated by the idea of getting $1,500 per ton, and challenged by the low yield of 2.5 tons per acre."

In 1983, the Zettlers bought the limestone Civil War-era house of Nicholas Smith, the stonemason for the original Kelley mansion and other grand houses. Adjacent to the vineyards, the farmhouse was first the winery, then later the bistro. "We applied for a license, opened the new Kelley's Island Wine Company (a name with a storied past that had never been trademarked), and started making wine," Kirt says. "We were convinced that the quieter island and beauty of Lake Erie would draw families, boaters, hikers, and collegians." The Zettlers also built an Australian Outback building with a sloping porch and rail fence that includes a restaurant, deli, and winery. Graced by pines and vineyards, the property has a pavilion, a picnic area, a playground, a volleyball court, and horseshoe pits.

Managers Brett and Lynn Maiers have created a seasonal menu of starters—smoked-chicken salad, heirloom tomato salad, and Prince Edward Island mussels—and entrees—veal chops, sautéed shrimp, and yellowfin tuna—in addition to deli appetizers, cheeses, dips, and spreads. Popular local Jimmy Buffet plays piano jazz and show tunes evenings and weekends.

After a particularly harsh winter in 1992, Kirt simplified the operation by leasing vineyards in addition to growing grapes.

The Lake Erie coastline at Kelleys Island

Lou Gardella

With annual production at 500 gallons, the Zettlers make small batches of wine on an as-needed-basis. "I average two to three tons a day, bottling ten, twenty, or fifty cases at a time," Kirt says. He uses a basket press, variable-capacity Italian stainless steel tanks, a natural cold room for wine stabilization, hand bottling equipment, and storage.

The Kelleys Island vinifera consist of Chardonnay, Johannisberg Riesling, Pinot Grigio, Merlot, and Cabernet Sauvignon. The blends include Inscription White, a Chardonnay and Vignoles blend; Indian Red, a Rhone-style Cabernet Sauvignon and Chancellor blend; Glacial White, a Germanic-style wine; Sunset Pink, a crisp blush blend; and Coyote, a sweet Niagara. "A good winemaker enjoys time with his friends, testing his products as well as drinking them," Kirt says.

Kelley's Island Wine Company

Directions From I-80, take exit 118/7 toward Cedar Point/Sandusky. Merge onto Ohio 2 west to 269 north (Marblehead/Lakeside exit) to Ohio 163 east, turn left on Frances Street and Kelleys Island Ferry. Travel 4.5 miles to Kelleys Island via the ferry boat line.

Hours June–August, Monday–Saturday 11a.m.–10 p.m.; Sunday 12–8 p.m.; September–October and April–May, Saturday–Sunday 12–8 p.m.

Tours Winery-viewing windows

Tastings Daily when open

Gifts Signature clothing, wine-related gifts, and pottery

Picnics No wine or food can be brought on property

Highlights at Winery Only winery on Kelleys Island; outdoor area featuring children's play area, volleyball, and horseshoes

Events Annual Spring Fling first Saturday in April

Restaurant Classic and regional culinary favorites; Wine Company Bistro: pizza, pasta, and the like; Deli: Imported and domestic cheeses, spreads, dips, sausages, fresh fruit, French bread, and house mustard

Prices $3.75–$4.50 by the glass; $10–$15 per bottle; 10 percent case discount; $4 off six-bottle purchase

Brand Names Kelley's Island Wine Company

Type of Production Full grapes to bottle

Method of Harvesting Hand

Pressing and Winemaking Bladder and cold fermentation

Aging and Cooperage Stainless steel tanks

Vineyards Founded 1981

County Erie

Appellation Lake Erie

Acreage 12

Waterway Lake Erie

Climate Temperate

Soil Limestone-based

Varieties Johannisberg Riesling, Chardonnay, Cabernet Sauvignon, Merlot, various French hybrids

Wines Chardonnay, Johannisberg Riesling, Cabernet Sauvignon, Merlot

Best Red Indian Red

Best White Chardonnay

Quote "A little vino would be keen-o!" —Kirt Zettler

Nearby Places to Visit Activities of Kelleys Island (tours, golf cart rentals, butterfly house, shopping); Sandy Beach State Park

Klingshirn Winery

33050 Webber Road

Avon Lake, OH 44012-2330

Tel: 440-933-6666

E-mail: info@klingshirnwine.com

Web site: www.klingshirnwine.com

Owners Corporation includes Allan and Barbara Klingshirn, Lee and Nancy Klingshirn

Winemaker Lee Klingshirn

Founded 1935

The story of Klingshirn Winery begins when Antone Klingshirn departed Bavaria's Wolfsig, a hamlet along the Mosel, and headed for Ohio's Avon Lake, a farming community along Lake Erie. In 1899, the patriarch of the American branch of the family purchased a farmhouse, barn, and vineyard. Over time, Klingshirn prospered and bought farms for each of his four sons. In 1919, Antone gifted the sixty-five-acre Klingshirn farm and vineyards to his son Albert R. Klingshirn. A surplus vintage in 1935 inspired Albert to establish a winery. He began to produce small batches of wine in 50-gallon wooden barrels in his home wine cellar.

By 1940, Albert broke ground for the two-tiered Klingshirn Winery. The all-purpose second floor was utilized for sales, bottling, and case storage. The downstairs production facility had room for two hundred 50-gallon wooden barrels. For decades, grapes were pressed at Antone's homestead.

In 1955, Albert's son Allan and his spouse, Barbara, purchased the Klingshirn Winery. Their growth strategy to invest in stainless steel tanks and large wooden barrels was timed to expand the overall product selection. "As the business grew, there was value in grapes and additional value in wine," says Lee Klingshirn, Allan's brother and the current winemaker. During the next two decades, the American wine business accelerated with limitless possibilities. Ohio caught the fever, and Allan, who anticipated future growth, quadrupled the Klingshirn Winery's sales room and production center.

"In 1978, there were twenty Ohio wineries, all hit by a major market shift in the opposite direction. Customers became 'wine savvy,' and competition from foreign and domestic wine pushed our product off its base," explains Lee, who in 1986 graduated from Ohio State University with a BA in enology and viticulture. To counter this trend, his father, his brother Allan, and several other Ohio vintners founded the Ohio Wine Producers Association.

The present Klingshirn property, an agricultural oasis of sorts, consists of the brown-shingled Klingshern Winery and adjacent buildings, twenty-three acres of prime vineyard, and two family homes. The dramatic change in zoning laws from agriculture to residential/industrial continues to challenge the future of the Klingshirn Winery. "We plan to stay put for the long term," Lee says. "We are global thinkers-marketers, and we value the reputation of the wine industry as a whole. As the industry grows, so shall we and always maintain our quality."

The silty, clay-soiled Klingshirn Vineyards is located on a peninsula between Cleveland's west side and the Lake Erie Islands. "This is a sunbelt, not a snowbelt," Lee says. "The weather is 10 percent to 15 percent drier here. In any typical season, any given variety grown here reaches harvestable maturity ten to fourteen days earlier than the same varieties grown in northeast Pennsylvania; and for the late-season premium grapes, this is a huge advantage. Our award-winning, twenty-year-old Riesling vines continuously produce good yield and consistent quality."

The 12,000-case Klingshirn Winery—with its 30,000-gallon capacity, stainless steel tanks, and oak cooperage—markets custom wine products and even has a personalized label program. "We sell 80 percent of our production at the winery and deliver the remaining 20 percent to Lorain beverage shops," Lee says.

Klingshirn consistently advocates practical winemaking and economic profitability. "We absolutely depend on the production of quality fruit from our vineyard. Smaller lots of premium grapes express both the character of the fruit and the nature of the vineyard. However, my energies are consumed with the production of labruscas, which continue to be the backbone of our operation," Lee says.

The Klingshirns have persevered with their age-old approach of quality with profit, and after six decades of implementing this practice, they are confident their approach works. Come visit and decide for yourself.

Klingshirn Winery

Directions Take I-90 west to exit 153 at Avon Lake at the State Route 83 interchange. Proceed north on State Route 83 for 1.6 miles. Turn left and west on Webber Road. Proceed 1/2 mile to the winery.

Hours Monday-Saturday 10 a.m.–6 p.m. Closed Sundays and holidays.

Tours/Tasting Formal tours with tasting for groups of up to 25 by appointment; informal tours and tasting provided staff available

Gifts Wine items

Picnics Encouraged for small groups

Highlights at Winery Site of one of most historic vineyards and urban wineries in Ohio; personalized labels for weddings, anniversaries, and holidays

Events Summer steak cookouts

Prices $4.26–$14.42; 10 percent case discount

Brand Name Klingshirn Winery

Type of Production All types of grapes and wine

Method of Harvesting Mostly mechanical except Lake Erie Iced Delaware

Pressing and Winemaking Screw-type press and improvisational winemaking

Aging and Cooperage Oak for Cabernet Sauvignon and Chardonnay; stainless steel for the rest

Vineyards Founded 1899

County Lorain

Appellation Lake Erie and Ohio

Acreage 17 (and 6 more soon to be planted)

Waterway Lake Erie

Climate Long, warm growing season

Varieties White Riesling, Chardonnay, Pinot Gris, Cabernet Sauvignon, Concord, Delaware, Chambourcin, Vidal Blanc

Wines Cabernet Sauvignon, Cabernet Franc, Chambourcin, Chardonnay, Pinot Grigio, White Riesling, Vidal Blanc, Country Blush, Catawba, Golden Chablis, Concord, Niagara, Vin Rose, Haut Sauterne, Pink Catawba, Sweet Concord, Cherry, Delaware Ice Wine, Champagnes: Contemporary Blend, White Riesling, Traditional Blend

Best Red Cabernet Sauvignon

Best White Riesling

Other Best White Iced Lake Erie Delaware

Quote "We are global thinkers-marketers, and we value the reputation of the wine industry as a whole." —Lee Klingshirn

Nearby Places to Visit Avon Antiques; Sunset Shores Bed & Breakfast

Mon Ami Restaurant & Historic Winery

3845 E. Wine Cellar Road
Port Clinton, OH 43452
Tel: (419)797-4445 or (800)777-4266
E-mail: info@monamiwinery.com
Web site: www.monamiwinery.com
Owners Lonz Winery, Inc. Includes John Kronberg and Claudio Salvador
Winemaker Claudio Salvador
Founded 1872

The most magnificent architectural treasure in the Lake Erie Islands' wine country is the Mon Ami Restaurant & Historic Winery in Port Clinton. Toledo stonecutter George Loeb built the winery in 1872 as a symbol of strength. From its foundation upward, it is constructed of six-foot limestone walls sealed with limestone mortar, sand from the lake shore, and walnut from the woodlands. It stands as a testament to the generations of winemakers who inspired fine winemaking in Ohio, guided the Catawba to regional prominence, and gave rise to the vinifera revolution.

Three growers and vintners—the Neals, the Landys, and the Ellithorpes—pioneered the 130,000-gallon Catawba Island Wine Company in 1873. At the time, it was said to be one of the largest of the four existing wine cooperatives in the district. By 1937, the winery complex was purchased by the Sandusky-headquartered Mon Ami Champagne Company. Taking its name from the French words for "my friend," Mon Ami was one of a few domestic wineries producing premium champagne in America. At its present location, forty workers produced 500,000 bottles of still wine and premium champagne. During the 1940s, the Mon Ami Restaurant was established to showcase Mon Ami wines with the local Zappone family's Italian cuisine.

In 1956, Norman Mantey, third-generation owner of Mantey Vineyards (now Firelands), purchased Mon Ami. Leon Adams, author of *Wines of America*, dubbed Mantey one of the busiest winemakers in America. His vaulted underground cellars were a tourist destination, and Mantey was a leading producer until he sold both Firelands and Mon Ami to

The winery, featuring stonework done
by George Loeb in 1872

designed in elegant comfort with a colorful décor, guests dine on American cuisine with a touch of French nouveau cuisine added to the mix. The menu pairs prime rib, grilled steak, rack of lamb, perch, walleye, and halibut with Mon Ami premium wines.

Tourists come from near and far for the Saturday seafood buffet and the Sunday brunch. They are dazzled with the Mon Ami California premium line— Chardonnay, Sauvignon Blanc, Shiraz, Merlot, and Zinfandel; they taste and compare it with the broader Mon Ami Ohio premium line—barrel-fermented Proprietor's Reserve Chardonnay, fragrant Riesling, spicy Gewürztraminer, full-bodied Proprietor's Reserve Cabernet, and berry Pinot Noir. Mon Ami also hosts banquets, celebrations, and weddings.

The Loretta Pagnini Cooking School at Mon Ami Restaurant & Historic Winery features classes and demonstrations taught by Pagnini, a chef and educator, in the teaching kitchen. Classes feature techniques, tips, and types of regional and worldwide cuisines. Guests may observe a chef at work, enjoy dinner while Pagnini (or an instructor) prepares a menu, assist as a sous chef, or take a cooking lesson.

Cincinnati's Meier's Wine Cellars in 1980.

In 2000, John Kronberg and Claudio Salvador formed Lonz Winery, Inc. and acquired Firelands and Mon Ami. "We wanted the place to come alive," they say. Firelands was modernized for vinifera wine production and for volume grape processing. "Our goal was to enhance and distribute Firelands, Mantey, and Mon Ami well and widely," Salvador says. "Currently, we retail 30 percent of our stocks and wholesale the remaining 70 percent of our stocks in Ohio, Michigan, Illinois, Kentucky, Nebraska, and Indiana."

At Mon Ami Restaurant & Historic Winery, landscapers spruced up the grounds and gardeners planted an arbor and rose garden. The interior was designed to offer customers authentic culinary and wine experiences. The existing kitchen was updated and a professional teaching kitchen was added. In the main dining room,

Mon Ami Restaurant & Historic Winery

Directions Take I-90 to Ohio 2 west. Exit at Ohio 53 and head right and north to Catawba Island. Turn left on Township Highway 238 east to Wine Cellar Road.

Hours Daily from 11–12 a.m.

Tours By appointment

Tastings Daily for individuals or groups

Gifts Log Cabin Gift Shop for jellies, jams, wines, and wine-related artifacts

Highlights at Winery Jimmie's Back Bar for original cocktails and menu; wine tasting bar; main dining room serving Saturday night buffets and Sunday brunches; Loretta Pagnini Cooking School on site

Events Fine dining, wine tasting, shopping, cooking classes, dancing, live entertainment, Sunday jazz on the lawn or by the fire

Restaurant American cuisine with emphasis on Mon Ami California and Mon Ami Ohio lines of wines, champagnes, and dessert wines; Chalet: Tuesday and Wednesday, steak; Thursday, pasta; happy hour 4–7 p.m.

Prices $5–$50; 10 percent case discount

Brand Names Mon Ami Ohio, Mon Ami California

Type of Production Classic and innovative

Method of Harvesting Mechanical Pressing and Winemaking: Bladder press for vitis vinifera and screw press for juice

Aging and Cooperage Stainless steel, temperature-controlled fermenters and tanks, American and French oak cooperage

Vineyards Founded 1950

County Ottawa

Appellation Lake Erie

Acreage 50

Waterway Lake Erie

Climate Moderating lake effect

Soil Clay loam

Varieties Chardonnay, Pinot Grigio, Riesling, Gewürztraminer, Cabernet, Merlot, Pinot Noir, Catawba, Niagara, Concord

Wines Proprietor's Reserve Chardonnay, Riesling, Pinot Grigio, Gewürztraminer, Chablis, Cellarmaster White, White Catawba, Haut Sauterne, Proprietor's Reserve Cabernet, Pinot Noir, Cellarmaster's Red, Concord, Reserve Cuvee, Brut, Extra Dry, Pink Spumante, Pale Cream Sherry, Rare Ruby Port, Spiced Wine, and others

Best Red Proprietor's Reserve Cabernet Sauvignon

Best White Proprietor's Reserve Chardonnay

Other Best Wine Methode Champenoise Champagne

Nearby Places to Visit Great Wolf Lodge indoor water park; Cedar Point Amusement Park

Sand Hill Vineyard and Winery

6413 South Hayes Avenue
Sandusky, OH 44870
Tel: (419)626-8500
E-mail: sndhvny@aol.com
Web site: www.ohiowines.org
Owner David Kraus
Winemakers David and Michael Kraus
Founded 2002

The enchanting Sand Hill Vineyard and Winery in Sandusky began as a boyhood vision of Ohio native David Kraus, now a New York resident and psychiatrist. "I had a lifelong dream to plant a vineyard and make wine," he says. After considering New York's Long Island and several other places, he returned home to plant his vineyard on fifteen acres of the Kraus family's 150-year-old farm.

His Sandusky calling was inspired by the area's lastingness and the benefits of a family-run wine venture. The winegrowing region surrounding Lake Erie was once dubbed the Lake Erie Grape Belt, and David was challenged by being a part of the Ohio wine revolution. "It has similarities to the Napa Valley and Bordeaux," says David, a self-taught viticulturist and enologist. The vineyard is appropriately named for the sandy ridge near Lake Erie where it is strategically situated. "Here the loamy sand with limestone subsoil and bedrock has proved ideal for wine grapes," David says. "The Catawba and Delaware grown here were similar to Chardonnay and Riesling." Sand Hill Vineyard was modeled after modern French vineyards, which David observed being planted on eastern Long Island. His brother Michael Kraus, who graduated with a BS in agronomy from Ohio State University, oversees the vineyards. Their goal is to produce high-quality wine grapes by densely planting the vines, spaced five feet apart and with six feet between each row, resulting in low yields of concentrated fruit with minimum irrigation and fertilization.

"We have one of the densest vineyards planted in Ohio, which contains varieties never, or rarely ever before, planted in Ohio," David says. The varietals are Viognier, Chardonnay, Riesling, Gewürztraminer, Sauvignon Blanc, Semillion, Cabernet Sauvignon, Cabernet Franc, Merlot,

Young vines at Sand Hill Vineyard and Winery

Phil Masturzo

two feet in width. Parts of the swinging thresher doors still remain on their original hinges.

When the barn was raised on supports to excavate the foundation, several discoveries were unearthed. Round glacial field stones were used as footers for the foundation wall with an overlay of limestone slabs. The livestock were protected from the elements by a solid limestone wall; the hay was aired and dried with construction of limestone pillars.

David takes a minimalist approach to winemaking. The grapes are machine harvested, then crushed and pressed and fermented. Long maceration on the skins extracts the maximum grape flavors. The wines are pumped, racked, and held in Italian stainless steel tanks. He practices minimal filtration for all wines, and only the white wines are sterile-filtered. Both the white and red wines are aged in stainless steel, with minimal oak aging for the red wines.

In 2005, Sand Hill Vineyard and Winery debuted its first wines, a spring release of white wines and a fall release of red wines.

Tempranillo, Touriga, Syrah, Italian Barbara and Nebbiolo, and three Sangiovese clones from Chianti, Brunella, and Romagna.

A renovated three-bay threshing barn with a silo serves as the tasting room and entertainment center. It was designed to meld the past with the present, resulting in one of the most unusual wineries in Ohio. When Ohio restoration experts Rudy Christian and Lindsay Graham authenticated the barn, they said it was one of the oldest timber-frame barns in Ohio, built between 1815 and 1820 on one of the earliest settlements in Sandusky. The enormous posts and beams were hand-hewn as timbers from the white oak trees in the virgin forests that the settlers found when they arrived, David says. The barn retains parts of the original polar siding, taken from virgin trees and cut in excess of

Sand Hill Vineyard and Winery

Directions From I-80, take exit 110/6A and proceed on Ohio 4 north to the winery on the left on Hayes Avenue.

Hours Monday–Thursday 11 a.m.–6 p.m.; Friday 11 a.m.–8 p.m.; Saturday 11 a.m.– 10 p.m.; Sunday 1–6 p.m.

Tours By appointment

Tastings Daily when open

Gifts Jellies, dessert toppings, cards, bags, jewelry, and gift baskets

Highlights at Winery Permanent facility is a restored early-1800s pioneer barn

Events Wine tastings; live music on weekends

Restaurant Breads, dipping oils, imported cheeses, and salads

Prices $9–$19; 10 percent case discount

Brand Name Sand Hill Vineyard and Winery

Type of Production Minimalist

Method of Harvesting By machine Pressing and Winemaking: Long maceration on the skins to extract maximum flavors

Aging and Cooperage Italian stainless steel and minimal oak aging

Vineyards Founded 2002

County Erie

Appellation Lake Erie Appellation of Origin

Acreage 15

Waterways Lake Erie, Sandusky Bay, and Pipe Creek

Climate Long and hot 200-day growing season, similar to Napa Valley or Bordeaux

Soil Loamy sand with limestone subsoil and bedrock

Varieties Viognier, Chardonnay, Riesling, Gewürztraminer, Sauvignon Blanc, Semillion, Cabernet Sauvignon, Cabernet Franc, Merlot, Tempranillio, Touriga, Syrah, Barbera, Nebbiolo, three clones of Sangiovese from Chianti, Brunello, Romagna

Wines Chardonnay, Riesling, Catawba, Merlot, Pink Catawba, Concord, Vidal Ice Wine

Best Red Syrah

Best White Chardonnay

Best Other Wine Riesling

Quote "Let the excellent site and clones express themselves." —David Kraus

Nearby Places to Visit Cedar Point Amusement Park; Lake Erie Islands

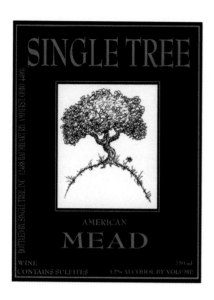

Single Tree Winery

12488 Baumhart Road
Amherst, OH 44001
Tel: (440)965-7777
E-mail: roby@singletreewine.com
Web site: www.singletreewine.com
Owners Todd and Keri Roby; Earl and
Sherry Winders
Winemaker Todd Roby
Founded 2004

Single Tree, a meadery and winery, was
established in 2004 in the farmlands along
Baumhart Road in Amherst, near the Lake
Erie grape belt. The winery was born when
Todd and Keri Roby partnered with their
neighbors Earl and Sherry Winders to
build a place that utilized the community's
people and resources.

The name Single Tree evolved from
family lore passed down from one
generation to the next. A "single tree" was
a two-pronged hitch that Keri's German
great-grandfather, Romie Urig, and
grandfather, Lester Urig, used to pull
their wagon through their Avon Lake
vineyards in the early twentieth century.
The "tree" was one that Todd's Scotch-Irish
grandmother, Alice Roby, a West Virginia
moonshiner, made famous when she
allegedly shot the sheriff and buried him
under it during Prohibition.

Todd's grandfather, Reynold "George"
Roby, was a jack-of-all-trades who taught
him how to make every wine imaginable
at home. Decades later, Todd, an infectious
disease specialist, and Keri, a McDonalds
Company employee, purchased the
seventeen-acre Roby family farm. "My
grandfather kept bees and gave his
beekeeping equipment to his friends,
Earl and Sherry Winders," says Todd,
"Bee experts, they gave us a gift of
honey. In 2001, I told them I made wine.
Later, they asked if we couldn't make
honey wine."

Over the next year, this enthusiastic
team researched mead, wine, and
equipment. Nick Mobilia, owner of
Arrowhead Winery in Westfield, New York,
encouraged them to open a winery. Ohio
vintners Lee Klingshirn of Klingshirn
Winery helped them find wine equipment,
and Dave Jilbert of Jilbert Winery allowed

them to use his ultra-filtration mead equipment.

Today, the work is divided four ways. Todd acts as president, winemaker, and marketer. Keri manages the inventory and the retail sales. Earl, who maintains the apiary, oversees the meadery/winery and its grounds. Sherry runs the office and does the accounting. "Everyone helps with the day-to-day operations," says Roby. His Western relatives introduced them to high-quality French and California wines, and the standard was set.

The Robys and Winders put in a gravel driveway, which passes through oak, hickory, ash, and maple trees to the pole barn, surrounded by farmlands and woodlands. They designed a spacious, high-ceilinged wine tasting room with lots of seating that is heated by a wood-burning stove. A large oak tasting bar, milled by the Amish from a downed tree on the property, dominates the room with its display of Single Tree mead, wines, and art posters. French doors lead to a grassy patio, a lovely place for picnics and dinners, then to a walking bridge through the woods.

The partners sourced honey from the Winders' apiary and blossoms from their seven acres of spelt. Roby planted grasses and wildflowers, also used in the mead. "We put in two acres of wetlands, an assortment of two thousand trees—many evergreens—and riparian buffers, which protected the natural waterways and provided habitat for pheasants," he explains. Winegrowers nearby provided grapes—Niagara, Concord, and Catawba.

An artisan producer, Single Tree makes two styles of mead. Traditional mead has a smelly bouquet that after three years transforms itself into a fragrant, clear gold, sweetened, honey-flavored wine. Honey wine/mead, a brilliant, delightfully fresh, pale clean beverage, is produced in 50-gallons lots utilizing ten-day ultra-filtration process. The popular dry Single Tree Riesling and Cabernet Sauvignon are augmented by the semi-sweet Concord, Catawba, Niagara, Vidal Blanc, and Blueberry wines. "We want to introduce everyone to our mead and wine and extend a warm welcome!"

Single Tree Winery

Directions From I-80, take exit 135 to Baumhart Road and travel south for 3.5 miles to the winery.

Hours Please call

Tours None

Tastings Daily when open

Picnics Guests are encouraged to bring picnics for outdoor patio

Highlights at Winery Picturesque farmland and woodlands; artisan meadery and winery

Events Themed outdoor picnics and festive barbeques during warm weather; live music—guitar, piano, jazz, and blues bands

Restaurant Simple fare—cheese, breads, snacks

Prices Moderate; 10 percent discount on case of wine

Brand Name Single Tree

Type of Production Modern winemaking; ultra-filtration method of mead-making

Method of Harvesting Hand-harvest grapes from Gore Orphanage Road vineyards in addition to blossoms and wildflowers

Pressing and Winemaking Basket press and traditional wine fermentation; ten day ultra-fermentation process for mead and aging processes

County Lorain County

Appellation American

Acreage Several acres of spelt and other wildflowers

Varieties Concord, Niagara, Catawba, Vidal Blanc, Mead, Blueberry, Cabernet Sauvignon, Riesling

Wines Same as varieties

Best Red Wine Cabernet Sauvignon

Best White Wine Riesling

Best Other Wine Mead

Quote "Our goal is to introduce everyone to wine!" —The Proprietors

Nearby Places to Visit Vermillion, small lakeside town with boating and fishing; Amherst, a quaint country town with shops, antiques, and curios

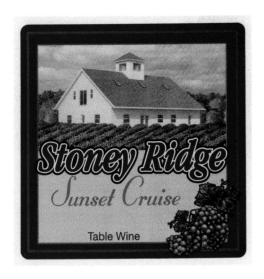

Table Wine

Stoney Ridge Winery

07144 County Road 16
Bryan, OH 43506
Tel: (419)636-3500
Fax: (419)636-7899
E-mail: stonridg@powersupply.net
Web site: www.stoneyridgewinery.com
Owners Phillip and Pamela Stotz
Winemaker Phillip W. Stotz
Founded 2002

Among the windswept farmlands and century-old New England houses in the northwest corner of the Buckeye State lies the
Stoney Ridge Winery in Bryan. The winery
adopted its name from the district's Stoney
Point schoolhouse, built on glacial stones
on the ridge of old Lake Erie.

A long, straight gravel road bisects stan-
chions of well-manicured, trellised vines
that take the visitor to a gabled, two-story,
stick-built Amish winery with an upstairs
loft and a spectacular viewing tower, which
affords a view of the ten-thousand-year-old
Indian Trail along the original beachhead of
Lake Erie. Beaver Creek, the site of an 1800s
flour mill, meanders east to old flood
plains, now planted in grapes and corn.
The residence of Phillip and Pamela Stotz,
Stoney Ridge's proprietors, and their
children sits to the south. Raised beds of
asparagus, cabbage, peppers, blackberries,
flowers, and herbs grow in front of the
vineyards to the west.

The Stotzes, locally born and bred, met
in the real estate business. Pamela expressed
to Phillip her interest in starting a farmer's
market on their forty-acre property. One
idea led to the next, and the market grew
into a plan to plant a vineyard and found a
winery. They tore out the soy beans and in
1996 planted the first acre of vines. New
vines have come every year thereafter. Their
concept was to provide their customers a
friendly and relaxing environment in which
to learn about wine. "Wine is meant to be
fun," Phillip says. "Friends and neighbors
like to stop by for an afternoon. Our business consists of 80 percent locals and 20
percent tourists."

People enjoy the harvest wagon tour
through the vineyard and flock to the rustic
tasting room. Shoppers crowd the gift store
in search of Stoney Ridge jams, jellies,
sauces, and pastas, or wines, cheeses, crafts,

and gift baskets. Others enjoy a glass of wine huddled by the stone fireplace in winter, or seated by the pond in summer. Cooks buy fresh estate-grown or local farm-raised organic produce one day a month, June to September.

Stoney Ridge Vineyards consist of twenty-nine varieties planted in productive, well-drained flood plains. "The silty loams are almost too productive, and minimize the grape production in the vines," Philip says. "So we prune back the leafy vines and utilize two types of vine placement. We grow grapes that can withstand the cold Midwestern climate."

Come fall, the Stotzes hand-harvest their French-American hybrids, starting in late August and finishing by late September. Their Chardonnay, Riesling, and Cabernet Sauvignon juice is purchased from Firelands Winery on North Bass Island. Other juice is bought from growers in Erie, Pennsylvania. The wines are processed in their modern wine-production center, which is equipped with Italian stainless steel, variable-capacity tanks, American oak cooperage, a hand-bottling line, a wine lab, and storage.

Stotz produces well-blended, ready-to-drink premium and table wines that undergo minimal to no aging. "We believe in the development of the right blend with the right degree of sweetness," he says. With aspirations to reach 10,000 gallons annually, Stotz turns over white wines in twelve to

fourteen weeks, red wines in fourteen to sixteen weeks (with the exception of the Cabernet), and sweet or fruit wines in ten to twelve weeks.

Stoney Ridge Winery produces sixteen different wines and categorizes 20 percent of its wines as dry to semi-dry. Some examples are the dry Chardonnay, the dry Riesling, and the two-year-old Cabernet Sauvignon. Some of their best-sellers include Sweet Barn Dance Red, Sunset Cruise, semi-dry Riesling, and Stormy Nights. "No wine drinker should apologize for their taste in wine," Stotz says. "Can it not be as varied as their taste in art?"

Directions From the Ohio turnpike, take exit 13/2, then go seven miles south on State Route 15 and two miles east on Road "G." Take a left on County Road 16 to the winery entrance.

Hours Tuesday–Thursday 12–6 p.m.; Friday and Saturday 12–7 p.m.; closed Sunday and Monday

Tours Yes

Tastings Daily when open

Gifts Farmer's market, produce, wine, Amish cheese, flowers, herbs, crafts, and gifts

Picnics Welcome at outside tables

Highlights at Winery Peaceful farm winery setting; unique country atmosphere by lakeside or fireside; circular staircase to owl's nest for view of vineyards; catered special events in upstairs loft

Events Summer steak fries; harvest wagon rides in vineyards

Prices $5.95–$14.95; 15 percent case discount; holiday specials

Brand Name Stoney Ridge Winery

Type of Production Traditional

Method of Harvesting By hand

Pressing and Winemaking Ratchet press

Aging and Cooperage Stainless steel with minimal American oak cooperage

Vineyards Founded 1996

County Williams

Appellation Ohio

Acreage 10

Waterway Beaver Creek

Climate Midwestern (first frost early October)

Soil Well-drained, productive silty loams

Varieties Chardonnay, Johannisberg Riesling, Cabernet Franc, Seyval Blanc, Marechal Foch, Vignole, Frontenac, Lacrosse, Traminette, and others

Wines Chardonnay, Johannisberg Riesling, Seyval Blanc, Barn Dance White, Cabernet Sauvignon, Marechal Foch, Barn Dance Red, Stormy Nights, Sweet Harvest, Golden Apple, Country Rhubarb, Blueberry Crisp, Cranberry Tart, Strawberry Blossom, Raspberry Patch, Sun-Ripened Peach

Best Red Barn Dance Red

Best White Riesling

Other Best Wine Sunset Cruise

Quote "No wine drinker should apologize for their taste in wine. Can it not be as varied as their taste in art?" —Phillip Stotz

Nearby Places to Visit Old Indian trail on Lake Erie beachhead; Amish country (Ohio, Indiana, Michigan corner)

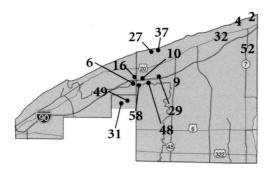

Lake Erie and Grand River Tour East

South River Vineyard at night

Biscotti Family Winery & Pasta

724 Whitney Road
Conneaut, OH 44030
Tel: (440)599-5555
E-mail: joepro@suite224.net

Joseph M. Biscotti's Family Winery & Pasta

2592 North Main Road
Hubbard, OH 44425
Tel: (330)534-8881

Owner Nancy Biscotti
Winemaker Joe A. Biscotti
Founded 2002

Located in a charming century house, the Biscotti Family Winery near Lake Erie in Conneaut is tucked into the contours of a lovely ninety-acre golf course and surrounded by one thousand maples and pines. This resort hamlet provides an escape from city life and a place to unwind.

Midwesterners Joe and Nancy Biscotti of Biscotti Restaurant fame left their many establishments in Greater Cleveland for a quieter lifestyle. "We thought of retiring," Joe says—but it was hard to keep Joe, a one-time PGA golf professional and instructor, idle, much less out of the kitchen where he has spent forty years as an Italian chef. And it was even more difficult to keep Nancy from her art or partnership as a woman entrepreneur.

In 1999, the Biscottis purchased a minority interest in Conneaut Shores, a golf club and restaurant. Next, they transformed the house on the property into their family home and converted the adjoining buildings, cellars, and decks into an Italian restaurant, a family winery, a gift shop, a logo design firm, and a gift basketry studio. "All the businesses complement each other," Joe says.

He also obtained a license to make wine. "I buy fresh juice and produce 2,000 gallons on site. We buy from different wineries to our taste in Ohio, Pennsylvania, and California and import wine from Italy." Biscotti makes wine in the old Italian style. "I am not a soulful winemaker like Arnie Esterer, but rather a marketing winemaker," he says. After Joe buys the fresh juice, he coddles the wine, adds yeast to commence fermentation, cold stablilizes the wine, then introduces basic ingredients and any residual sugars. Once aged appropriately, Biscotti wines are held in a variety of small cooperage in the cellars below the restaurant.

"Both the Sangiovese (which is aged in Hungarian oak) and the Muscatel have no residual sugar. I stick-stir each wine," he says. "A 12 to 14 percent fortified wine, the Old Italian Red is wine in the style Old Italians would make." Made from Chambourcin, Tony Soprano Red, a deep red, dry wine goes well with pasta.

"I always loved to cook, make wine, and run golf courses," says Joe, who started as a chef at age twenty-one. During the nineteenth and twentieth centuries, his Italian grandparents had a mountainside restaurant with stone-carved booths in Fogia near the Adriatic Sea. His parents came to the United States in the early 1900s.

"Traditionally our family invited someone to dinner almost every night," he says. "My mom always asked my friends if they were hungry."

The Biscotti Italian culinary legacy continues. Weekdays, Joe makes wine. Weekends, he cooks at Biscotti Family Winery & Pasta in Conneaut or their second establishment, Jos. M. Biscotti Winery & Pasta in Hubbard. "We serve old-fashioned Italian, Depression food—big portions of spaghetti with meatballs and great salads. Two people can have a great meal and wine for $35," he says with pride.

A porch with overhead pull fans and a pot-bellied stove serves as the restaurant. Dining options include cozy booths, cafe tables, a tasting bar with a fireplace, a wine cellar, intimate porch rooms, and deck tables with umbrellas on the golf course. Wine artifacts—a Biscotti stained-glass window, a basket press, a wine cask, and photographs of the Italian wine country—give character to the room. Celebrity shots of Johnny Desmond of the Glen Miller Band, baseball Hall-of-Famer Bob Feller, Chi Chi Rodriguez, Bryant Gumbel, Tim Conway, and Dean Martin highlight the picture gallery.

"We run five creative and integrated cottage industries," Joe says. While Joe makes wine for Merrill Lynch (one of their big national clients along with the Museum Shop, Disney Stores, and Harley Davidson), Nancy hand-paints wine glasses or puts up Nancy's Preserves, Jellies, Jams, and Marinara Sauce. Joe Pro Enterprises, Biscotti's design firm, customizes logos for golf gifts—putters, tees, ball markers, and divot tools—or theme gift baskets—gardening, beauty, travel, sports, and culinary arts—that Nancy designs as Grace Kelly Gift Baskets. There is no doubt about it—this place is a real adventure!

Biscotti Family Winery & Pasta

Directions Take I-90 to Conneaut. Go north on State Route 7 for eight miles, then left and west on State Route 531. Turn left on Whitney Road to the winery.

Hours 12–7 p.m. daily

Tours Daily

Tastings Daily

Gifts Variety of hand-crafted, painted, and designed wine glasses, jellies, jams, preserves, sauces, wine gadgets, and golf items

Picnics Welcome

Highlights at Winery Old World Italian atmosphere with good food and good wine; scenic golf course near Lake Erie with one thousand old-growth maples and pines

Events Spaghetti night; clambake

Restaurant Family-style Italian cuisine with interesting wine list

Prices $7.50–$20.00

Brand Name Biscotti Family Winery

Type of Production Hand-crafted old Italian style; 2,000 gallons in Conneaut and 1,000 gallons in Hubbard from grapes that are purchased; rest of wine custom-produced

Pressing and Winemaking Bladder press and old world methods

Aging and Cooperage Variety of small cooperage

Appellation Lake Erie and American

Varieties Niagara, Catawba, Concord, Chambourcin, Chardonnay, Riesling, Pinot Gris, Cabernet, Merlot, Zinfandel, Sangiovese, Berry sources

Wines Niagara, Riesling, Pinot Gris, Chardonnay, Catawba, Nancy's Blush, Pink Rose, Tony Soprano Red, Concord, Old Italian Red, Merlot, Cabernet Sauvignon, Elderberry, Peach, Strawberry

Best Red Old Italian

Best White Nancy's Blush

Other Best Wine Tony Soprano Red

Quote "Winemaking is an art similar to making love. Go slow and easy and enjoy yourselves." —Joe Biscotti

Nearby Places to Visit Conneaut Shores Golf Course; charter fishing at Conneaut Marina; Railroad Museum

Buccia Vineyard

518 Gore Road

Conneaut, OH 44030

Tel: (440)593-5976

E-mail: bucciwin@suite224.net

Web site: www.bucciavineyard.com

Owners Joanna and Fred Bucci

Winemaker Fred Bucci

Founded 1975

Just south of Lake Erie, the road to Buccia Vineyard in Conneaut takes the traveler through northeast Ohio farmlands and past the Conrail Crossing to an unexpected country getaway. Proprietors Joanna and Fred Bucci established the Buccia Vineyards in 1975 and added Buccia Bed and Breakfast in 1986.

"One stormy February night in the seventies, Fred, originally from North Kingsville, started home from AT&T and got stuck in a two-hour traffic jam. He decided it was time for a change," remembers Joanna, a native of Conneaut, who agreed wholeheartedly with her husband. They relocated to Ashtabula County.

"I was a home winemaker," Fred says. "We often tasted and talked wine with Arnie Esterer at Markko Vineyard. "So, planting a vineyard and making wine as a livelihood didn't seem far-fetched. I began to seriously study and to attend winemaking conferences at Ohio State University."

By 1975, the Buccis purchased a picturesque six-acre farm with a cottage and pastureland once used for beef cattle. They reconfigured the cottage into a modern family home. A series of odd buildings was magically transformed into a gabled winery, romantically reminiscent of Italy, with a patio for picnics, pink flower baskets, a grape trellis, and a vineyard.

A hand-carved wood-and-glass door leads to a vaulted hall decorated in a festive grape motif. Visitors have many choices for a good time. A library with books, brochures, and maps provides information on what to do and where to go in the area. A gift shop sells wine, shirts, and gadgetry for the aficionado. An oak upright player piano belts out tunes from the corner. Round and square tables for tasting wine or gathering with friends fill the hall. Murals of people, life, and events at the winery cover the walls. Daily (except Sunday),

Courtesy of the Ohio Wine Producers Association

color and taste." He notes the four-and-one-half-acre vineyard planted to Baco, Seyval Blanc, Steuben, and Vignoles. "We also grow Agawam, a red grape that makes a white wine. We acquired some two hundred grape cuttings from one of the last growers of Agawam in Madison, Ohio."

Buccia Vineyard has a reputation for producing wines in a classic manner with flair. "We make the best wines from the best grapes. We do the best job possible," Fred says. The hand-harvested grapes are brought to the winery, where they are crushed and pressed in a bladder press. The white wines are cold-pressed and fermented in stainless steel, then pumped over and held in stainless steel and other cooperage. The red wines are fermented on the skins in stainless steel, then pumped over and held in stainless steel and other cooperage.

"My goal is to make wine for people to enjoy," Fred says. Fairly priced, Buccia wines are sold at the winery for $6.84 to $12.26 a bottle. Buccia Vineyard produces Baco, Seyval Blanc, Reflections, Riesling, Vignoles, Agawam, Catawba, Maiden's Blush, Terrace White, Terrace Red, Pinot Gris, and Chambourcin. "Different winemakers make different styles of wine," he says, explaining that he tries to satisfy the changing tastes and demands of his target market.

For almost two decades, the Buccis have

guests stop by the winery to taste Joanna's delicious breads and assorted cheeses with Buccia wines.

"We offer visitors a total wine experience," Joanna says. "People book in advance over the Internet." The bed and breakfast extends from the winery's center. The rooms advertise comfy beds, hot tubs, high-tech stereos and TVs, microwaves, fridges, coffeemakers, and a patio with an arbor. The loft, reached by a ladder, has one of the only waterbeds in the wine country. The honeymoon suite features its own den and fireplace, a private patio with a fountain and hot tub, and an upstairs master suite.

The Buccia Vineyard, located in the Lake Erie Appellation of Origin half a mile from the water, has a long, cool growing season. Here the soils consist of four feet of sand with an underpan of twelve feet of gravel. "The soils are very well-drained," Fred says. "Our grape varieties have good won the hearts and minds of fiercely loyal customers. Recently, Joanna and Fred redesigned the Buccia Vineyard and Buccia Bed and Breakfast on a somewhat grander scale. They have a stately new entrance, an outdoor patio, and an expanded tasting room with a stone floor. The Buccis eagerly await your arrival and a chance to extend their hospitality to you!

Buccia Vineyard

Directions Take I-90 east for 62 miles to exit 235. Proceed north on State Route 193 toward North Kingsville. Turn right on East Center Street/U.S. Route 20, then left on Poore Road, then right on Gore Road to the winery.

Hours 12–7 p.m., except Sundays

Tours Upon request

Tastings Daily when open

Gifts Complete and wine-oriented

Picnics Welcome

Highlights at Winery Relaxed and romantic getaway; fun-filled activities; good atmosphere and friendly people; unique accommodations with hot tubs

Events Steak fry; ox roast

Restaurant Homemade breads and assorted cheeses

Prices $6.84–$12.26; 10 percent case discount

Brand Name Buccia Vineyard

Type of Production Classic winery

Method of Harvesting By hand

Pressing and Winemaking Bladder press with emphasis on good winemaking

Aging and Cooperage Stainless steel and other cooperage

Vineyards Founded 1975

County Ashtabula

Appellation Lake Erie

Acreage 4.5

Waterway Lake Erie

Climate Temperate, cool spring and summer, lake breezes, cold winters

Soil Sandy with underpan of gravel

Varieties Baco, Seyval Blanc, Steuben, Vignoles, Catawba, Agawam, Chambourcin, Riesling, Pinot Gris

Wines Baco, Seyval Blanc, Reflections, Riesling, Vignoles, Agawam, Catawba, Maiden's Blush, Terrace White, Terrace Red, Pinot Gris, Chambourcin

Best Red Baco

Best White Vignoles

Other Best Wine Agawam

Quote "We make good wine for people to enjoy!" —Fred Bucci

Nearby Places to Visit Conneaut Marina; covered bridges

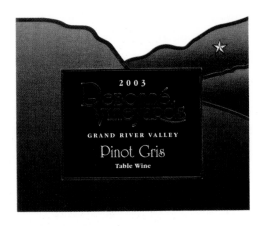

Chalet Debonné Vineyards

7743 Doty Road
Madison, OH 44057
Tel: (440)466-3485
Fax: (440)466-6753
E-mail: info@debonne.com
Web site: www.debonne.com
Owners Anthony P., Tony J., Rose M., and
Beth A. Debevc
Winemaker Vincent Negret
Founded 1972

The country road to Chalet Debonné Vineyards turns and bends, passing Mill Creek (part of the Grand River Valley Watershed) before it bursts with the beauty of emerald green vineyards and purple grape clusters.

In 1916, Anton Debevc departed Ljublana, Yugoslavia, an area rich in grapes and lumber, and migrated to West Virginia before finally settling in Madison, Ohio and establishing a farm with apples, pears, peaches, raspberries, grapes, and animals. He sold Concord and Niagara grapes to local farmers and customers in Cleveland. Anton's son, Tony J. Debevc, eventually purchased land next door and raised cattle and planted corn, wheat, and grapes.

Today, Tony P. Debevc recalls his grandfather, Anton, who entertained friends on his farm with chicken dinners and homemade wine. "During the Depression, those picnics were how he made a living," says Tony P., a 1969 Ohio State University horticulture major and pomology specialist. "An old inspector who knew Anton made wine then said my grandfather never took advantage of the situation. But that was how he fed his family and also farmed."

The heyday of Concord and Niagara grapes in northeast Ohio lasted from the mid-forties to the late sixties. The Debevcs gained name recognition and increased sales as grape growers to Smucker's and Welch's, producers of juice, jams, and jellies. In 1970, two enterprising generations of Debevcs embarked on a venture that dramatically changed their lives. Tony P., his spouse, Beth, and his parents, Tony J. and Rose M., pooled their resources and invested in Chalet Debonné Vineyards. "Our dream was to start a family-owned and -operated farm market on our vineyard estate," Tony P. says. In 1971, they crushed 5,000 gallons of their first Chalet Debonné wines. "We did well with Pink Catawba and River Rouge, hybrid blends. Our customers, many Slovenians, preferred sweet wine. A Slovenian highball was 50 percent dry Concord and Niagara sweetened with 50 percent soda." As the customers changed, their tastes changed, and they began to buy dry wines.

The hilltop Chalet Debonné has windowed atriums accented by a red bottle pattern. A draftsman of sorts, Tony P. Debevc designed the Chalet from his own drawings. He created a warm environment and a practical, modern winery. A wooden door opens to a great room with a brick fireplace, rustic barn walls, brick floor, an oak tasting bar, and wine-gift shop. People gather for grand banquets, simple summer fare, or a mid-winter escape to taste Debonné Vineyards premium varietals or Chalet Debonné Vineyard Select house wines. An open-air pavilion for parties and dances leads to a lawn and gazebo with unrivaled vineyard views.

The Debevc family has a reputation as both growers and vintners. Tony P. attributes this to Chalet Debonné's attention to detail in the vineyard and its high standards of sanitation in the winery. "We bring quality fruit and varietal character in from the field. Because Ohio has a European climate with four distinct seasons, the quality of our grapes is consistent, but the vintages can vary from year to year."

Vineyard manager Gene Sigel oversees 110 acres of vineyards comprising twenty-one varieties. He uses John Deere tractors and a mechanical harvester to implement the latest practices, such as high-cordon trellising, irrigation, leaf removal, crop thinning, use of micronutrients, and improved drainage. Enologist Vincent Negret oversees the technical winemaking procedures in the 26,000-case, state-of-the art wine production center. It is equipped with Bucher presses, stainless steel, temperature-controlled, jacketed fermentors and Southern Great Lakes, Demptos, Canton, and Radoux American white oak cooperage. Vincent does the crushing, pressing, processing, and wine aging.

Debonné Vineyards has won Double Gold and Gold Medals in major competitions around the world for Chambourcin, its signature Riesling Reserve, Pinot Gris, Chardonnay, Chardonnay Reserve, and Lake Erie Riesling.

A bottle of blush wine framed by the arched wooden doors of Chalet Debonné

Phil Masturzo

Chalet Debonné Vineyards

Directions Take I-90 to Madison. Go south on State Route 528. Go left on Griswold Road, left on Emerson Road, then right on Doty Road to winery.

Hours Tuesday 12–6 p.m.; Wednesday and Friday 12–11 p.m.; Thursday and Saturday 12–8 p.m.; Sunday 1–6 p.m. (Sunday hours June–October only)

Tours Upon request

Tasting Tasting trays daily when opened; private tasting by appointment

Gifts Wine gifts and casual clothing

Highlights at Winery Beautiful grounds and quality wines made from estate-grown fruit

Events Hot air balloon rally; candlelight cellar dinners

Restaurant Light fare, specialty sandwiches and dips

Prices $6.99–$12.99; 10 percent case discounts

Brand Names Chalet Debonné; Debonné Vineyards

Type of Production Traditional

Method of Harvesting Machine-harvested; ice wine grapes by hand

Pressing and Winemaking Vaslin Press and traditional winemaking

Aging and Cooperage Stainless steel tanks and American oak cooperage

Vineyard Founded 1916

County Lake

Appellation Lake Erie and Grand River Valley

Acreage 110

Waterways Grand River Valley and Lake Erie

Climate Lake Erie and Great Lakes microclimate influence

Soil Clay

Varieties Concord, Niagara, Catawba, Delaware, Reliance, Vidal Blanc, Seyval Blanc, De Chaunac, Foch, Chambourcin, Vincent, Rosette, Chardonnay, Riesling, Cabernet Franc, Pinot Gris, Pinot Noir

Wines Chardonnay, Chardonnay Reserve, Pinot Noir/Syrah, Merlot, Cabernet Franc, Chambourcin, Harmony, Riesling, Riesling Reserve, Vidal Blanc, Classic White Chablis, Classic Red, Country Selections Red, Delaware, River Blush, River Rouge, River Blanc, Pink Catawba, Classic Rose

Best Red Chambourcin

Best White Pinot Gris

Other Best Wine Vidal Blanc ice wine

Quote "Of course I don't look busy; I did it right the first time." —Tony P. Debevc

Nearby Places to Visit President Garfield's Mentor home; Geneva-on-the-Lake

Farinacci Winery, Ltd.

3951 West State Route 307
Austinburg, OH 44010
Tel: (440)275-2300
Fax: (440)275-1255
Web site: www.farinacciwinery.com
Owners Michael and Dawn Farinacci
Winemaker Michael Farinacci
Founded 2003

The Farinacci Winery, on thirty-eight acres of farmland, was named for generations of Farinaccis who made wine in their native Gildone, Italy, by the Adriatic Sea before migrating to Canada, Venezuela, and America.

Antonio Farinacci brought the family tradition of winemaking to Cleveland's Little Italy, where he settled in 1912. He later passed the practice on to his son Dominic. In 2004, Antonio's grandson, Michael, and his spouse, Dawn, broke ground for the first commercial Farinacci Winery in the country. The name "Farinacci," which means "miller of wheat" in Italian, recognizes not only their family's name but also their interest in agriculture.

As a boy, Michael Farinacci often accompanied his grandfather Antonio to the flat, fertile vineyards along Lake Erie. "They would bring home fresh grape juice," recalls Dawn, whose Eastern European family introduced her to wine. "Michael kept a five-gallon container for wine in the kitchen. One day when it was ready to drink, his father asked him, 'How is that wine?' Michael never realized his father knew he was secretly making wine."

Michael's grandfather and father made wine and vinegar. "They made wine from whatever grapes they purchased. There were no commercial wine yeasts for fermentation," he says. "They all were strict traditionalists with limited knowledge of wine chemistry. The wine was predicated on sugar content of grape juice in that particular year. If the sugar was high, it was wine. If the sugar was low, the wine was unstable."

Michael and Dawn purchased an old farm with a house and barn along State Route 307 and converted the barn into a modern winery with a patio, gardens, and walkways. The interior has a warm Italian décor accented by a fireplace and a curved tasting bar. A great room—used for wine tastings and live performances—is illuminated by candlelight and is furnished with comfortable chairs and tables. There is also a stainless steel fermentation center and storage area.

"We want to offer our customers a cross-section of different types and styles of wine.

No wine will be sold before it is ready," Michael says.

"We concentrate on wine," says Dawn, the office manager. The winery markets home winemaking supplies and kits, wine casks, and a premium line of Farinacci wines.

Farinacci Winery sources grapes from Italy, British Columbia, Washington, Oregon, and California. "The whole world is our vineyard," says Michael, a traditional winemaker. The grapes will eventually come from his estate vineyard. The juice is blended, balanced, and held in stainless steel tanks to which oak chips and staves are added for complexity. "We like our wines to be consistent."

Farinacci Winery, Ltd.

Directions Take I-90 to Ohio State Route 45 south toward Austinburg for 1/4 mile. Go right on State Route 307 west through Austinburg for 1.5 miles to a right turn at Farinacci Winery.

Hours Monday–Thursday 12–5 p.m. for home winemaking supplies; Friday 5–8 p.m.; Saturday 10:30 a.m.–7 p.m. at winery

Tastings By the glass

Gifts Winemaking supplies, kits, books, and wines

Events Fine and performing arts; country dancing and live music (classical, jazz, rock and roll); themed food events

Highlights Bucolic Grand River Valley setting; outdoor patio with wine-country views; wine casks in three-liter and five-liter boxes

Restaurant Italian fare—biscotto; focaccia biscotto; biscotti, cannoli, and cheeses

Prices $9.99–$19.99; 10 percent case discount; modest food prices

Brand Name Farinacci Winery, Ltd.

Type of Production Traditional

Aging and Cooperage 100 percent held in stainless steel and oak barrel

Appellation American

Varieties Cabernet Sauvignon, Merlot, White Merlot, Chardonnay, Pinot Grigio, Riesling, Muscat, Vidal Blanc

Wines Cabernet Sauvignon, Merlot, Luna Rossa, White Merlot, Chardonnay, Pinot Grigio, Riesling, Matrice White, Piesporter, Late Harvest Vidal, Riesling Ice Wine

Best Red Cabernet Sauvignon

Best White Riesling

Best Other Wine Chardonnay

Quote "People with great minds drink great wines." —Michael Farinacci

Nearby Places to Visit Geneva State Park in Austinburg; Shandy Hall in Unionville

2003
GRAND RIVER VALLEY
Cabernet
Franc

Ferrante Winery & Ristorante

5585 State Route 307
Geneva, OH 44041
Tel: (440)466-8466
Fax: (440)466-7370
E-mail: info@FerranteWinery.com
Web site: www.FerranteWinery.com
Owner Peter Ferrante
Winemaker Nick Ferrante
Founded 1937

The imposing Ferrante Winery & Ristorante in Harpersfield Township has a stone entrance with French doors, a peaked roofline with a cupola, and a garden and wrought-iron fence. A back terrace with gazebos is lit by lanterns for entertaining. The original farmhouse remains, and the barns are used for wine-making. Rows of well-tended emerald vineyards surround the property as far as one can see.

In 1937, Nick and Anna Ferrante, whose families sailed from Italy to the United States, lived in Cleveland's Collinwood district. Nick was a tailor by day and a winemaker by night at the Ferrante Winery. Anna saved their money and invested in land in South Euclid and Harpersfield Township. On weekends, the Ferrantes, accompanied by their sons, Peter and Anthony, drove to their Ashtabula country retreat—a farmhouse and barn where they also had gardens and vine-yards. In 1955, Peter married a woman named Josephine, and they relocated to Mentor. In 1957 Nick Ferrante died, followed in 1958 by Anna. This marked the end of an era.

Peter was both a carpenter and a wine-maker. On weekends, the Ferrantes packed their car and their eight children and motored to Harpersfield Township. In 1973, the Ferrante Winery in Collinwood formally closed. Peter, with the help of his brother, Anthony, hand-built the wood-and-stone Ferrante Winery, which opened in Harpersfield Township in 1979. Peter's daughter, Mary Jo Ferrante, recalls the operation: "My father made four different wines: Russo, Bianco, Concord, and Niagara. We also built a small Italian ristorante, where he made pizza to go with his Italian wines." A key decision maker in the family business,

Mary Jo handles winery and restaurant finances and, with her sister Carmel, oversees public relations and marketing.

Through the eighties, Peter and his son, Nick, expanded the Ferrante Winery. They purchased new equipment and planted new vineyards. "Then, the winery and restaurant were run as a small business," Mary Jo says. "By 1989, the family opened a full-service Italian restaurant and featured Josephine Ferrante's original recipes—wonderful lasagna, rolled meatballs, and spaghetti." The younger Ferrante women assumed increasingly more responsible executive positions in running the wine venture; the men managed the vineyard and winemaking.

In November 1994, a horrific fire gutted the restaurant but not the wine-production center or aging cellars. Undaunted, the Ferrantes redefined their life's dream. They hired Willoughby architect Joe Meyers to design a wine complex and Geneva contractor Raymond Builders to implement it. "We showcased Italian wine and food in a place with an Italian Old World feel. We wanted an open and airy restaurant with spectacular vineyard views and needed a functional winery," Mary Jo says.

Since 1995, when the Ferrante Winery & Ristorante reopened, business has boomed. The wine gift shop is crammed with merchandise and jammed with buyers. The fireside café with a wine bar and outdoor patio attract customers year-round. The more formal Ferrante dining room, with its floor-to-ceiling brick fireplace and overhanging balcony, boasts views from almost any table.

The Ferrante Winery produces classic vinifera and labrusca wines from its excellent 140-acre Ferrante Vineyards. "We emphasize practical winemaking," Mary Jo says. "We do minimum filtering and fining. Forty percent of the wines are sold off-premises, and 60 percent of the wines are sold in the restaurant or at the winery."

A winery of distinction, Ferrante is known for its Cabernet Franc and Cabernet Sauvignon, its Pinot Grigio, and its signature Grand River Valley Riesling. Generations of customers return, sold on the Ferrantes' commitment to quality wine and service to their customers.

Gazebos at Ferrante Winery

Courtesy of The Ashtabula County Convention and Visitors Bureau

Ferrante Winery & Ristorante

Directions Take I-90 to Geneva. Go south on State Route 534, then go right on State Route 307 to winery.

Hours Monday–Tuesday 10 a.m.–5 p.m.; Wednesday–Thursday 10 a.m.–8 p.m.; Friday–Saturday 10 a.m.–10 p.m.; Sunday 1–6 p.m.

Tours Educational and historic led by tour guide; tour and tasting $3 per person

Tastings Daily when open

Gifts Extensive gift shop

Highlights at Winery Great wine, great food, Great Lakes!

Restaurant Full-service Italian cuisine

Prices Wine $12–$32; 10 percent case discount

Brand Name Ferrante

Type of Production Vitis vinifera

Method of Harvesting Mechanical

Pressing and Winemaking Bladder press and traditional winemaking

Aging and Cooperage Stainless steel and American white oak

Vineyards Founded 1937

County Ashtabula

Appellation Grand River Valley

Acreage 140

Waterways Grand River and Lake Erie

Climate: Long, cool growing season

Soil Clay

Varieties Chardonnay, Riesling, Pinot Gris, Cabernet Franc, Cabernet Sauvignon, Merlot, Catawba, Concord, Niagara, Vidal Blanc

Wines Chardonnay, Chardonnay-Lake Erie, Pinot Grigio-Lake Erie, Riesling, Grand River Valley, Vidal Blanc-Grand River Valley, Bianco, White Catawba, Rosato, Jester's Blush, Pink Catawba, Cabernet Sauvignon Lake Erie, Cabernet Franc-Grand River Valley, Merlot, Rosso, Vidal Blanc Ice Wine-Grand River Valley

Best Reds Cabernet Sauvignon and Cabernet Franc

Best White Pinot Grigio

Other Best Wine Grand River Riesling

Quote "We showcase Italian food and wine." —Mary Jo Ferrante

Nearby Places to Visit Ashtabula County rivers, lakes, parks, and covered bridges

HARPERSFIELD
V I N E Y A R D
2002
PINOT NOIR
clos mes amis
Grand River Valley

Harpersfield Vineyard

6387 Route 307

Geneva, OH 44041

Tel: (440)466-4739

Fax: (440)466-4896

E-mail: info@harpersfield.com

Web site: www.harpersfield.com

Owners Patricia and Adolf Ribic; Joe and Tony Logan

Winemaker Wes Gerlosky

Founded 1979

The back country roads in Geneva roll past meadows, hayfields, tree farms, and a century-old village before they reach Harpersfield Vineyard in the heart of the Grand River Valley. A gravel driveway, which passes through rows of tended vineyards brilliant with mustard, statis, and clover, turns left at the bend toward an imposing stucco mission with wooden doors, a tower with a purple fleur-de-lis, and extensive grounds. Inside the large hall with beautiful hand-hewn beams and wrought-iron chandeliers lies a seating area that faces the lighted sandstone hearth and brick il fornaio. Here people relax by the fire as they taste wine paired with French cheeses, artisan breads, focaccia, and tortes fresh from the oven.

"*La vie est bonne*," booms Wes Gerlosky, a big man whose hair stands upright. He makes a sweeping gesture with his hand. Originally, this picturesque apple farm, orchard, and press house was the retirement home of Gerlosky's father. But unbeknownst to Wes, his wife, Meg, and his father had conspired otherwise. They convinced Wes the farm was the ideal place for home and family.

The younger Gerloskys purchased the property from Wes's father in 1979. Their introduction to fine French wine—Chablis and Chassagne Montrachet—by their tasting partner David Skiba inspired them to found a vineyard estate that same year. "We planted Chardonnay and Riesling, made wine, and sold grapes to vintners," Gerlosky says. "I made wine in the house until my wife said it was time to construct a building."

In 1985, with shovels in hand, Gerlosky and a friend used their architectural imagination and sweat equity to build a two-story winery. The upstairs consists of a system for bottling and corking by hand and case storage; the downstairs houses an underground stone cellar with tiers of American oak puncheons for winemaking and aging. Recently, the Gerloskys and partner Patrick Vautrin

steel, then aged in small oak barrels. "We are non-interventionists," Gerlosky says. Of its annual 4,000 cases, 75 percent of the wines are sold at the winery and 25 percent at wholesale only in Ohio.

Noted for his outstanding Burgundian-like Pinot Noir, Gerlosky follows traditional practices, fermenting the grapes 100 percent on the stems in big open stainless steel fermentors. Then the wine is held in American oak barrels. The cherry Pinot Noir, Clos Mes Amis, tastes of raspberries and cranberries, with medium tannin and a silky acidity. The deep garnet Pinot Noir, Clos Mes Amis Reserve Cuvee, is deep garnet with a rich, berry aroma and full spiciness.

Chardonnay St. Vincent, named for the patron saint of winegrowers, is rich, opulent, and full-bodied with intense perfume and fruit flavors. Named for Joseph the carpenter-father, the Chardonnay St. Joseph is a fresh, delicate, grassy blend, leaner in style and austere, with good acidity. A smoky blend with fruit flavors, Chardonnay Isidore, noted patron of gardens, has pronounced personality and acidity. Elegant richness, Chardonnay St.

sold their majority interest in Harpersfield Winery to Patricia and Adlof Ribic, Ohio wine lovers, and to Joe and Tony Logan, who had formerly held interest in the company.

Harpersfield has a bucolic atmosphere and a French outlook. "We have a distinct vision to make quality-oriented, estate-bottled wines from grapes reflective of the *terroir*—the characteristics of the land, the soil, the climate, and the grapes. The wines are magical and mysterious. We are both iconoclastic and slightly insouciant," Gerlosky says.

At harvest, the grapes are hand-picked into twenty-five-pound lug boxes. Grapes are lightly pressed using a low-tech Howard Rotapress, fermented in Canton Cooperage American oak and/or stainess

Vincent "Le Coeur du Cote" originated from grapes along the heart of the slope. Other Alsatian powerhouses include the Riesling, the Gewürztraminer, the Pinot Gris, and Auxerrois, dubbed the child of Pinot Gris.

"I am not a renegade," says Gerlosky says. "I am a traditionalist making wines from vinifera grapes that have grown around the world for centuries. If one works, it is a miracle what one gets in returns," quips this extraordinary winemaker.

Harpersfield Vineyard

Directions Take I-90 to Geneva. Go south on Route 528, then left and east for four miles on Route 307.

Hours Thursday 4–10 p.m.; Friday–Saturday 1–11 p.m.; Sunday 1–10 p.m.

Tours By appointment

Tasting Daily when open

Gifts Shirts and caps

Highlights at winery High-quality, estate-bottled vinifera wines; bucolic atmosphere; sustainable viticulture practices

Events Mapleleaf Theatre (live outdoor summer theatre); call for other events

Restaurant Wood-fired oven specialties —homemade breads, tortes, and foccacia; selection of international cheeses

Prices $12–$25; 10 percent case discount

Brand Names Harpersfield Vineyard

Type of Production Vinifera grapes

Method of Harvesting By hand into 25-pound lug boxes

Pressing and Winemaking Light pressing and non-intervention

Aging and Cooperage American oak and stainless steel

Vineyards Founded 1979

County Ashtabula

Appellation Grand River Valley

Acreage 18

Waterway Grand River

Climate Cool growing region, moderated by Lake Erie

Soil Platea silt loam

Varieties Chardonnay, Pinot Noir, Pinot Gris, Gewürztraminer, Cabernet Franc, Riesling, Auxerrois, Muscat Ottonell, Kerner

Best Red Pinot Noir

Best White Chardonnay and/or Riesling

Other Best Wine Pinot Gris and/or Cabernet Franc

Nearby Places to Visit Canoeing on the Grand River; Shandy Hall, home of Alexander Harper

The Lakehouse Inn Winery

5653 Lake Road
Geneva-on-the-Lake, OH 44041
Tel: (440)466-8668
Fax: (440)466-2556
E-mail: lakehouse@ncweb.com
Web site: www.thelakehouseinn.com
Owners Fagnilli family
Winemaker Sam Fagnilli
Founded 2002

State Route 534 travels north through the red-brick town of Geneva (an antique collector's dream), past its clock tower on Main Street and through a residential area before the road bends past small cottages and tall condominiums. It is here in Geneva-on-the-Lake where the white of the sun and the blue of the sky meet the gray-blue of Lake Erie. And it is here that The Lakehouse Inn Winery was situated to capture one of the most spectacular, breathtaking views—especially at sunset—in all of northeast Ohio.

Since 2000, proprietors Karen and Sam Fagnilli and their children, Andrea and Nathan, have envisioned this wine-country escape. Karen, who updates their picturesque Web site daily, says, "The majority of our bookings come over the Internet. We tried to appeal to people who cherish the leisure of reading a book or the quiet of their surroundings."

During the spring, summer, and fall, guests flock to this old-fashioned resort community, where they can pair good wine with delightful fare or play an afternoon game of backgammon. During the winter, visitors nest by the warm fire to taste wine with hors d'oeuvres or homemade soup and listen to classical music. Families can also enjoy swimming, fishing, boating, cycling, kayaking, walking to nearby attractions, covered-bridge and winery tours, horseshoes, bocce ball, croquet, and sunset bonfires at the beach.

The Fagnilli family renovated and furnished the 1940s Collinger Hotel and cottages in New England green and white. Andrea, who manages the inn, artistically decorated and furnished the guest rooms, suites, beach house, and cottages. The suites and beach house feature Jacuzzis and lake views. The great room doubles as a living room and dining room. The special-occasion dinners—pork or beef tenderloin and grilled salmon—and the hot breakfasts have great appeal for the guests.

A lakeside building, the beach house, an atelier of sorts, consists of a luxury cottage upstairs and a winery, cellars, a tasting room, and a deck downstairs. The tree-lined lawns—dotted with red cascading geraniums, picnic tables, viewing benches, and flower gardens—sweep to the beach. "We are open to the public as a year-round bed and breakfast. People tour the wine country with us, taste our wine and food, and stay the weekend," say Sam, who also is the winemaker.

A self-taught enologist, Sam regularly attends winemaking classes at Ohio State University and Purdue University. He names Arnie Esterer of Markko Vineyards as his mentor. The first year, 2001, the Fagnillis purchased finished juice, which they blended and bottled. Ready for 2002, the first wines released included Lakehouse Inn Winery Grand River Valley Appellation Riesling, Cayuga, and Chambourcin. They also continue to purchase grapes from Chalet Debonné and other vineyards. "We try to purchase mostly Grand River Valley or Lake Erie Appellation grapes, but due to the supply and demand, we also purchase some California and Oregon grapes," Sam says.

Once the grapes arrive at the winery, they are crushed and fermented. The Chardonnay, for example, is barrel-fermented in small, 60-gallon French Nadalie oak barrels, and the Pinot Grigio and Riesling are fermented in stainless steel. The Merlot, Pinot Noir, and Cabernet Franc, however, are fermented in stainless steel and barrel-aged. The Chardonnay and Cabernet Franc are aged in barrel for eighteen to twenty-four months before additional aging in bottle. Similarly, the Riesling is held in stainless steel tanks for up to twelve months, with additional bottle age. Typically, the Merlot is oak-aged for eight months in barrel, then the balance held in stainless steel tanks. "Less is more," Sam says of his approach to winemaking. "Patience is my teacher. Sometimes a wine will taste good, and sometimes it will taste off. With patience, the wine usually improves."

Courtesy of the Ohio Wine Producers Association

The view from The Lakehouse Inn Winery

94

The Lakehouse Inn Winery attracts customers from as far away as Columbus and Cincinnati. Of course, southern Clevelanders are their big supporters. Patrons' tastes vary from dry to semi-dry to sweet. They typically order a dry Cabernet Franc or a dry Pinot Grigio, followed by Summer Breeze, a light and fruity blend of Riesling and Cayuga.

The Lakehouse Inn Winery

Directions Take I-90 to Geneva, then head north on State Route 534 for 6 miles to winery.

Hours May–October, Thursday–Friday, 6–9 p.m., Saturday–Sunday, 1–9 p.m.; November–October, Saturday–Sunday 1–6 p.m.

Tours Educational tours of local wineries by appointment

Tastings $1 per taste, $5 for five tastes and a complimentary glass

Gifts Small gift area

Picnics Snacks and meals with advance notice

Highlights at Winery Spectacular views and sunsets of Lake Erie; small family-owned and -operated; comfortable bed and breakfast and cottages on Lake Erie

Events November Vino Novello Italian Dinner celebrates the new Harvest wines; May Bacchus Festival features barrel tasting with Italian cuisine and hors d'oeuvres

Prices $8–$24; 10 percent case discount

Brand Name The Lakehouse Inn Winery

Production Traditional but drinkable

Method of Harvesting Mechanical

Winemaking Minimal

Aging and Cooperage French Nadalie small oak barrels and stainless steel tanks

Vineyards Purchased grapes from local vineyards

County Ashtabula County for Lake Erie grapes; Geauga County for Grand River Valley

Appellations Lake Erie and Grand River Valley

Waterways Lake Erie

Climate Long, cool growing season

Soil Mixture of sandy topsoil and rocky clay in Lake Erie; sandy loam in Grand River

Wines Cabernet Franc, Merlot, Chambourcin, Pinot Grigio, Chardonnay, Riesling, Cayuga

Best Red Cabernet Franc

Best White Pinot Grigio

Other Best Wine Summer Breeze

Quote "Less is more." —Sam Fagnilli

Nearby places to visit Geneva State Park and Marina; Ashtabula Harbor

Laurello Vineyards

4573 State Route 307 East
Geneva, OH 44041
Tel: (440)415-0661
E-mail: wineabite@laurellovineyards.com
Web site: www.laurellovineyards.com
Owners Larry and Kim Laurello
Winemaker Larry Laurello
Founded 2002

Named in honor of the Laurello family, Laurello Vineyards in Geneva is derived from the Italian word meaning "laurel tree." As the tradition goes, Olympians were honored by their peers by being crowned with laurel wreaths. In that same spirit, the Laurello family salutes its guests and visitors by inviting them to share in the authentic Laurello wine experience.

"The secret to a good life is passion, hard work, and the love of family," says Larry Laurello, winemaker, who with his wife, Kim, manager, started the winery in 2002.

In 1944, Larry and Kim's grandparents, Josephine and Cosmo Laurello, ran a small winery in Ashtabula. Decades later, when Larry and Cosmo were driving past a vineyard along I-90, Cosmo asked his grandson to stop for grapes. Larry jumped the fence and returned with several clusters. During the nineties, when that same eighty-six-acre Burkholder Orchard and Vineyard came up for auction, the Laurellos bid on the property and won.

They renovated the former Burkholder open-air market into a Tuscan-style mission. "Our goal is to make people feel welcome and part of our family," Kim says. A step inside the winery is like an escape to Italy. A grand hall with gold walls, tiled floors, and a terra-cotta ceiling features a painting of the island of Capri above the bandstand. On weekends, live music fills the room. "We have clients who like to talk or to listen to music over good food and wine," Kim says. Others guests enjoy the tasting bar, the café, the gift shop, and the photo gallery. On Fridays, the family bakes homemade pizzas in their Italian il fornaio. On Saturdays, they prepare appetizers and panini sandwiches, or grill chicken and steak. A wooden door opens to a room that was once an ice cooler and now is booked for private wine-cellar parties.

"Friends and family have donated their time and creativity," Kim says. "Multiple generations have given of themselves in the tradition of being a family." Her late uncle gave his dining room table, her mother-in-law designed the swags and banners, and her children and their friends painted the winery and cellar.

Laurello Vineyards owns eighty-six acres of Niagara and Concord vines planted in tight clay soils. These estate grapes are used to make one wine, Naso Rosso, which means "red nose" in Italian. The rest of the grapes are sold to Welch's. Grower Tony Debevc provides the other grapes—Chardonnay, Pinot Noir, Cabernet Franc, Chambourcin, and Vidal—and grower Arnie Esterer supplies the Riesling. California growers ship whole bunches of Sangiovese and Merlot in refrigerated trucks.

Another wooden door leads to the wine-production center. The grapes are crushed and pressed in a Vaslin Press, then fermented in stainless steel and/or oak cooperage. All the wines are held and aged in either stainless steel and/or American or French oak barrels with

A selection of Laurello Vineyards wines

Courtesy of the Ohio Wine Producers Association

additional time in bottle. Larry takes a minimalist, somewhat eclectic approach to fine winemaking.

Another relaxation spot is the outdoor patio, with its umbrella-covered tables and chairs surrounded by green lawns and perennial gardens. Customers gather in the open air or under the new canopy to taste the Laurello Vineyards Cabernet Franc, Cosmo, and Pinot Noir (a Gold Medal winner), their favored reds, or the Laurello Vineyards Chardonnay or Rieslings, their favored whites. Cosmo, an outstanding California blend of 75 percent Sangiovese and 25 percent Merlot, is named for their grandfather. Sweet Genevieve, an ice wine, is dubbed for Kim's mother. Every Easter Kim's father gave Genevieve, his spouse, and his daughters a gardenia. "My mother loved that fragrant flower," Kim says, "and this memory continues through the gardenia on the label of this wine."

Laurello Vineyards

Directions Take I-90 east to exit 218 at Geneva. Go south on State Route 534 and left on State Route 307 for 1.5 miles to the winery on left.

Hours Monday–Tuesday open for private functions only; Wednesday–Thursday 1–8 p.m.; Friday–Saturday 1–10 p.m.; Sunday 1–6 p.m.

Tours Educational tours of the wine-production center

Tastings Scheduled in advance for any size group

Picnics Backyard patio and lawn suitable for picnics

Highlights at Winery Italian family welcomes public to their cantina; high-quality dry wines; authentic Italian cuisine; top entertainment

Events Laurello Vineyard-Lakehouse Inn and Winery Progressive Dinner "Vino Novello" Bacchus Fest: Springtime Opening of the Wine Cellars

Prices $7.50–$35.00; 10 percent case discount

Brand Name Laurello Vineyards

Type of Production Vinifera and French hybrids

Method of Harvesting By hand and by machine

Pressing and Winemaking Traditional

Aging and Cooperage American, Hungarian, and French oak

Vineyards Founded circa 1930s

County Ashtabula

Appellation Grand River Valley

Acreage 86

Waterways Lake Erie and Grand River

Climate Long, cool growing season

Soil Clay

Varieties Cabernet Franc, Merlot, Sangiovese, Chardonnay, Pinot Grigio, Niagara, Catawba

Wines: Late Harvest Vidal Blanc, Ice Wine, Chardonnay, Pinot Gris, Chambourcin, Riesling, Vidal Blanc, Naso Rosso, Niagara, Concord, Catawba

Best Red Cabernet Franc

Best White Chardonnay

Other Best Wine Pinot Noir

Quote "The secret to a good life is passion, hard work, and the love of family." —Larry Laurello

Nearby Places to Visit Seventeen covered bridges; Geneva-on-the-Lake

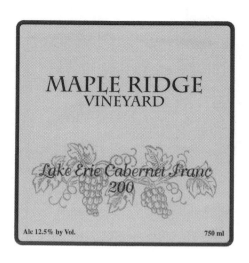

Maple Ridge Vineyard

6326 Dewey Road
Madison, OH 44057
Tel: (440)298-3290
E-mail: mapleridgev@ncweb.com
Owners Jim and Patti Iubelt
Winemaker Patti Iubelt
Founded 1994

The road to Maple Ridge Vineyard in Madison is a paradise for people who love animals, farms, and a natural lifestyle. Come spring or fall, visitors who stop by this charming vineyard estate are greeted by Paint horses, Navajo Churro sheep, Alpine goats, Italian honey bees, Rhode Island Red Hens, and wolf hounds that freely roam the grounds.

A beige farmhouse with green trim, accentuated with purple and yellow flowers, adjoins the tasting room, the winery, and a patio with a green umbrella and café tables and chairs. A red barn looms in the distance. This is as ecologically as pure a home as owners Patti and Jim Iubelt could create for their children, Jessica, Tricia, and Jim.

A registered nurse in pediatrics, Patti descended from several generations of agriculturists. Her father, an organic farmer and an advocate of Rodale Press, taught her how to farm cool-climate conditions. Her husband Jim, an applications engineer and marketing guru, has toured small world-class wineries and vineyards and passionately read about and tasted wine. Their paths crossed over a mutual love of wine, and they settled in the Ohio wine country.

The Iubelts built a totally self-sustaining wine farm in the old European tradition. "Maple Ridge is a diversified, organic-certified farm that is more a lifestyle than a method of production. The farm depends on the synergistic environment where all the farm activities contribute to the entire operation," Jim says. Friends and visitors are invited to buy their farm products—wine, fruits, vegetables, honey, vinegar, poultry, lamb, and wool—at the farm or at Cleveland's North Union Farmer's Market.

In 1994, the Iubelts purchased twenty acres of farmland forty-five miles from Cleveland and eight miles from the water. In the southernmost part of the Lake Erie Appellation of Origin, Maple Ridge Vineyard stands at 1,200 feet above sea level, the highest altitude of any vineyard in Ohio. Along the top of the property, a treeline breaks the wind off the lake and results in warmer temperatures over the vineyard. Mean temperatures equal Burgundy and Bordeaux, averaging 2,300 mean degree days. The soil consists of six feet of packed clay, with a base of shale. This winning combination adds soil nutrients and amplifies grape flavors.

The Iubelts consulted with Herman Amberg, a viticulturist active in wine education at Cornell University, on the preparation of their northwesterly-sloped three-acre vineyard. At the onset, Gold Seal Winery imported plants from France, and the cuttings were sent to Amberg, who grafted them onto 3309 rootstock, which he sold to Maple Ridge Vineyard. Clonal blocks were planted to Chardonnay, Riesling, Pinot Gris, Cabernet Franc, and Pinot Noir. The vines are trellised at a height of thirty-six inches, then shoots are positioned vertically. This creates a higher fruit zone for grape maturation and increases the survival of the vine during the harsh winters. "We are the only winery in Ohio making wine from certified grapes," Jim says.

Maple Ridge Vineyards uses a tractor with a mechanical grape hoe to weed around surrounding vines. The Iubelts fertilize the vines with seaweed, kelp, humic acid, mined rock powders, and manure. "We strive for the perfect nutrients," says Patti, who manages the vineyard operations. A recipient of a Sustainable Agricultural Research and Education grant, Patti studies the impact of a natural compost tea and its benefits for their vineyard, as well as for Markko's and Tarsitano's. Every seven to ten days during the growing season, a Bordeaux mix of copper and lime or sulfur is sprayed on the vines to control fungus.

Since 1999, the Iubelts have followed the highest organic winemaking practices. By October, the last grapes are hand-harvested into lug boxes with a yield of two tons per acre. All the wine fermentation and barrel aging takes place in a combination of Italian stainless steel and French oak cooperage. Once blended, both the red and white wines are bottled unfiltered and given up to one year additional time in bottle. The popular Cabernet Franc comes in three styles: a berry-flavor wine and two reserves wines, one a French Pomerol style and the other a French Bordeaux style (with lamb orders only), starting at $25. The exquisite Chardonnays include two reserve wines, one a White Burgundy style and one a French Montrachet style, a library reserve, French Chablis style wine, and a Sauterne, from $21 to $35. The best Chardonnays are barrel-fermented in 60-gallon or 120-gallon French Allier oak barrels, then blended, bottled, and aged.

As a 400-case producer of small lots of high-quality American-certified organic wines, Maple Ridge Vineyard has carved out an excellent reputation. "Our wines are made in the vineyard; therefore, we are concentrating on caring for the life in our soil, which allows our wines to exhibit their true varietal characteristics," they say.

Maple Ridge Vineyard

Directions Take I-90 toward Madison. Go south on State Route 528 for four miles, then west on Mosley Road; head left and south on Dewey Road to third drive on right.

Hours Friday 1–6 p.m.; Saturdays, 2–7 p.m.

Tours Guided, certified organic farm with sheep, goats, horses, and chickens

Tastings During hours when open

Gifts Produce, honey, vinegar, and wine

Picnics Bring your own

Highlights at Winery Small, diversified organic farm; certified organic European-style wines

Events Wine and produce sold at Cleveland's North Union Farmer's Market on Shaker Square, Saturdays, April–December, 8 a.m.–12 p.m.

Prices $15–$50; 10 percent case discount

Brand Names Maple Ridge Vineyard

Type of Production Small lots

Method of Harvesting Hand-harvested; two tons per acre

Pressing and winemaking Bladder press; some French oak barrel fermentation; some Italian stainless steel fermentation

Aging and Cooperage Some French Allier and Nevers oak barrel-aging and Italian stainless steel; additional bottle age

Vineyards Founded 1996

Appellation Lake Erie

Acreage 3

Climate Cool climate

Soil Clay

Varieties Cabernet Franc, Chardonnay, Pinot Gris, Pinot Noir, Riesling

Best Red Cabernet Franc

Best White Chardonnay

Other Best Wine Pinot Gris

Nearby Places to Visit Pioneer Waterland; Geneva State Park; Geneva-on-the-Lake

Markko Vineyard

4500 South Ridge Road
Conneaut, OH 44030
Tel: (440)593-3197 or (800)252-3197
Fax: (440)599-7022
E-mail: markko@suite224.net
Web site: www.markko.com
Owner Arnie Esterer
Winemakers Arnie Esterer and
Linda Frisbie
Founded 1968

As you wind your way off I-90 in Kingsville and head north, a turn on South Ridge Road leads to a jewel of a winery. Here the road passes through a splendor of woodlands, interspersed among century-old farmhouses with green pastures and leafy vineyards. Just as South Ridge becomes a country dirt road, stone pillars mark the entrance to Markko Vineyard.

The rustic winery founded in 1968 by Arnie Esterer and Tim Hubbard was named for its original Finnish dairy owners. Markko was the first Ohio winery to pioneer vitis vinifera varieties: Chardonnay, Cabernet, and Riesling. For more than thirty-five years, this two-thousand-case producer has championed these classic, estate-bottled, vintage-dated wines.

Wine grapes have grown in this historic viticultural district called the Lake Erie Appellation of Origin for more than 150 years. The cold winters on Lake Erie are one of struggle and survival for Markko Vineyard. The vines often face ten-below-zero temperatures that test the life of the vine and the vigor of the budwood. Markko Vineyard reflects the *terroir*, a French expression that defines all physical aspects that influence the personality of the wine.

The fourteen-acre Markko Vineyard sits atop a ridge with a three-mile view to Lake Erie. Markko trellising is characterized by five-foot-high wire cordon, which creates great exposure to sunlight and thus better fruit and an improved grape climate. "How we manage the trellis system and the cultivation process is very important in maximizing the quality of the fruit," Esterer says. The low crop yield imparts a distinct character to the wine—one of depth, complexity, and intrigue. "Each wine speaks for itself, and the aroma, flavor, and body vary from harvest to harvest."

How did Esterer learn to produce a world-class Chardonnay? He exchanged his time for the tutelage of one legendary wine

Arnie Esterer

Phil Masturzo

figure, New York wine expert Dr. Konstantin Frank. Esterer was also inspired by Maryland's Boordy Vineyard winemaker Philip Wagner, a red wine specialist, and California winemaker Andre Tchelistcheff of Georges de Latour fame. But it was Dr. Frank who most influenced Esterer's philosophy.

"Quality in wine, grapes, and soil with honest winemaking practices are the classic components that Dr. Frank emphasized," Esterer says. Applying this approach, he established a demonstration vineyard consisting of Chardonnay, Cabernet, Riesling, Pinot Noir, and Pinot Gris. "Chardonnays from different vintages produce a rainbow of wine with no preconceived style," he says. Dr. Frank advocated three marriages for a

vineyard to be successful: the soil with the rootstock, the rootstock with the scion, and the scion with the climate. Markko Vineyard's Homage Chardonnay was made as a tribute to Dr. Frank.

Wagner believed that red wine grapes produced better wines when blended. Tchelistcheff emphasized that the earlier one made the marriage of grapes in red wine, the better the marriage. "It is this unity that gives wine its personality," Esterer says.

All winemaking and barrel aging at Markko take place below ground in a Burgundian environment, including a heavy cellar mold brought from France. Esterer and vineyard manager Linda Frisbie work as a team to make the wine. The Chardonnay is barrel-fermented and aged in fifty-nine-gallon, lightly toasted, air-dried, American white oak barrels. The Cabernet and Pinot Noir are fermented in stainless steel, then aged for two years in similar American white oak barrels. The Riesling is fermented and held in stainless steel for aging. "The lighter toast provides more expression in the wine, and the taste of the fruit comes forward," Esterer says.

The late Leon D. Adams, author of *Wines of America*, told the American Wine Society Conference that Esterer made the finest Johannisberg Riesling in North America in 1972. Adams wasn't sure if the winemaker could repeat it. In 1997, the American Wine Society presented the Award of Merit, its highest honor, to Esterer.

Markko Vineyard

Directions From I-90 at exit 235, head one-half mile north on State Route 193 to Kingsville, then right for three miles on South Ridge Road to the winery driveway back into the woods.

Hours Monday–Saturday 11 a.m.–6 p.m.; closed Sunday

Tours Self-guided

Tastings Daily when open

Gifts Wine-related

Picnics Welcome

Highlights at Winery Lovely wooded setting; outdoor tasting deck; great destination for dog-lovers; earthy experience tasting some of Ohio's best vitis viniferas

Events Blessing of the Vines, third Saturday in May; Odds & Ends Sale, third Saturday in September

Prices $12–$54; 10 percent case discount

Brand Name Markko Vineyard; Covered Bridge; Excelsior Champagne

Type of Production Traditional

Method of Harvesting: Hand-harvested into cart-mounted lug boxes; two to three tons per acre

Pressing and Winemaking Vaselin press and Burgundian winemaking

Fermentation Barrel-fermented Chardonnay in American oak casks, stainless steel, temperature-controlled, fermented Cabernet, Pinot Noir, and Riesling

Aging and Cooperage Traditional, 59-gallon American, oak-aged Chardonnay, surlees; Pinot Noir and Cabernet also American oak-aged for two years; Riesling held in stainless steel

Vineyards Founded 1968

County Ashtabula

Appellation Lake Erie

Acreage 14

Waterway Lake Erie

Climate Temperate growing season, cool spring and summer, lake breezes just right for wine production; cold winters one of struggle and survival

Soil Elongated plateau comprised of silty, loamy soil and glacial till

Varieties Chardonnay, Riesling, Pinot Gris, Cabernet, Pinot Noir

Wines Excelsior Brut Methode champenoise Champagne, Chardonnay, Riesling, Pinot Gris, Cabernet, Pinot Noir

Quote "Each wine speaks for itself." —Arnie Esterer

Nearby Places to Visit Covered bridges at Creek Road, State Road, and Middle Road

Lake Erie
SEYVAL BLANC
A Semi-Dry Table Wine

Old Firehouse Winery

5499 Lake Road

Geneva-on-the-Lake, OH 44041

Tel: (440)466-9300

Fax: (440)466-8011

E-mail: info@oldfirehousewinery.com

Web site: www.oldfirehousewinery.com

Owners Dave Otto, Joyce Morgan, and Don Woodward

Winemaker Don "Woody" Woodward

Founded 1988

Situated in the resort town of Geneva-on-the-Lake, the Old Firehouse Winery captures the imaginations of guests and visitors who long for a taste of nostalgia. The red-shingled winery, once the town's first fire station, and "Old Betsy," the 1924 Graham Brothers fire truck, are an invitation to experience life along ‾ the Lake Erie shore.

What enticed David Otto, Joyce Morgan, and Don Woodward to start a wine venture? They loved the rambling nineteenth-century firehouse with a big red barn and open space. The town had a storied reputation as a fashionable 1920s resort, and the region had a legacy for producing fine wine. "We only make wines we like, and we only make what sells," says Don Woodward, an advocate for quality grapes from the Lake Erie Appellation.

The story of the Old Firehouse Winery is deeply linked to the history of the town's first firehouse. Woodward's grandfather, "Pop" Pera, was one of seven businessmen who formed the Geneva-on-the-Lake Fire Department in 1924. "After fruitlessly battling blazes with a bucket brigade, the seven businessmen purchased a 1924 Graham Brothers fire truck," says Don, a third-generation volunteer firefighter, EMT, and former assistant fire chief.

With the arrival of the fire truck, the firemen needed a barn and a chief. So, one Emory Tyler, a fireman, happily donated his barn, which became the fire station. By 1987, the story had come full circle, when Dave Otto, Joyce Morgan, and Don Woodward purchased an old red barn and a rusty fire truck. "We had the formula for the Old Firehouse Winery!" Woodward says.

Old Firehouse customers come from near and far to reach this favorite outpost, where there is something for everyone—

especially families with children. They often escape to adjacent Erieview Park, with its rides, slides, roller coaster, train tour, video arcade, and billiard parlor. Shoppers head for Nature's Touch, which offers an assortment of novelties and gifts. But most guests begin their visit with a good meal accompanied by Old Firehouse wines and a tour.

Set amongst a stand of tall pines, the winery and restaurant consist of a series of decks, patios, a gazebo, and walkways. A bandstand features live music throughout the summer. Small and large groups sit at tables in the open, under red and white tents, in the latticed gazebo, or under green umbrellas. "The atmosphere is both informal and friendly, a place for fun and relaxation," Woodward says. Distinguished

by variety and price, the full-service restaurant features Mexican and American cuisine on the outdoor grill, as well as appetizers, barbequed chicken and ribs, healthy salads, and hearty sandwiches.

As winemaker, Woodward follows three cardinal rules handed down by Tony Carlucci, the winemaker who made the winery's first six wines. "He said there is no mystery in making wine. Use sound grapes, clean premises, and watch for light and air," he says. The Old Firehouse and Firehouse Cellars brands consist of 45 percent vitis vinifera grapes and 30 percent vitis labrusca grapes and other fruit. "Close to 70 percent of the grapes come from Tony Debevc, a local grower, and 30 percent of the grapes and fruit come from New York," Woodward says. "Ninety percent of the wine is made at the eight-thousand-gallon Geneva-on-the-Lake Winery, and all the wine is sold in Ohio."

During harvest, the white grape juice is bought outright and then finished and held in stainless and oak barrels. Some red grapes are crushed, pressed, and fermented on the premises and held in stainless and oak barrels. Select wines, such as The Firehouse Cellars Chardonnay and the Firehouse Cellars Cabernet Sauvignon, are crafted and bottled by hand at the winery. So, the next time you visit Geneva-on-the-Lake, be sure to experience the "heart of it all" at the Old Firehouse Winery.

Old Firehouse Winery

Directions Take I-90 to Geneva. Go north on State Route 534 for seven miles. State Route 534 becomes State Route 531. The winery is 1/5 mile east on State Route 531.

Hours May–September, 12 p.m.–1 a.m. daily; October–December, Sunday-Thursday 12–7 p.m., Friday–Saturday 12 p.m.–12 a.m.; January–April, Friday–Saturday 12 p.m.–12 a.m., Sunday 12–7 p.m.

Tours For pre-booked groups of 50 or more

Tastings During regular hours; sweet or dry tasting trays or individual tastings available

Gifts Full line of firehouse and wine gifts at winery and online

Highlights at Winery Beautiful decks, patio, and gazebo overlooking Lake Erie; restored country firehouse; full-service restaurant, space to accommodate groups up to three hundred; motor coach friendly

Events Northeast Ohio Polka Fest (first weekend in June); Celtic Feis (weekend before Labor Day)

Restaurant Casual American and Mexican

Prices $7–$20; 10 percent off full case; 5 percent off half-case (can mix and match wines)

Brand Names Old Firehouse and Firehouse Cellars

Type of Production All hand-bottled

Pressing and Winemaking On-site by hand

Aging and Cooperage American oak and one-quarter French oak, two years on Chardonnay

County Ashtabula

Appellation Lake Erie

Varieties Labrusca, French hybrids, vinifera, fruit wines, ice wines

Wines Sweet Concord, Pink Catawba, Grape Jamboree, Spiced Apple, Red Raspberry, Blackberry, Frosty Peach, Lighthouse Niagara, Firehouse White & Red, Sunset Blush, Reflections, Syval Blanc, Vidal Ice, Delaware Ice, White Zinfandel, Riesling, Country Cabernet, Chardonnay, Merlot, Chambourcin, Spumante Champagne

Best Red Merlot

Best White Riesling

Other Best Wine Reflections of Lake Erie, blend of Lake Erie viniferas and French hybrid grapes

Quote "We only make wines we like, and we only make what sells." —Don Woodward

Nearby Places to Visit Geneva-on-the-Lake, with two amusement parks, a golf course, and 100 attractions

South River Vineyard

6062 South River Road
Geneva, OH 44041
Tel: (440)466-6676
E-mail: info@southrivervineyard.com
Web site: www.southrivervineyard.com
Owners Gene and Heather Sigel
Founded 2000

The elegant simplicity of this tall white stark chapel surrounded by beautiful well-tended vineyards on South River Road in Geneva stirs the soul. This church, more than a century old, marks the site of one of the most spectacular views in the Grand River Valley, where the quiet of the moment magically transports the first-time visitor to an earlier time in the history of Ohio viticulture.

Proprietors Gene and Heather Sigel met while they were employed at Chalet Debonné Vineyards, Gene managing the vineyards and Heather working the tasting room. Later, they married and merged their natural talents. "We were growing grapes and selling wine, so we decided to make wine for ourselves," Heather says.

The Sigels leased a small two-acre vineyard in 1995 and purchased their present thirty-two-acre estate in 1998. They dubbed it South River Vineyard and commenced tearing out the Concord vineyards there and rejuvenating the land. The tight, heavy clay soils were bulldozed and tile-drained in preparation for a state-of-the-art vitis vinifera vineyard. High cordon trellises were installed to promote vertical shoot positioning. The twenty-four-acre vineyard was planted to Chardonnay, Riesling, Pinot Gris, Cabernet Franc, Cabernet Sauvignon, Merlot, Syrah, and Sangiovese. The dense and manicured vineyard plot reflected Sigel's commitment to modern farming practices: fertilization, draining, and canopy management. "Our strategy is to create low yields of intense and concentrated fruit," Gene says.

The Sigels learned about an abandoned 1892 Victorian chapel situated in nearby Portage County, and they thought it would be a perfect home for their winery. In early 2000, the Sigels began the artful process of dismantling the chapel one nail at a time. Each piece of the building was identified and packed for the fifty-mile road trip back to Geneva. "The reconstruction was a labor of love; we did most of the work ourselves," Heather says. The vaulted ceilings create space and light, contrasted by stained glass windows and rows of chestnut pews and small tables grouped for tastings. Outside, a lovely summer pavilion with comfortable Adirondack chairs overlooks the vineyards.

South River Vineyards opened in 2000 as a small artisan winery with an emphasis on quality vineyards. A meticulously detail-oriented farmer and consultant, Gene spends most days outside maintaining the vineyards. "Our wines are made in the vineyard," says Gene, an economist with a PhD from the University of Massachusetts. "We thin the fruit, select the best, and harvest by hand." The Sigels lease the tractors and their equipment from Chalet Debonné Vineyards, where Gene is still the vineyard manager. He received his formal viticultural training under the tutelage of its owners, the Debevc family, which began growing

grapes in the Grand River Valley in 1916. Gene oversees one hundred acres of prime vineyards for South River Vineyards and Chalet Debonné Vineyards combined.

Gene describes himself as a minimalist winemaker. "Our wines are lightly filtered, pressed, matured, aged in American Demptos and Canton oak cooperage and oak chips, then served," he says. "I produce 200 gallons to 300 gallons, sometimes 800 gallons, of a specific variety at a time. Our goal is become known for our special lots of fine wines."

South River Vineyards, known for its signature cold-winter Riesling Vineyard Reserve and Riesling Vintner Select, attracts educated consumers, many vitis vinifera devotees. Its Chardonnay, Pinot Gris, and Cabernet Franc have brought it success. The proprietary Trinity consists of

equal parts Pinot Noir, Chambourcin, and Cabernet Franc. Temptation, aptly named, is a 100 percent, semi-sweet Cabernet Franc. Hand-harvested on December 6, 2002, at 2 a.m., at 11 degrees Fahrenheit, the Concord Ice Wine was produced from frozen Concord grapes, which by dawn had been pressed from 70 gallons of rock-hard berries. This is a highly floral, intensely rich, sweet nectar, harvested at 35.4 brix and finished at 13.2 brix. This is the Ohio wine country at its best!

South River Vineyard

Directions Take I-90 east to Geneva. Go south on State Route 528, take a left on Griswold Road, and turn left again on Emerson Road. Turn right on Doty Road, which turns into South River Road and leads to the winery on the right.

Hours Monday–Thursday 2–6 p.m.; Friday 1–11 p.m.; Saturday 1–11 p.m.; Sunday 1–7 p.m.

Tours By appointment

Tastings Daily when open

Gifts Wine-related

Picnics Welcome

Highlights at Winery Historic Victorian church; Grand River Valley at its finest

Events Weddings

Prices $14–$26

Brand Names South River Vineyards

Type of Production Classic

Method of Harvesting By hand

Pressing and Winemaking Vaslin and minimal filtering and fining

Aging and Cooperage American oak

Vineyards Founded 1998

County Ashtabula

Appellation Grand River Valley

Acreage 24

Waterways Grand River Valley watershed and Lake Erie

Climate Long, cool growing season

Soils Heavy clay

Varieties Riesling, Chardonnay, Pinot Gris, Cabernet Franc, Cabernet Sauvignon, Merlot, Syrah, Sangiovese Wines: Chardonnay, Pinot Gris, Riesling, Trinity, Cabernet Franc, Temptation, Concord Ice Wine

Best Red Cabernet Franc

Best White Chardonnay

Other Best Wine Pinot Gris

Quote "Our wines are made in the vineyard." —Gene Sigel

Nearby Places to Visit Downtown Cleveland; Lake Farmpark

St. Joseph Vineyard

6060 Madison Road

Thompson, OH 44086

Tel: (440)298-3709

E-mail: Stjosephvineyard@alltel.net

Web site: www.saintjosephvineyard.com

Owners Art and Doreen Pietrzyk

Winemaker Art Pietrzyk

Founded 1987

The Grand River Valley has a reputation for being one of Ohio's finest viticultural districts for growing vitis vinifera grapes. After experimenting with winegrowing at other locations, Clevelanders Art and Doreen Pietrzyk came to this prestigious sub-appellation to plant St. Joseph Vineyard, named after their son Joseph. Their objective was to create nothing less than the best vineyard possible.

The Pietrzyk family has a history of winegrowing that dates from 1972. Their wine appreciation began during the eighties at Chalet Debonné, where they tasted River Rouge. "We wanted to learn," says Art, an engineer, who made wine at home from concentrate and grapes. "Then, my wine never met my expectations. We needed to start with quality grapes." By 1982, the Pietrzyks invested in Bill Worthy's Grand River Winery. They experimented with a Pekin Road vineyard, 50 percent French hybrids and 50 percent vinifera, but ran into frost problems every third year. "We grew grapes, we made wine, and we were passionate for certain wines, especially Pinot Noirs," they say.

Determined, the Pietrzyks researched information from Ohio State University, where they learned of the Lake Erie Appellation of Origin as a top place to grow grapes. They consulted with Arnie Esterer of Markko Vineyard, who in 1968 planted Ohio's first cold-climate vinifera grapes. They talked with Doug Moorehead, proprietor of Presque Isle Winery, one of the first to grow vinifera in Pennsylvania. With the Lake Erie Tasting Group, the Pietrzyks tasted Grand Cru Pinot Noirs from France's most highly rated vineyards and vintages. At La Tache, they observed, there were no great wine-makers, just generations of agriculturists committed to maintaining great vineyards, from which came great wines.

By 1986, the Pietrzyks had purchased twenty acres of farmland along Madison Road in Thompson. A curving road meanders past the lush, rolling vineyards to the family home and pole barn. From April to October, it isn't unusual to see Art tending vines. At the back of the property stands the winery, built in 1999, showcasing a colorful stained-glass window of the vineyard. Upstairs in the cedar tasting room with its displays of wines and medals, Doreen, an accountant, oversees the wine education, taking visitors through flights of St. Joseph Vineyard wines. Outside, the terrace offers comfortable places to gather or picnic next to the gorgeous open spaces. Downstairs, the winery consists of the fermentation center, the bottling room, and the aging cellar.

The St. Joseph Vineyard philosophy parallels Mathew 7:16: "Where-fore ye shall know them by their fruits. The good vine bears good wine." High quality is the emphasis here. "We bring intensity and complexity to our wines. There is vibrance in the vineyard, in the winery, and in the wines," Art says. His vineyard differentiates itself by offering its patrons a heightened wine experience, where they are encouraged to arrive with curiosity and leave with knowledge.

Education begins in the vineyard with those natural characteristics that give St. Joseph wines their sense of place, which the French call *terroir*. The wines are the combination of the parts: the cultivar, the gravel and sandstone with its sandy topsoil, the warm mornings and cool evenings that moderate the long growing season, the classic viticultural practices, and the traditional winemaking.

The vineyards comprise seven acres of predominately red grapes in Thompson's Geauga County Grand River Valley Appellation, and an additional six acres of white grapes under contract in Conneaut's Ashtabula County Lake Erie Appellation. The vineyards include Pinot Blanc, Chardonnay, Sauvignon Blanc, Riesling, Pinot Noir, Cabernet Franc, Merlot, Shiraz, and one French hybrid, Vidal Blanc. "We start tasting dry whites, dry reds, then finish with sweet wines," Doreen says. Typically the whites and the reds are fermented and held in Italian (with a variable-top tank) and American stainless steel, plus time in bottle. Both the Chardonnay and the Pinot Noir are aged in 60-gallon French Nevers oak barrels, plus time in bottle. Recently, the Pietrzyks purchased an additional sixty acres with plans to expand.

The wines of St. Joseph Vineyards are recognized nationally and internationally. Recently, the St. Joseph Vineyard Pinot Noir won a Gold Medal at the Riverside International Wine Competition in Riverside, California. The St. Joseph Vineyard Riesling was awarded a Gold Medal at the Tasters Guild Internal Wine

Competition in Grand Rapids, Michigan. "Since entering competitions recently, our Pinot Noir has consistently won medals in national and international competitions, and may prove to be the red wine that puts the Grand River Valley on the map as a great region," Art says.

St. Joseph Vineyard

Directions Take I-90 east toward Madison. Go south on Route 528 for four miles to the winery.

Hours Friday 5–8 p.m.; Saturday 1–8 p.m.

Tours By appointment

Tasting Daily during above hours

Gifts Hats, T-shirts, glasses, cork pullers, and wine-related items

Picnics Bring from home

Highlights at winery Internationally and nationally recognized wines; wine quality at boutique winery; personal attention; wine education

Restaurant Light fare—selection of cheese, crackers, and fruit

Prices $8.99–$34.99

Brand Names St. Joseph Vineyard

Type of Production Vinifera grapes and one French hybrid

Method of Harvesting By hand into 25-pound lug boxes

Winemaking and Pressing Traditional

Aging and Cooperage French Nevers oak barrels

Vineyards Founded 1986

County Geauga

Appellation Grand River Valley

Acreage 7

Waterway Farm pond

Climate Cool, long growing season

Soil Rock and gravel

Varieties Chardonnay, Riesling, Pinot Blanc, Sauvignon Blanc, Pinot Noir, Cabernet Franc, Merlot, Shiraz, Cabernet Sauvignon and one French hybrid, Vidal Blanc Ice Wine

Best Red Pinot Noir

Best White Riesling

Other Best Wine Sauvignon Blanc

Quote "You will know us by our fruit." —Doreen Pietrzyk

Nearby Places to Visit Geneva-on-the-Lake; Shandy Hall

Tarsitano Winery

4871 Hatches Corners Road
Conneaut, OH 44030
Tel: (440)224-2444
Fax: (440)224-2444
E-mail: info@tarsitanowinery.com
Web site: www.tarsitanowinery.com
Owner/ Winemaker Kenneth Tarsitano
Founded 2001

Conneaut's Tarsitano Winery, a gabled, cedar-sided building with French doors, stands atop a knoll overlooking rolling vineyards. The Conneaut River lies to the east, and Beaver Creek flows to the south. The winery, established in 2001 by Ken Tarsitano, symbolizes the will of two branches of the family: the Finnish Ahos and the Italian Tarsitanos.

"The farm is a gathering place. When we all get together, we are very strong-willed," Ken says. "We have connected the land with the history of a traditional farm that grows, develops, and produces an end product."

The family's belief in these lands as a premiere growing district began almost a century ago. Ken narrates the story of Issac Aho, his great-grandfather, who migrated from Finland to northeast Ohio. There, he established a successful dairy farm that lasted until the 1980s. Every summer, Aho's grandchildren, Marsha and Tim, visited from Parma, Ohio, to partake in the ritual of baling hay. From the onset, the farm had a magnetic pull on the family and each successive generation. When Marsha married Ralph Tarsitano, they shared the same custom with their children, Ken and Michele.

"I followed in the same tradition," affirms Ken, the one-time advertising executive and computer whiz. A career change in the mid-nineties inspired him to tap his creative muses and explore his world. With his camera in tow, Ken set off to photograph life in China for three months. Upon his return, he took to the open road to hike the Appalachian Trail from Maine to Georgia. In his absence, the family farm remained vacant for seven long years.

Once Tarsitano returned home to Conneaut, he divided his time pursuing two separate but parallel career paths. He worked both for the Ohio State University Grape Research Center in Kingsville and as an organic farmer on his property. "On fifteen acres, I farmed seventy-two different fruits, nuts, and vegetables, which I sold directly to the Community Sponsored Agricultural Programs, to the North Union Farmer's Market, and to the Willoughby Farmer's Market. Mother Nature knew she wanted to grow grapes," he says. So, he took the first step in that direction.

By the late nineties, Tarsitano had talked to vinifera guru Arnie Esterer from Markko Vineyards and French hybrid advocates Joe Biscotti of Biscotti's Family Winery, Fred Bucci of Buccia Vineyards, and Nick Ferrante of Ferrante Vineyards. "I asked questions and listened," he says.

Tarsitano chose the vitis vinifera route, planting two acres of Chardonnay; Bianca, a Hungarian hybrid; and Lemberger, a Blaufrankish vinifera (from the same town that produces Limburger cheese). "Our reasoning was practical," he says, explaining that the Bianca tolerates cold and the Lemberger resists disease.

Tarsitano Winery produces hard-to-find specialty wines with unique tastes and flavors. "We are showcasing the land," says Ken, the principal, CEO, and winemaker of this small artisan winery. The diversity of the grapes is highlighted by meticulous field-blending and artful barrel blending,

which makes wines of depth and complexity. "We pick, crush, and press by hand, we ferment both our white and red grapes in oak, and we craft our wines with care."

Great variety in Ken's line of Chardonnays is a source of pride. "With this variety, we emphasize the clonal mix, and some wines are made surlees, filtered, unfiltered, lightly oaked, or heavily oaked. Of the seven Chardonnays we produce, two are aged in French oak, two in German oak, two in American oak, and one in Hungarian oak," he says.

On Covered Bridge Weekend in October, Tarsitano Winery draws a crowd, and friends volunteer to help conduct tastings and tours for guests and visitors. In the winter, guests can enjoy an afternoon of cross-country skiing through vineyards and woods, then relax by the fire with a glass of wine. (There are cross-country ski trails less than two miles long between Tarsitano and Markko vineyards.)

"Our motto is by sharing, we learn," says Ken, who envisions a second phase of his dream that includes building a new winery and tasting room with a bed and breakfast.

Tarsitano Winery

Directions From Erie, take I-90 to Conneaut. Take State Route 7 south and turn right on Hatches Corners Road to the winery. From Cleveland, take I-90 to State Route 193 and continue straight ahead. Proceed east on State Route 84 for 2.9 miles, left on State Road for 1.5 miles, then right on Hatches Corners Road to the winery.

Hours Monday–Thursday 12–6 p.m.; Friday–Saturday 11 a.m.–9 p.m.

Tours By appointment only

Tastings Daily when open

Gifts Arts, crafts, wine artifacts, gizmos, gadgets, jams, jellies, nuts, and fruits

Highlights at Winery Beautiful location with terrace views of vineyards and farmlands; boutique style of winemaking for adventurers; Kenneth Tarsitano's photography; ski trails from Tarsitano via vineyards and woodlands to Markko

Events Covered Bridge Weekend in October; Valentine's Day dinner

Restaurant Café with light fare—bruschetta, veggie burgers, gourmet pizza, cheeses; gourmet dinners for two or more upon request

Prices $15–$35; 10 percent case discount

Brand Name Tarsitano Winery

Type of Production Interpreting wine, mixing artistic and natural elements

Method of Harvesting Hand-harvested into lug boxes

Pressing and Winemaking Ferment primary and secondary reds; some whites in oak barrels

Aging and Cooperage New and used American, French, Hungarian, and German oak

Vineyards Founded 1998

County Ashtabula

Acreage 13

Waterways Lake Erie, Conneaut River, and Bear Creek

Climate Long, cool growing season on north-facing slopes called Pinnacles; influenced by three water sources that create cool spring and warm fall

Soil Heavy platea loam

Varieties Auxerrois, Cabernet Sauvignon, Chardonnay, Gewürztraminer, Lemberger, Bianca, Pinot Gris, Pinot Noir, Riesling, Seyval

Wines Auxerrois, Bear Creek Red, Caberenet Sauvignon, Chardonnay, Inaugural, Lemberger, Pinot Gris, Pinot Noir, Riesling, Seyval

Best Red Cabernet Sauvignon

Best White Chardonnay

Other Best Wine Inaugural

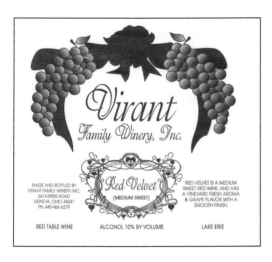

Virant Family Winery, Inc.

541 Atkins Road

Geneva, OH 44041

Tel: (440)466-6279

E-mail: virantfamilywinery@mailbag.net

Web site: www.virantfamilywinery.com

Owners Virant family

Winemakers Frank and Charlie Virant

Founded 1998

The view at sunset over the rolling hillside vineyards at the Virant Family Winery in Cork is unrivaled. The winery sits atop a knoll within sight of one of Ohio's oldest Slovenian agricultural communities. Two farmsteads, one new and one old, are nestled into the verdant vineyards, home to five generations of the Virant family who have made agriculture their livelihood.

At the turn of the twentieth century, Lewis Virant immigrated to the United States from Slovenia, where winemaking began some 2,400 years ago with the Celtic and Illyrian tribes of northeastern Slovenia before the Romans arrived in the first century AD. During the 1930s, employment was scarce in Cleveland, so Virant moved his family east to the countryside and established a farm with his son Frank. From sunrise to sunset, the family ran the farm with its vineyards, orchards, gardens, cattle, and chickens. "We made milk, butter, meat, and poultry. We produced wine for fun for our friends and neighbors," says Frank's son, third-generation Charles Virant.

In 1962, Frank and Charles planted an eleven-acre vineyard left of the present Virant Family Winery. A year later, Charles and Martha Virant purchased an eight-acre vineyard opposite the former Claire's Grand River Wine Company in Thompson. Charles and his son, also named Frank, the fourth generation, grew up managing these Lake Erie Appellation vineyards. They were selected for their excellent location and growing conditions between the north ridge (State Route 20) and the south ridge (State Route 84) of old Lake Erie, their clay soils, and their warmer temperatures than areas farther south.

"Along this corridor, there were flower nurseries and truck farms," Charles says. "Farmers grew grapes, peaches, apples, melons, corn, tomatoes, and blackberries." By 1998, Charles and Frank purchased

Charles Virant toasts his family's vineyard

Phil Masturzo

the vineyards they had managed next to the Virant Family Winery. Concord and Niagara, dominant varieties at both sites, are used to produce the Virant wines or are sold to the Welch's Grape Juice Company.

The opening of the Virant Family Winery, also in 1998, drew on the family's rich Slovenian heritage. They emphasized traditions, inclusiveness, delicious food, and good wines with music and entertainment in a beautiful setting. "We appeal to ordinary people who want to taste wine and enjoy food. We treat everyone like family members," Charles says.

The Virant Family Winery produces eight wines. The fresh, sweet Red Velvet, the best-seller, has won many awards. At the Ohio State University Wine Competition in Wooster, it won a Gold Medal as Best American Red out of 238

wines. At the Los Angeles State Fair, an international competition with 778 wineries featuring 3,000 entries, it won a Bronze Medal. And the dry, red Midnight Chambourcin, with its peppery, plum flavor and oak nuances, won a commendation at the Ohio State University Wine Competition. The Virants also have introduced a dry Cabernet Franc, their first vitis vinifera varietal.

Banks of purple and pink petunias interspersed with milk cans and oak cooperage flank the entrance to the peaked brick Virant Family Winery. Upstairs is a large open room with photos and memorabilia for tasting, dining, buying gifts, and listening to music. Spacious windows bring the gorgeous vistas indoors like a painting. An outdoor dining area and tented picnic area overlook the vineyards. Downstairs, the winery houses fermentation equipment, a bottling line, and a variety of cooperage for the production and aging of wine.

The winery hosts monthly events: pig and beef roasts, clambakes, and ribs and steak cookouts with jazz, polka, or light rock. The annual celebration "Christmas in July," with holiday music, Christmas trees, wreaths, food, wine, and Santa Claus, attracts crowds. The Virants invite you to visit throughout the year to meet the family and join the fun!

Virant Family Winery, Inc.

Directions Take I-90 toward Geneva. Go south on State Route 534. Turn right on Cold Cork Springs Road, then right onto Atkins Road to the winery.

Hours Wednesday–Thursday 2–9 p.m.; Friday: 2–11 p.m.; Saturday 1–11 p.m.; Sunday 1–5 p.m.

Tastings Daily when open

Gifts Wine-related articles and gifts

Highlights at Winery Everyone treated like family; good wine, good food, and good service

Events Clambakes; steak and rib dinners

Restaurant Light fare

Prices $8.50–$12.50

Brand Names Virant Family

Type of Production Innovative and adaptive

Method of Harvesting Mechanical harvesting

Pressing and Winemaking Normal

Aging and Cooperage Two to three years

Vineyards Founded 1962 and 1963 respectively

County Ashtabula County

Appellation Lake Erie Appellation of Origin

Acreage 19

Waterway Grand River

Climate Long, cool growing season

Soil Clay

Varieties Concord and Niagara

Wines Midnight Chambourcin, Fancy Seyval, Red Satin, White Lace, Red Velvet, White Silk, Chiffon, Delightfully Delaware, Pink Delight, Chantilly Blush

Best Red Red Velvet

Best White Chiffon

Other Best Wine White Silk

Quote "Treat people like you like to be treated." —Charlie Virant

Nearby Places to Visit Lake Erie and Grand River; covered bridges

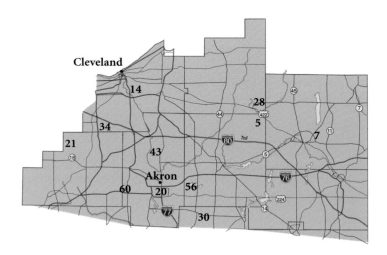

Canal and Lock Tour

A glass of Sweet Revenge framed by silhouetted grapevines at The Winery at Wolf Creek

Candlelight Winery

11325 Center Street
Garrettsville, OH 44231
Tel: (330)527-4118
Fax: (330)527-4118
E-mail: cconkol@candlelightwinery.com
Web site: www.candlelightwinery.com
Owners Chris and Amanda Conkol
Winemaker Chris Conkol
Founded 2002

The Candlelight Winery along Tinkers Creek, located in the gently rolling hamlet of Garrettsville, is the town's newest rising star. From the time of the town's first Silver Creek grist-sawmill in 1805, this corner of the Western Reserve has appealed to farmers, artists, writers, poets, and entrepreneurs. And now, since Chris and Amanda Conkol founded Candlelight in 2002, its first winemakers. "Our goal is to educate, entertain, and enrich the lives of anyone who enjoys a glass of wine," Chris says. In the nineties, Chris was completing a BA at Kent State University's School of Architecture while Amanda, his high school sweetheart, was finishing a BS in computer science at Bowling Green State University. "I went to Italy, where I studied wine more than I did architecture," Chris says. Upon his return, Chris and Amanda married, and she became a software quality insurance manager while he became an architect. But Chris pursued his interest in wine, taking winemaking classes at Viking Vineyards and Portage Hills Winery. The first year, he made wine from a concentrated Chianti blend. The second year, he made wines from Concord, Niagara, and Marechal Foch juice from a winery. The third year, he made both dry and sweet wines from fresh grapes.

Chris started making wine in his apartment, later in his house, and finally in his garage. "I had a five-gallon wine container in the bedroom, and my wife told me that it was time I did something about it," he says. In 2002, the Conkols purchased fifteen acres of land, part of an old farm, with a road and site for a creek-side winery in the backcountry of Portage County. Earlier that year, they had planted a two- to three-acre vineyard between Burton and Chesterland in Geauga County.

While maintaining their regular jobs, the Conkols hand-built their winery themselves. Chris designed a two-story modified pole barn with a great room with French doors that opened onto a deck overlooking a field by Tinkers Creek. He installed stainless steel, jacketed fermentors with variable capacity and other new equipment.

The inside of Candlelight Winery mirrors the Conkols' good taste in art and wine. The captivating great room has laminated wooden floors contrasted with a midnight-blue ceiling dotted with twinkling stars that light up, three pale-yellow walls covered with the work of regional artists, and one sienna-red wall. "Wine just isn't grapes; it is the atmosphere or mood of what's going on when one drinks it," Chris says. "Wine tastes different under candlelight." A tasting bar features the newest Candlelight wines and light fare while shelves hold wine-oriented baskets and

gifts. A hall table features a calendar of events—Italian dinners or holiday festivities—along with live music—jazz, folk, blues, and featured guitarists and harpists. In addition to the Geauga County vineyards, the Conkols planted a one-acre vineyard on their Garretsville property in 2002. On the edge of the snowbelt, the vineyards are planted in sandy clay soil to Vidal Blanc, Marechal Foch, Chambourcin, Niagara, Concord, and Riesling. The Candlelight wines include Chardonnay, Reflection, Riesling, Illumination, Cabernet Sauvignon, Chambourcin, Luminare, Afterglow, and First Light. Plans are under way to make a Late Harvest Ice Wine.

Chris takes a traditional approach to winemaking, using a bladder press to process the grapes. He checks the wine hourly and lets the sediment settle out before he commences with the fermentation. The reds are typically fermented on the skins while the whites are not. "We let

Chris Conkel

the wine run its course, check it daily for any necessary adjustments such as acid or sugar," Chris says. "The wines are bottled very young; five out of seven have residual sugar. As we grow, we will produce more dry wines until we reach a happy medium."

So, the next time you want a romantic evening and a place to share a lovely bottle of wine with a friend, stop by Candlelight Winery!

Candlelight Winery

Directions Take I-422 to State Route 88 south to Garrettsville. Go left and east on State Route 82 in Garrettsville 500 feet, then turn left (north) on Center Street for two miles to the winery on the left.

Hours Tuesday–Thursday 12–9 p.m.; Friday and Saturday 12-11:00 p.m.

Tours By request

Tastings Daily when open

Gifts Wine-related gifts

Picnics Outdoor deck and special events

Highlights at Winery Romantic atmosphere and personalized ambiance; stars light up on dark-blue ceiling

Events Live music (blues, folk, guitar, harp, holiday music); themed dinners (Italian, New Year's Eve); summer hot dog roast

Restaurant Light fare—crackers, chips, fruit, cheese

Prices $8–$15; 10 percent discount on case of wine

Brand Names Candlelight Winery

Type of Production Traditional

Method of Harvesting By hand

Aging and Cooperage Stainless steel, variable-capacity tanks

Vineyards Founded 2001, Burton and Chesterland; 2002, Garrettsville

Counties: Geauga and Portage

Appellation American and Ohio

Acreage 3–4

Waterway Tinkers Creek

Climate Harsh winters on edge of snow-belt

Soil Heavy clay

Varieties Vidal Blanc, Marechal Foch, Chambourcin, Niagara, Concord, Riesling

Wines Reflection, Riesling, Illumination, Chardonnay, Chambourcin, Luminaire, Afterglow, Blush, First Light, Cabernet Sauvignon, Chianti, Sangiovese, Ice Wine

Best Red Wine Chambourcin

Best White Wine Riesling

Other Best Wine First Light

Quote "Wine isn't just grapes. It is the atmosphere and the mood of what is going on when one drinks it. Wine tastes different under candlelight than fluorescent."
—Chris Conkol

Nearby Places to Visit Garrettsville clock tower; James A. Garfield Historical Society

Cicero's Winery

4248 North River Road
Warren, OH 44484
Tel: (330)856-4144 or (800)416-3920
E-mail: info@ciceros.com
Web site: www.ciceros.com
Owners Peter Cicero Sr. and
Peter J. Cicero Jr.
Winemaker Peter J. Cicero Jr.
Founded 2003

Along North River Road in Warren, a row of century trees graces the driveway to Cicero's Winery. Established by founder Peter Cicero Sr. and his son, Peter J. Cicero Jr., in 2003, the winery is located in a wooden roadhouse on two acres of sparsely wooded valley property.

Cicero descends from three generations of Italian delicatessen owners who settled in Warren at the beginning of the twentieth century. There, the family established a reputation as purveyors of high-quality Italian products. Cicero's Spaghetti Sauce, an original family recipe, launched a popular Italian-American tradition there. Gradually, Cicero's Winery developed a selection of fancy foods for its custom gift baskets—gourmet fruit, imported cheeses and meats, homemade sauces, delicious pastas, desserts, and Italian-style California wines. Over time, the Cicero family developed national recognition as a marketer of wine and food.

For more than twenty years, Peter J. Cicero Jr. has sold grapes, juice, and produce. In 1984, he acquired a wholesale produce company that had an intriguing grape and juice component. "Many of my customers made wine at home," says Peter Jr., adding that he viewed his segue into wine as a natural progression. His venture now includes wine and food production, the sale of California grapes, juice, class instruction, gift baskets, banquet and catering services, tastings, and entertainment.

A black-and-white awning over the entrance to the roadhouse welcomes guests and visitors. The doorway leads to a foyer and a peach room with a curved oak wine bar, metallic stools, and hardwood floors lit by glowing, dangling lights and track lighting. The lemon-yellow great room and entertainment center is designed for small groups. French doors open onto a stone patio surrounded by antique oak barrels and tall pine trees. During the warmer months, this setting is used for wine tastings, light dining, barbeques, and live music events.

Years ago, Peter J. sourced grapes and juice from Central Valley grape grower Frank Pantaleo in Madera, California. There the long, hot growing season produced quality grapes with abundant flavors. These wine grapes are harvested and either chilled as whole berries or cooled as fresh juice, then shipped by refrigerated trucks to Ohio. Cicero's Winery then makes its famous Regina juice from fresh grapes that are crushed, pressed, and extracted as juice, then held at a constant temperature in monitored stainless steel tanks across the country. The winery offers more than thirty-five varietal juices—Chardonnay, Chenin Blanc, French Colombard, Muscat, Pinot Grigio, Cabernet Sauvignon, Carignane, Gamay, and Merlot just to mention a few. The juices are available in six-gallon pails, fifty-five-gallon drums, and partial or full stainless steel tankers.

"Our Regina juice is consumer-ready," Peter J. says. "An enologist balances it for acid, pH level, color, sugar content, and yeast prior to its sale. All the buyer must do is open the container and transfer the juice into the proper fermentation barrel."

Peter J. suggests that his clients follow the procedures he uses for making the Cicero wines—100 percent California Chardonnay, Cabernet, Zinfandel, and Ruby Cabernet. Over eighteen to twenty-four days, the wine ferments depending on its sugar content and its temperature. A slight drop in temperature will result in a slower or halted fermentation. Using a hydrometer, he measures any drop in sugar content, which serves as a guide for when to do the first racking. Because some wines are better dry than sweet, he recommends consulting with an expert regarding the proper sugar content suitable for a particular variety and its taste.

Fermentation is followed by racking, a process that separates the clear wine from the cloudy sediment, or lees, which settles at the bottom of the tank. For maximum clarity, Peter J. recommends racking wine a second, or even a third, time. The white wines are held in stainless steel, while the red wines are kept in stainless steel with a maximum of one year in oak. Once Cicero achieves the desired taste and clarity, he sterilizes the bottles and corks. Next, the wine is bottled to the top of the neck, then corked and capped with foil. Cicero's Winery keeps its corked wines moist and stored on their sides at 64 degrees Fahrenheit.

In the decades to follow, Cicero sees great growth in the Ohio wine movement. "We wish you years of happy winemaking, and the good health to enjoy it. From our family to yours, Salud!"

Cicero's Winery

Directions Take I-80 east to exit 209/14. Turn east onto Ohio 5, then take the Elm Road ramp toward Warren. Turn left on Elm Road NE. Turn left on North River Road/CR 142 to the winery.

Hours Winter, 4–10 p.m. daily; Summer, 4 p.m.–2 a.m. daily

Tours By appointment only

Tastings Daily when open

Gifts Gift baskets featuring Italian products; premium fancy fruit (oranges, red, green, and gold apples, Bosc and d'Anjou pears, tangerines, grapefruit, and grapes); premium pastas and sauces; cheeses; salamis; sesame bread sticks; Cicero's wines; and desserts

Highlights at Winery Wine and food tastings; suppliers of quality California grapes, juice, and instruction; Italian gourmet wine and food gift baskets; catering and banquet services

Events Themed barbeques; live music and bands

Restaurant Light fare and catered affairs

Prices $10–$14; 10 percent case discount

Brand Name Cicero's

Type of Production Traditional

Pressing and Winemaking Wine juice ready for fermentation stage of development

Aging and Cooperage Stainless steel for whites and reds with French oak barrel aging for some reds

Appellation California

Varieties More than 35 varieties of grapes and juice available for sale

Wines Cicero's Chardonnay, Cabernet Sauvignon, Zinfandel, Ruby Cabernet

Best Red Cabernet Sauvignon

Best White Chardonnay

Best Other Wine Zinfandel

Quote "We wish you years of happy winemaking, and the good health to enjoy it. From our family to yours, Salud!"
—Peter J. Cicero Jr.

Grande Wine Cellars

4653 Warner Road
Garfield Heights, OH 44125
Tel: (216)441-4439
Owner/Winemaker Paul Grande
Founded 1999

The Grande Wine Cellars in Garfield Heights is one of a handful of small family-owned and urban-operated wineries in Greater Cleveland. Located in one of the city's early Italian-Polish neighborhoods, the winery was established by Ohioans Paul and Linda Grande and their dentist son, Paul S. Grande, in 1999 as a natural outgrowth of their shared Italian heritage.

"We take pride in being a small winery and making wine and food for our family and friends," Paul Sr., now semi-retired, says. "If I invite you over, it is the same as inviting you to my house. I expect you to be respectful."

The Grandes were both born into Italian families that possessed a legacy of winemaking passed down from one generation to the next. "As a boy I grew up in the Collinwood district," Paul Sr. says. "I would sneak down to the basement cellars of my friends' parents and watch them make wine. Almost forty years ago, I started to make my first wine." Linda's parents owned a restaurant across the street from the winery. "Both my grandfathers made wine," she says. Continuing in that tradition, the Grandes purchased twin red brick buildings close to the Ohio Canal District. One was for the winery; the other was for the tasting room.

The Grandes purposely designed the Grande Wine Cellars tasting room for small groups of people. "Our thought was to create a small, cozy, friendly place with lots of ambiance," says Linda, also a Cleveland Clinic registrar. The décor, lit by lanterns, has an Italian flair, with a dash of 1920s Hollywood thrown in. Straw fiaschi wine bottles from Chianti Classico, lovely Italian scenes, photos of famous movie stars, and artifacts decorate the walls. The wooden bar, mirror, and stools, all hand-crafted by Paul Sr., are the focal point of the room. Tables, covered with red-and-white checkered tablecloths, and wooden chairs fill the room.

The Grandes make and sell authentic Italian foodstuffs. Paul Sr. follows old family recipes, which use ingredients characteristic

dry wines. Then Claudio Salvador, my friend and now the winemaker at Firelands Winery, suggested I add several sweet wines to the list," he says. The sweeter wines have done well, especially their best-selling Lake Erie White.

Paul Sr. has enjoyed how the whole process of winemaking has changed. Demand has caused him to introduce new practices and different wine styles.

of another era. "I prepare dried Italian sausage; Italian prosciutto, a dried, banjo-shaped, whole leg of ham; dried capicollo, a loin of ham; and red pasta sauces, made with pork neck bones. For me, this is a hobby—a true pleasure," Paul Sr. says.

The winery emphasizes the value of working with hand-picked varietals of the best quality. "I buy my wine grapes from the very best winegrowers in the Buckeye state. [He mentions Tony Debevc of Chalet Debonné.] If I don't like something, I send it back. My Zinfandel is the only wine grape I purchase from California," Paul Sr. says.

Paul Sr. frankly admits that he has tried just about everything when it comes to winemaking. "I started out making all

Typically, the wine grapes are crushed and pressed in a bladder, basket press. The juice is fermented in stainless steel, pumped over, racked, and held in either stainless steel or oak. The whites are kept in stainless steel or oak, and the reds are aged in American or Hungarian oak barrels. "I make small batches of European-style wine with a French and Italian influence."

Today, Grande Wine Cellars produces just under 5,000 gallons annually of an Ohio Chardonnay, Pinot Noir, Cabernet Franc, Merlot, Burgundy, Shiraz, Lake Erie White, Lake Erie Red, and a California Zinfandel. "If a wine doesn't meet my standards, I won't sell it," says Paul Sr.

Grande Wine Cellars

Directions From I-77, exit at 157 toward Ohio 17/Granger Road. Proceed right and east on Granger Road/Ohio 17. Go left on Warner Road to winery.

Hours Friday–Saturday 12–10 p.m.

Tours None

Tastings Daily when open

Gifts Gift baskets

Picnics This is a city winery with a small outdoor patio.

Highlights at Winery Best wines under $10 a bottle; small, friendly tasting room with lots of ambiance

Events Christmas Eve Feast of the Seven Fishes (traditional Italian meal including seven different fish courses); clambakes

Restaurant Limited Italian fare: cheese, crackers, antipasto, and sandwiches

Prices $6–$10 wines; $6–$10 food; 10 percent case discount

Brand Names Grande Wine Cellars

Type of Production European-style wines with a French and Italian emphasis; also vitis viniferas

Method of Harvesting Purchase only hand-picked grapes of the best quality

Pressing and Winemaking Bladder, basket press

Aging and Cooperage American and Hungarian oak barrels

Appellation All Ohio with exception of California Zinfandel

Varieties Niagara Concord, Cabernet Franc, Merlot, Zinfandel, Pinot Noir, Shiraz, Chardonnay, Riesling

Wines Chardonnay, Cabernet Franc, Pinot Noir, Merlot, Burgundy, Shiraz, Lake Erie White, Lake Erie Red

Best Red Cabernet Franc

Best White Chardonnay

Other Best Wine Zinfandel

Quote "If a wine doesn't meet my standards, I won't sell it." —Paul Grande Sr.

Nearby places to visit Rock and Roll Hall of Fame; Great Lakes Science Center

It's Your Winery

2855 West Market Street
Fairlawn, OH 44333
Tel: (330)864-2939
Fax: (330)865-0211
E-mail: itsyourwinery@sbcglobal.net
Web site: www.itsyourwinery.com
Owners/Winemakers John and
Shelli Scurka
Founded 2003

It's Your Winery has quickly earned a reputation as one of Ohio's classier wine establishments. It offers its patrons a captivating challenge—to create their own designer label and fine wine. Proprietors Shelli and John Scurka, residents of Rootstown, came up with the concept for marketing wine experientially after learning about the popularity of wine-on-premises in Canada.

Earlier, the Scurkas, who had read magazines and books on wine, embarked on "self study." In the early nineties, they started as wine hobbyists. "We made fruit wines and purchased our equipment from Home Brew in Kent," says John, who is also an electrician. "We graduated to juice concentrate, producing Cabernets and Merlot."

What feelings did winemaking provoke? "There was the anticipation of waiting for the wine to develop," Shelli says. "And there was the satisfaction of making the wine ourselves," John adds. As the wines improved, the Scurkas' friends encouraged them to consider entrepreneurship. "We took pride in making our own wine and sharing the idea with others by founding our Ohio store," Shelli says.

In 2003, the Scurkas opened the doors to their upscale, full-service boutique, earmarked for people with discriminating tastes in luxury goods and fine wines—and with curiosity about making their own wine. "Customers drop by, sample our wine, and then learn how to use the winery," Shelli says. "Later, when they are making wine, they figure out the meaning of the name It's Your Winery."

Once inside, people are struck by the winery's understated elegance. The classic décor consists of white walls offset by one purple wall and a slate-gray carpet. Napa Valley photos by Phil Masturzo, photographer for the Akron Beacon

Journal, hang in a gallery.

The retail area includes hand-crafted wine racks, Mikasa wine glasses, accessories, and gift baskets. Customers sit at the tasting bar (which looks through French doors into the wine center), settle in at a wrought-iron table and chairs, or relax in leather arm chairs.

The owners pour a line of thirty-five wines that they both have perfected. All are candidates for customers' typical order of a twenty-eight- to thirty-bottle personal cellar (the minimum sale), which breaks down to $4–$7 a bottle. "We cater to brides and people who label and make their own wine as favors for weddings, anniversaries, or special events," Shelli says.

They include the Vintner's Reserve at $149, Chardonnay, Riesling, Liebfraumilch, Merlot, White Zinfandel, and Chianti; the Selection Reserve at $159, Muller Thurgau, Luna Bianca or Cabernet Sauvignon, and Pinot Noir; the International Vintage Reserve at $169, French Chardonnay, Italian Pinot Grigio or Spanish Rioja, and Australian Cabernet/Shiraz; and the Estate Selection at $179, Washington Columbia Valley Riesling or Napa Valley Stag's Leap Merlot; plus Fruit Wines at $99 (Green Apple Riesling or Blackberry Cabernet) and the Riesling Ice Wine at $199.

Once customers select a variety, they are invited into the production center to start the wine. A grape concentrate or grape juice is combined with ingredients and yeasts to activate the primary fermentation in six-gallon bins. They design a label from templates, write the text, choose the fonts, and add a picture. During the next four to six weeks, the Scurkas track the fermentation, then rack, filter, fine, and age the wine in glass carboys. Shelli calls the customer one week before the wine is ready to book a final get-together (often a pre-bridal event) where participants bottle, cork, and label their wine.

"Customers find the process immensely rewarding and depart with a product they produced. We believe it is our role to supply our customers with the best service and wine that we possibly can," the Scurkas say.

It's Your Winery

Directions Take I-77 to the Miller/Ridgewood exit. Proceed north on Miller and turn right on West Market to the winery.

Hours Tuesday–Thursday 11 a.m.–7 p.m.; Friday–Saturday 11 a.m.–9 p.m.; closed Sunday–Monday

Gifts Mikasa wine glasses, backpacks, racks, wine, gift baskets, and wine accessories

Tastings Daily when open

Highlights at Winery Opportunity to make your own wine; full-service wine establishment; opportunity to design your own labels for all occasions and events

Events Participants in Ohio Wine Festival

Prices Wine made by customers ranges $4–$7 per bottle

Brand Name: IYW—custom

Type of Production: Traditional

Pressing and Winemaking: Traditional winemaking

Aging and Cooperage: Glass carb

Appellation: American and European

Varieties 35 varieties

Wines Chardonnay, Riesling, Liebfraumilch, Merlot, White Zinfandel, Chianti, Muller Thurgau, Sauvignon Blanc, Johannisberg Riesling, Luna Bianca, Cabernet Sauvignon, Pinot Noir, Luna Rossa, White Merlot, Barolo, French Chardonnay, Italian Pinot Grigio, French Merlot, Spanish Rioja, Australian Cabernet/Shiraz, Italian Barberesco, Australian Shiraz, Italian Montepulciano, Washington Columbia Valley Riesling, British Columbia Chardonnay, Woodridge Ranch 11 Cabernet Sauvignon, Lodi Old Vines Zinfandel, Napa Valley Stag's Leap Merlot, Peach Apricot Chardonnay, Green Apple Riesling, Tropical Fruit Gewürztraminer, Exotic Fruit White Zinfandel, Wildberry Shiraz, Strawberry White Merlot, Blackberry Current, Riesling Ice Wine

Best Red Napa Valley Stag's Leap Merlot

Best White French Chardonnay

Other Best Wine Fruit wines

Quote "To supply customers with the best service and wine that we possibly can." —Shelli and John Scurka

Nearby Places to Visit Cleveland Zoo; Geauga Lake Amusement Park

Jilbert Winery

1496 Columbia Road
Valley City, OH 44280
Tel: (216)781-4120 or (330)483-5949
Fax: (216)241-5720
E-mail: dbjilbert@ aol.com
Web site: www.ohiohoneywine.homestead.com
Owners David and Lisa Jilbert
Winemaker David Jilbert
Founded 1999

At first glance the stone fence and farm along Columbia Road at Jilbert Winery in Valley City might be mistaken for a romantic seventeenth-century sheep and dairy farm on Martha's Vineyard. But clearly this is not Massachusetts! Instead, it is a very rare Ohio find.

The gorgeous ten-acre Walnut Hill Farms, with its tall timbers and elegant pines, has the distinction of being the only pure meadery in the Buckeye State. Lisa and Dave Jilbert discovered a twentieth-century farm with good bones that had fallen into disuse. In the mid-1990s, they purchased the property and settled there with their children.

The Jhelbare meadery (the French translation for their surname, Jilbert) and craft shop (beeswax candles and pure honey) are housed in a 1905 wooden barn with a sandstone foundation next to a fenced pasture. Daffodil, their beloved sheep, is the sole resident. Nearby, a stately 1913 blue-gray farmhouse with red shutters was renovated for the family home. Behind the carriage house, now called the Honey House, a steep ravine leads to their beehives and the Rocky River, which divides their property.

"We are primarily beekeepers who produce pure honey as a farm commodity," the Jilberts say. "We then value add that commodity (honey) to a retail product (wine)." During the week, Dave is an environmental engineer for a Cleveland firm, and Lisa works as an IT project coordinator for Westfield Insurance. Their professional work supports the winery and gift shop, their hobby.

As a child growing up, Dave Jilbert's father, then a marketer of wine-crafting

The Jilbert family home (left) and seventeenth-century barn

products, gave his son a beehive. "Because of this, I knew making mead was possible," he says. Then, he was captivated by the role of the queen and the labor of the drones and worker bees to build combs. "We make something out of nothing," Dave says. Lisa's sentiments are similar: "Making mead is a labor of love."

The Jilberts make honey wine, also called mead, from wildflower honey gathered from beehives Dave tends on the farm and from around Medina County. The honeycombs are transported to the Honey House, where David meticulously extracts honey from the combs by hand and by centrifuge. The process creates a concentrated brown honey mash, which he racks into fifty-pound plastic containers and hauls to the winery for filtration.

Dave studied winemaking under the late professor Robert Kimes at New York's Cornell University Agricultural Experiment Station in the Finger Lakes. They exchanged ideas about the process.

Kimes was concerned about the science, and Jilbert was concerned about opening a winery and the practicalities of the process.

"Historically, honey wines have not been popular in the U.S. because they leave a bitter aftertaste," Dave says. "This bitterness comes from the wine yeast metabolizing bacteria, molds, pollens, and waxes found in the honey. Our method filters out these materials prior to fermentation." Typically, vintners mask this bitterness in honey wine by adding fruit or spices or by producing a very sweet wine.

Because of the long shelf life of honey, the Jilberts are able to manufacture their product year-round. They filter a honey-water mixture to a tenth of a micron. At this level of filtration, the mixture is considered sterilized. "There are no competing wild yeasts or bacteria," Dave says. "After filtering five hundred pounds of honey, we are left with a five-gallon bucket of sludge. This is all the stuff found in honey greater than a tenth of a micron." After filtration, a pale, straw-colored liquid remains to be fermented. This method ensures the consistent production of honey wine/mead from batch to batch, fermentation within ten days, no bitter aftertaste, and no protein hazing. The four-thousand-bottle Jilbert Winery produces honey wine using state-of-the-art equipment—stainless steel floating-lid fermentation and holding tanks. All bottling and labeling are done by hand.

The Jilberts produce two versions of the same wine under the Jhelbare label: the Jhelbare Summer Solstice Honey Wine and the Jhelbare Midsummer Moon Mead. The bright golden 11-percent-alcohol honey wine/mead has a floral bouquet, a clean but not cloying taste, low 8 percent residual sugar, and a lively citrus finish. Served slightly chilled, this delicious honey wine/mead goes well with pork or beef tenderloins, wild game, lobster, or crab. The Jilberts sell it on-site and throughout Ohio through Heidelberg Distributors.

Jilbert Winery

Directions Take I-71 to Route 303 West to Route 252; turn left, and look for the winery sign on the right.

Hours Saturdays 12–6 p.m.; other days by appointment

Tours Educational and historic nature

Tastings Daily when open

Gifts Hand-crafted beeswax candles, honey, and arts and crafts

Highlights at Winery Only pure meadery in Ohio; state-of-the-art methods of honey wine manufacturing

Prices $6–$8; 10 percent case discount

Brand Name Jhelbare

Type of Production Honey wine/mead manufacturing

Pressing and Winemaking Cornell University state-of-the-art winemaking techniques

County Medina

Acreage 10.5

Waterway West Branch of the Rocky River

Wines Jhelbare Midsummer Moon Mead, Jhelbare Summer Solstice Honey Wine

Quote "We are the only pure meadery in the state of Ohio." —David Jilbert

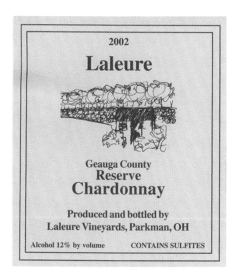

2002

Laleure

Geauga County
Reserve
Chardonnay

Produced and bottled by
Laleure Vineyards, Parkman, OH

Alcohol 12% by volume   CONTAINS SULFITES

Laleure Vineyards

17335 Nash Road
P.O. Box 738
Parkman, OH 44080
Tel: (440)548-5120
E-mail: rich@laleurevineyards.com
Web site: www.laleurevineyards.com
Owners Richard and Betsy Hill
Winemaker Richard Hill
Founded 2003

The Laleure Vineyards in Parkman, with its gently rolling vineyards and thickly wooded forests, conjures up visions of farming in the heart of Amish Country in times gone by. Proprietors Richard and Betsy Hill lovingly named their wine estate for their grandmother, Jeanne Marie Laleure Hill, a native of France's Loire Valley. A woman with great *joie de vivre*,

she inspired them to choose a quieter family lifestyle centered around a farm winery.

In 1997, they purchased the thirty-acre 1860s Stoll dairy farm. They were intrigued by the century farmhouse, the milking barn, and the acres of pastureland. In the spring of that year, they broke ground for a small vineyard. "I dug the first 250 holes in clay, twelve inches wide and sixteen inches deep," recalls Rich, a technical director. Thus, the Betsy-West Vineyards were christened in honor of his partner, Betsy, once owner of Ohio and New York cookware stores.

The Hills reinvented themselves as farmers. They attended courses at Ohio State University Agricultural School and Grape Extension, consulted with the Ohio Wine Growers Association, and read lots of wine books. "We were advised by our grape vendor to experiment with hardy, winter-resistant varieties because we were inland of Lake Erie. We planted grapes such as Vignoles, Bianca, Chardonnay, and Pinot Noir," Rich says.

Encouraged by the results of their initial experiment, the Hills harvested a small quantity of quality grapes in 1999. Next, they expanded their Geauga appellation hillside vineyards, noted for their excellent air circulation and frost protection, and added two acres of Riesling, Seyval, Cabernet Franc, and Chambourcin. They called it Jeanne-East

Vineyards in tribute to their daughter and her namesake, Rich's grandmother. "We grow grapes with tender loving care, and we are particular," Rich says. In 2003, Laleure Vineyards was established.

A 250-case Ohio artisan producer, Laleure Vineyards practices a classic style of farming and winemaking. "We believe that good fruit makes good wine," Rich says, "and we strive to make wines we like. Winters are colder—as low as -15 degrees Fahrenheit—because we are not on the lake. Summers we get more heat because we are not cooled by the lake. Our Chardonnay grapes, for example, get more heat value, producing fruit with higher sugars and more intensity."

The grapes are hand-harvested, then crushed and pressed in a basket press, followed by a traditional fermentation in stainless steel with no use of additives. The wines are racked four to five times with little or no fining or filtering, with the exception of one plate-frame filtering just before bottling. All the wines remain in stainless steel with the exception of the Reserve wines, which are aged in American small oak barrels. "Our wines are dry, simple, straightforward, and well balanced. The taste of the fruit comes through in our wines," he says.

Guests and visitors who travel to Parkman are struck by the natural beauty of the setting. The Hills have renovated their home, a New England cedar farm-house with open porches. A gravel drive-way leads past a huge dairy barn with a tall silo to the former milk house, now a charming tasting room. The white-washed interior has a pine tasting bar and high wicker chairs, oriental rugs, photos, a picture of the Alps, and an iron stove. A gift shop displays wine-related items.

The wines from Laleure Vineyards offer the consumer a step up in the quality department. The Hills are committed to making dry wines, and they find that fewer consumers are requesting sweet ones. "We see a very interested and educated group of people stopping by," says Betsy, who oversees the wine tasting room on any given weekend. The room's intimate nature allows for good wine discussion.

The Chardonnay Reserve, by far their best wine, has big, pronounced Chardonnay flavors, with fourteen months in small, American oak barrels before bottling. The aromatic Chardonnay, also of note, has a great bouquet and overall gusto. The Vignoles bursts with bright color and fresh, slightly tart, captivating taste. Their Pinot Noir has ranked among the top three in Ohio. "We are dedicated to producing high-quality wines from our top-quality fruit and simple processes," Rich says.

Laleure Vineyards

Directions From the west, take U.S. Route 480 east to U.S. Route 422 east toward Warren. After passing State Route 44, cross La Due Reservoir and continue five miles to Parkman. Go left and north on State Route 528 for one mile. Go right on State Route 88 for 1.9 miles to the winery on the right. From the east, take U.S. 422 west to Parkman. Go right and north on State Route 528 for one mile. Go right on State Route 88 for 1.9 miles to the winery on the right.

Hours Friday 5–9 p.m.; Saturday 11 a.m.–5 p.m.; also by appointment

Tours Educational

Tasting On weekends or by appointment

Gifts Wine accessories

Picnics Encouraged to bring picnics

Highlights at Winery Dry, high-quality wines; beautiful country setting and views

Prices $9–$18

Brand Names Laleure Vineyards; Parkman Hill

Type of Production Traditional

Method of Harvesting By hand

Pressing and Winemaking Light pressing in stainless steel tanks

Aging and Cooperage American oak cooperage

Vineyard Founded 1997

County: Geauga

Appellation Geauga County

Acreage 3

Waterways Streams on property lead to Grand River

Climate Typical northeast Ohio, but more heat value in summer than wineries on Lake Erie, which is an advantage. Hillside vineyard location provides good air circulation and frost protection.

Soil Clay

Varieties Chardonnay, Vignoles, Pinot Noir, Riesling, Bianca, Seyval, Cabernet Franc, Chambourcin

Wines Chardonnay, Vignoles, Pinot Noir, Riesling, Bianca, Seyval, Cabernet Franc

Best Red Pinot Noir

Best White Reserve Chardonnay

Other Best Wine Seyval

Quote "We are dedicated to producing high-quality wines from our top-quality fruit and simple processes." —Richard Hill

Nearby Places to Visit Geauga County Swine Creek Park; Middlefield Cheese Factory

Maize Valley Winery

6193 Edison Street NE
Hartville, OH 44632
Tel: (330)877-8344
Fax: (330)877-0915
E-mail: mr.maze@maizevalley.com
Web site: www.maizevalley.com
Owners Kay and Donna Vaughan,
Michelle and Bill Bakan, and Todd Vaughan
Winemaker Todd Vaughan
Assistant Winemaker Michelle Bakan
Founded 2004; family farm since early
1800s

The Maize Valley Farm & Winery in Marlboro Township rests near the original 1800s land grant deeded to pioneer Joseph Vaughan, a teacher and farmer, signed by then President James Monroe. Vaughan's great-great-great-grandson Kay Vaughan and his wife, Donna, along with fifth-generation grandson Todd Vaughan, granddaughter Michelle Bakan, and her husband, Bill, established the Maize Valley Winery in 2004 as a tribute to their forbearers.

"Earlier generations understood reality," Bill Bakan says. "Joseph is said to have put up bear skins across the doorway of the original farmstead to keep it warm during winter. He carved out a subsistence lifestyle growing fruits and vegetables and raising livestock, which was traded for basic essentials such as food, clothing, and shelter." Succeeding generations of Vaughans and Bakans have worked hard to build a strong foundation that melded tradition with modernity.

After graduation from Ohio State University, Michelle, a dairy science major, and Bill, an education and an agribusiness major, married. They returned to Marlboro Township in 1985 and lived on the Vaughan family farm, which consisted of 120 parcels totaling 3,000 acres of corn, wheat, and soy beans; 150 registered Holstein milking cows and fifteen registered prove bulls; a grain elevator; an agriculture supply business; and a trucking business.

"Suddenly, we were impacted by global competition. To succeed in commodity crops, we needed to be low-cost producers," Bakan says. Kay Vaughan, Bill's father-in-law, planted twelve rows of sweet corn as a trial in the early 1990s; he wholesaled the corn for sixty cents a dozen, but it retailed for as high as four dollars a dozen. "We started doing direct marketing in 1997. We set up a roadside fruit and vegetable stand and realized its potential."

A pathway leads to the renovated tan antique barn with the sloping green roof. Outside, hanging baskets and potted plants in pinks, purples, and yellows surround a brick patio perfect for picnics. Inside the entry are displays of grapes, apples, peaches, pears, and local cabbages, lettuces, tomatoes, carrots, broccoli, asparagus, and other produce. The corridor opens to the barn with its sandstone and oak walls; beech, oak, and chestnut hand-hewn cross beams; tiled floor; and upright posts. The great room houses a bistro and tasting bar with tables and chairs, a fancy deli showcasing Holmes County cheeses and meats, gourmet foods, and a bakery.

A walkway leads from the farm market through the greenhouse, which is used as a spring potting shed, to the Maize Valley Winery. It is managed by Todd Vaughan, the winemaker, and his sister Michelle, the assistant winemaker. At the onset, they purchased juice and hand-harvested grapes. "We do some crushing and use a wooden basket press. We are starting at 1,250 cases our first year, with considerable growth by our third year," says Bakan, who anticipates investing in larger-capacity stainless steel equipment. "Our emphasis is quality in the grapes and the winemaking process."

Four acres of Maize Valley are now planted to Chardonnay, Chambourcin, Riesling, Concord, Vignoles, and New York 73 in addition to strawberries, red raspberries, cherries, and blueberries. Todd and Michelle are looking for the right grapes for this location with plans to increase their vineyard acreage incrementally.

Meanwhile, he states, "We are a farm market and winery, taking a simple, not a sophisticated, approach to all we do." White wines are fermented, racked, and held in plastic containers; red wines are fermented, racked, and held in new 60-gallon Keystone American oak barrels. The wines undergo careful filtering and fining. The Maize Valley Winery produces a sweet style of white wine and a dry style of red wine.

The proprietors invite everyone to experience an Ohio farm winery. Activities they host include wine and food pairings, wagon rides, balloon liftoffs, helicopter rides, corn and haunted mazes, and a seasonal greenhouse, petting pasture, and pumpkin picking. "We focus on the farm, families, and fun," Benkan says.

Maize Valley Winery

Directions Take State Route 224 (76) to State Route 44 south to State Route 619 West for 1 mile to winery on north side.

Hours Seasonal, Monday–Saturday 10 a.m.–6 p.m., Sunday 10 a.m.–5 p.m.

Tours Educational tours for groups by appointment

Tastings By the glass or bottle, seating inside market or out on porch or patio

Gifts Year-round wine-oriented gifts; others vary by season

Picnics Yes

Highlights at Winery Great home-grown goodness from a local family farm and vineyard; offers more than forty types of meats, cheeses, salsas, dips, curries, relishes, olives, jams, jellies, honeys, seasonal fresh fruits and vegetables, baked goods, and seasonal flowers

Events Balloon liftoffs, helicopter rides, May days of wine and roses, October harvest happenings, campfires, wagon rides, kids' play area, petting pasture, greenhouse, corn maze, haunted maze, pumpkin picking

Restaurant Menu varies from steaks to sandwiches, with occasional hog roasts

Prices $9–$25; 10 percent case discount

Brand Names Maize Valley Winery

Type of Production Grape and fruit wines

Method of Harvesting By hand

Aging & Cooperage Limited, more as time progresses

Vineyards Founded 2004

County Stark

Acreage 4 acres of vineyards; more than 700 acres of farmland

Waterways Schwartz's ditch & Minishellin Creek

Climate Moderate

Soil Sandy hilltops to high organic mulch

Varieties Chardonnay, Chambourcin, Riesling, Concord, Vignoles, New York 73, strawberries, red raspberries, cherries, blueberries

Wines Chardonnay, Riesling, Cabernet Sauvignon, Chambourcin, Fredonia, Niagara, Catawba, strawberry, red raspberry, cherry, blueberry

Best Red Chambourcin

Best White Riesling

Other Best Wine Red raspberry

Nearby Places to Visit Pro Football Hall of Fame; McKinley Museum

Metrillo Wine Cellars

9841 York Alpha Drive, Suite B
North Royalton, OH 44113
Tel: (440)582-7000
Fax: (440)237-1130
E-mail: metrillowinecellars@yahoo.com
Web site: www.metrillowinecellars.com
Owners Susan and David Metro
Winemaker David Metro
Founded 2002

Metrillo Wine Cellars, located in a red brick building on York Alpha Drive in North Royalton, is part of the Western Reserve, a remnant of the land grant given to the colony of Connecticut by King Charles II of England in 1662. Susan and David Metro founded Metrillo in 2002 as one of northeast Ohio's first urban wineries. "The winery was formally named Metrillo Wine Cellars, a derivation of David's surname, Metro, and my family name, Mutillo," Susan says.

"I used to watch wine grapes, shipped by truck, arrive at the Joseph Mutillo family home. My grandfather produced red table wine in fifty-gallon barrels. Then, a grape was a grape and a wine was a wine," says Susan, a recreation center specialist. At Mutillo family gatherings, Susan's grandmother Marie often told stories of her grandfather's wine escapades while the family shared a glass of his wine with a meal.

Earlier, Susan Metro's grandfather had escaped Mussolini's wrath to arrive in America. A long period of writing to the U.S. government was necessary to enable the rest of the family to immigrate here. The Mutillos settled in Ashtabula, then later moved to Garfield Heights.

But it was David's avocation as a wine hobbyist that led to the Metros' discovery of their own Italian wine heritage. "I joined an amateur wine club," says David, president of D. J. Metro Mold and Die Company, just five doors down from the winery.

"We made more wine for fun," Susan says, "and even my grandmother got interested." Eventually, the Metros decided to introduce Clevelanders to an authentic and modern Ohio wine experience.

The winery was designed to offer guests and visitors hospitality in a casual, friendly environment. "We've created a homey place, where people can enjoy a reasonably priced evening out with their friends," Susan says. Customers buy five tastes of wine or one wine taste with an appetizer—brie and fresh fruit, Italian meatballs, or fresh crab dip. Light dinners, such as seafood bisque or quiche, are offered regularly, in addition to special nights featuring steak, scampi cookouts, and clambakes.

The Metros created a grand gathering hall reflective of Susan's creativity. They painted the interior white, adding lighting and a grand staircase. Pine and oak tables are accented with candles and comfortable chairs. They hung a floor-to-ceiling grape tapestry opposite the oak wine-tasting bar, which David designed. A grapevine tiered on a trellis serves as a reminder of where the wine comes from. Metro and Mutillo family portraits are interspersed in the art gallery with photos of the younger generation. Susan designs wine gift baskets for birthdays, anniversaries, and weddings; they are sold at retail with Metrillo wines, foods, novelties, candles, and accessories.

A self-taught winemaker, David began by buying grapes and juice from growers in Ohio and California. In 2000, the Metros purchased fifty-seven acres of farmland in Jefferson in Ashtabula County with plans to grow a vineyard and eventually retire there. The two-acre Metrillo Vineyards, located in the Lake Erie Appellation of Origin, has clay soils and a short, hot growing season. In 2001, the Metros planted 500 vines of Agawan, Cabernet Franc, Vidal Blanc, Chambourcin, and Vignoles; in 2002 they added 325 vines; and in 2003 they cultivated 150 vines of Traminette. Soon, the Metros will make estate-bottled wines from their own vineyards, which they hope will serve as a legacy to the next generation.

Metrillo Wine Cellars has a modern wine-pressing area, a stainless steel production facility, a wine lab, and a storage area. "I make 500 gallons annually—whatever tastes good," David says. "We buy all our white grape juice, cold stabilizing most white wines, such as the Riesling. We ferment the red wines on the skins, giving our Cabernet Sauvignon Reserve, for example, up to two years in small French oak barrels."

As the winemaker, David takes pride in the Metrillo Wine Cellars' premium table wines. The list comprises dry Chardonnay, Riesling, slightly off-dry Pinot Grigio, Niagara, Pink Catawba, Chambourcin, Merlot, Old Vines Zinfandel, Cabernet Sauvignon, an oak-aged Cabernet Sauvignon Reserve, Sangiovese, Barbera, Frosty White Ice Wine, and Metrillo Wine Cellars Sparkling Wine. With each vintage, the Metros are one step closer to fulfilling their vision of bringing family winemaking to the general public. They are intensely dedicated to providing quality for many years to come.

Metrillo Wine Cellars

Directions From I-71, take State Route 82 east, then turn left on York and left on York Alpha Drive to the winery. From I-77, take State Route 82 west, then turn right on York and left on York Alpha Drive to the winery.

Hours Wednesday–Friday 4–8 p.m.; Saturday 1–8 p.m.; also by appointment

Tours Educational tours with the winemaker

Tastings Tasting when winery is open or by reservation

Gifts Wine artifacts and related items, decorative candles, shirts, and gourmet foods

Highlights at Winery Modern urban winery with historic roots; homey setting designed with taste and flair; casual but friendly smoke-free atmosphere; reasonably priced evening out with friends

Events Chef Wally's cookouts; Friday Lenten dinners

Restaurant Light fare—simple appetizers and light dinners by request

Prices $9–$15; 10 percent case discount for shipping within Ohio

Brand Name Metrillo Wine Cellars

Type of Production Emphasis on quality vitis vinifera and vitis labrusca

Harvesting By hand

Pressing and Winemaking Bladder press

Aging Stainless steel tanks and 60-gallon French oak barrels

Vineyards Founded 2001

County Ashtabula

Appellation American and Lake Erie

Acreage 2 (57 total available)

Waterways Pond for watering vines

Climate Short, hot growing season

Soil Clay

Varieties Agawan, Cabernet Franc, Vidal Blanc, Chambourcin, Vignoles, Traminette

Wines Chardonnay, Riesling, Pinot Grigio, Niagara, Pink Catawba, Cabernet Sauvignon, Sangiovese, Barbera, Old Vines Zinfandel, Frosty White Ice Wine

Best Red Chambourcin

Best White: Traminette

Best Other Wine Vidal Blanc

Quote "Our Metrillo wines are somewhere in between being not too dry and not too sweet." —David Metro

Nearby Places to Visit Geauga Lake Park; Cleveland museums of art and natural history

Sarah's Vineyard

1204 West Steels Corners Road
Cuyahoga Falls, OH 44223
Tel: (330)929-8057
E-mail: mike@svwinery.com
Web site: www.svwinery.com
Owners Margaret and Mike Lytz
Winemaker Mike Lytz
Founded 2002

Sarah's Vineyard—a hybrid of a winery, art gallery, and studio that is scheduled to open late in 2005—is tucked in gently rolling hills on sixty-eight acres in the beautiful Cuyahoga Valley National Park. Proprietors Mike and Margaret Lytz named the site for their late daughter, Sarah Katherine Bertsch. The farmstead was founded in 2002 to capture her spirit of excitement for the creative arts.

Mike, a teacher with the Akron Public Schools, and Margaret, a nurse with the Akron City/Summa Health, have long pursued their avocations. Mike, a home winemaker for twenty-five years, dabbles

with his grandfather Miguel Archangelo Cerrone's recipe for dry Muscat, Aligante, and other wines. Margaret, a ceramicist, designs pottery and mosaic tiles in her studio.

For years, the Lytzes dreamed of a business that combined their loves of wine and art. They frequented country roads in search of affordable land. "We envisioned a place in northeast Ohio where people could stop by and we could sell our wine," Mike says. "We felt that undeveloped land at $15,000 to $25,000 an acre in this region was too expensive." They temporarily put their dream on hold.

One day, the Lytzes learned of the Cuyahoga Valley Countryside Initiative in the *Akron Beacon Journal*. It was a program to bring small farmsteads (which the government had purchased at the outset) to the Cuyahoga Valley to preserve its rural landscape. Cuyahoga Valley National Park Superintendent John Debo had studied the English agricultural practices. He learned that the British government owned 80 percent of the farms in the United Kingdom and leased them back to the farmers.

"We pursued this idea, wrote a competitive proposal, and won the bid," Mike says. "We emphasized sustainable agriculture using limited chemicals and fertilizers, mechanical weeding, integrated pest management, organic fungus control, and no application of herbicides or insecticides."

In 2002, the Lytzes moved into the original white farmhouse, accentuated by tall stands of trees. The property had no barn or significant out-buildings. They built a structure to house farm machinery, which they used to cultivate their hillsides. In 2003, they planted a two-and-a-half-acre Summit County vineyard in silty loam to Vidal Blanc, Cabernet Franc, Frontenac, Chambourcin, Traminette, Niagara, Rubiana, Seyval Blanc, and Cayuga. Their production features three white wines, three red wines, several fruit wines, and a dessert wine. "We believe good fruit makes good wine," Mike says. "We researched the possibilities with viticulturists and winegrowers."

"We settled on nine varieties," Margaret says, "with 2005 being our first vintage."

A sign along West Steel Corners Road reads "Sarah's Vineyard." The driveway leads to an antique, three-story, timber-framed building situated in a beautiful meadow with views of the vineyards. The winery was designed as a gathering place for friends and neighbors.

A large doorway opens to a vestibule, which leads to a 1,200-square-foot high-ceilinged art gallery and overhead loft. Colorful works—pottery, paintings, textiles, photography, and mosaics by local and regional artists—are displayed throughout the facility. The wine tasting bar introduces patrons to the winery's selections.

Customers are free to sip wine as they stroll through the gallery and around the grounds. An outdoor patio is planned to connect the gallery to the vineyard, the site of seasonal art shows, and to an herb and flower garden, which attracts butterflies and humming birds.

One staircase leads up to classrooms, where students receive instruction in quilting, woodworking, stained glass, and other mediums. "We encourage adults and children to take art classes," Margaret says. Behind the art gallery is her 1,200-square-foot art studio, where she teaches pottery. Another staircase leads down to the 2,400-square-foot wine center and aging cellar. Sarah's Vineyard produces wines that appeal to everyone, from dry to sweet to semi-sweet. Their approach blends tradition and innovation.

Sarah's Vineyard

Directions From State Route 8, exit at Steels Corners Road and go west for 3.8 miles. Sarah's Vineyard is just west of the Blossom Music Center on the opposite side of road. From I-271, exit at State Route 303 Richfield-Peninsula and go east 3 miles through Peninsula. Turn right (south) on Akron-Peninsula Road. Turn left on Steels Corners Road to Sarah's Vineyard.

Hours Call for hours

Tours Educational tours

Gifts Gallery and art studio

Picnics Will provide light fare, or bring your own food

Highlights at Winery Winery in park; high-quality art and fine wines; beautiful, enjoyable, and educational experience; personalized customer service

Events Summer Solstice Art Show & Wine Tasting; Fall Harvest Festival

Restaurant Light fare, fresh soups, homemade breads, cheeses, and desserts

Prices Moderate

Brand Names Sarah's Vineyard

Type of Production Both traditional and innovative

Method of Harvesting By hand

Pressing and Winemaking Natural

Aging and Cooperage Oak barrels and stainless steel

Vineyards Founded 2003

County Summit

Appellation American

Acreage 68

Waterway Cuyahoga River

Climate Temperate

Soil Silty loam

Varieties Vidal Blanc, Cabernet Franc, Frontenac, Chambourcin, Traminette, Niagara, Rubiana, Seyval Blanc, Cayuga

Best Red Wine Cabernet Franc

Best White Wine Seyval Blanc

Quote "Good fruit makes good wine."
—Mike Lytz

Nearby Places to Visit Ohio and Erie Canal Towpath Trail; Hale Farm and Village

Wolf Creek Vineyards

SUMMIT COUNTY
CABERNET FRANC
2002
ALCOHOL BY VOLUME 12.0%
750 mL

The Winery at Wolf Creek

2637 South Cleveland-Massillon Road
Norton, OH 44203
Tel: (330)666-9285 or (800)436-0426
Fax: (330)665-1445
E-mail: info@wineryatwolfcreek.com
Web site: www.wineryatwolfcreek.com
Owners Andy and Deanna Troutman
Winemaker Andy Troutman
Founded 1980

The steep hills and deep valleys among century-old farmsteads are one of the many great sights to behold in Summit County. The glass and wooden Winery at Wolf Creek, framed by elegant white pines, is yet another sight to see. An expanse of some five hundred acres of cherry and sugar maple, interspersed with rows of vines, swoops down a dramatic hillside to the raging Wolf Creek below. In the dis-

tance, the Akron skyline lingers.

The first thought that comes to mind is: What a spectacular place to live! The second: What a great place to build an Ohio winery. Fifty years ago, Andrew Wineberg purchased thirty-five acres of land here as an escape from his career as a chemist. He built a brick house on the ridgeline of the property, distinguished by its New England stone walls, and raised two sons, Andrew and Mike. Andrew Wineberg Jr. inherited the property, and later founded the vineyard and filled the role of winemaker. His brother, similarly inspired, established Pleasant Valley Vineyards in Mt. Vernon.

In 1996, Andy Troutman graduated from the Ohio State University School of Agriculture with a BS in horticulture and food microbiology. Recipient of the Lonz Winery Fellowship, he studied at the Ohio Agricultural Research and Development Center in Wooster before Andrew Wineberg hired him as the vineyard manager for The Winery at Wolf Creek. By 1998, Andy and his wife, Deanna, had expanded and started Troutman Winery and Vineyards, a farm winery in Wooster.

The next few years were tumultuous. Andrew Wineberg and his wife divorced, and he died unexpectedly. "I was the only person who knew how the cellar worked," Andy says. "Suddenly, I was the winemaker."

By 2002, the Troutmans purchased The Winery at Wolf Creek and employed their extended family. Andy made the wine; Deanna marketed it; Sara, Andy's sister, promoted it; and Bob, his father, oversaw the winery's maintenance and grounds.

There are five acres of vines (75 percent vertical shoot positioned and 25 percent bilateral cordoned) planted in sandy loam, clay loam, and gravel in Summit County. Similar to the climate in the Loire Valley, with the moderating Wolf Creek nearby, the vineyards consist of 20 percent red—Cabernet Franc and Chambourcin—and 80 percent white—Pinot Gris, Leon Millot, and Vignoles.

The grapes are harvested by hand and machine. Afterward, they are transferred into one thousand bins and sorted. The grapes are put into the destemmer-crusher and then into an Italian membrane press. The winery does mostly cold-fermentation fixed-capacity stainless steel tanks. "We age our wines on an average of six to eight months in 80 percent American oak and 20 percent French oak," Andy says, adding that they add new oak barrels every year.

He believes that Cabernet Franc has great potential in Summit County. Its full capacity as a varietal has yet to be explored. "We do no filtering of our Cabernet Franc," he says. "It is a very stable wine." He points out that their estate-grown Cabernet Franc is by far the winery's best red.

"We serve a diverse group of consumers from twenty to eighty years old. Their preference ranges from dry to semi-sweet to sweet," Andy says.

The Winery at Wolf Creek was designed to offer guests and visitors many possibilities. Some come and spend the day outdoors, hiking the woods and vineyards, then enjoying a hillside picnic with a great view. Some gather in the elegant tasting room to pair wine and food. Still others come to celebrate graduations, anniversaries, or weddings in the more formal great room. But regardless of how guests spend their time at Wolf Creek, they all share this magical experience in Ohio wine country.

The view of the vineyard from The Winery at Wolf Creek

Courtesy of the Ohio Wine Producers Association

The Winery at Wolf Creek

Directions From the north, take I-77 to State Route 21 south. Turn left at Minor Road and follow it to Cleveland-Massillon Road. The winery is 1 mile on the left. From the south, take I-77 to I-76 west. At exit 14, head north on Cleveland-Massillon road 1.5 miles to the winery on the right.

Hours January–March, Thursday 12–9 p.m., Friday–Saturday 12–10 p.m., Sunday 1–9 p.m.; April–December, Monday–Thursday 12–9 p.m., Friday–Saturday 12-11 p.m., Sunday 1–9 p.m.

Tours Cellar tours by appointment for ten or more

Tastings Daily when open

Gifts Wine accessories, clothing, and gift baskets

Picnics Picturesque grounds and romantic vistas for lovely picnics and gatherings

Highlights at Winery Incredible view for miles of reservoir and Akron skyline; quality packaging and quality line of wines

Prices $11–$23

Brand Names The Winery at Wolf Creek

Type of Production 80 percent white wine and 20 percent red wine

Method of Harvesting By hand and mechanical

Pressing and Winemaking Membrane press, mostly cold-fermented white wine

Aging and Cooperage 80 percent American oak, 20 percent French oak; one-third new oak per annum

Vineyards Founded 1979

County Summit

Appellation American

Acreage 5

Waterway Wolf Creek

Climate Similar to the Loire Valley soil, sandy loam, clay loam, and gravel

Varieties Cabernet Franc, Pinot Gris, Vignoles, Chambourcin, Leon Millot

Wines Cabernet Franc, Pinot Gris, White Lies, Original Sin, Rhapsody, Vignoles

Best Red Cabernet Franc

Best White Vignoles

Quote "Cabernet Franc has great potential here." —Andy Troutman

Nearby Places to Visit Downtown Akron attractions; Fairlawn shopping complex

Viking Vineyards

Glacier Myst

WHITE TABLE WINE
ALCOHOL 11% BY VOLUME   CONTAINS SULFITES
PRODUCED AND BOTTLED BY
VIKING VINEYARDS & WINERY, L.L.C., KENT, OHIO 44240

Viking Vineyards and Winery

268 Old Forge Road
Kent, OH 44240
Tel: (330)678-2080
Fax: (330)678-6364
E-mail: Viking@vikingvineyards.com
Web site: www.vikingvineyards.com
Owners Jeff and Dana Nelson
Winemaker Jeff Nelson
Founded 1999

Just off of Old Forge Road in Kent, a one-lane road passes by two lakes surrounded by wetlands and woodlands and leads to Viking Vineyards and Winery. The wine estate commemorates the Scandinavian heritage of founders Jeff and Dana Nelson and the North American Norse settlement Vinland, described in Icelandic Sagas as rich in grapes, timber, and wheat.

In 1997, the Nelsons contemplated departing the rigors of travel and corporate life for a more fulfilling existence. "We decided on the wine business," says Dana, a former manager with the Timken Company. They designed their lives around people who shared their love of viticultural and vinification. In 1998, they purchased a twenty-acre property with a house, a pole barn, and lakes. Viking Vineyards and Winery was transformed into a country residence with a rustic winery, an estate vineyard, and water vistas.

The Nelsons consulted a viticulturist from the Ohio Agricultural Research Center to evaluate their Portage County land, soil, and climate and its suitability as a vineyard. "We dug holes and discovered sandy loam, perfect for hardy winter-resistant varietals," says Jeff, who doubles as an environmental consultant for J. Nelson Enterprises. In 1999 the Nelsons planted one-and-a-half acres of Vidal Blanc, Traminette (a first-generation hybrid off of Gewürztraminer), and Lemberger on a northerly, gently sloping vineyard. The trellises are vertical shoot positioned, and the typically hot Midwestern climate has no lake effect to moderate it. Additional juice—Chardonnay, Riesling, Pinot Gris, Cabernet Sauvignon, Chambourcin, and Marechal Foch—originates from growers in Ohio and New York.

Viking Vineyards offers striking lakeside views

A descendant of Illinois dairy farmers, Jeff produced his first wine while he was a student at the University of Illinois. Later, he experimented at home. But the real test of his skills began in 1999 with his first one thousand gallons at Viking Vineyards. "I specialize in small-batch, limited-production wines," he says, pointing out that the pole barn winery had no electricity, water, insulation, or even a floor until they rebuilt it. The wine grapes are harvested by hand, then pressed and crushed in a small bladder-basket press. The wines are fermented in stainless steel tanks with either a variable capacity, a floating lid, or a fixed capacity. Oak staves are used to age some whites and reds.

"Viking Vineyards wines are made crisp, dry, and refreshing in the style of Alsatian wines from France," Jeff says. "Typically they are characterized as very drinkable and lighter than other wines on the market, especially the reds."

Dana has used her prior career experience to analyze their wine products and define their target market. "Our wines are fruit-forward and palate-friendly," she says. "And for consumers with wonderful memories of Niagara and Concord, we have other styles of wines we produce."

The Nelsons' strategy to build market share was twofold. They built the reputation of Viking Winery with a good-tasting Viking product. In 1999, they started with a white, thirty-seat, view-oriented tasting room. Jeff's photography of landscapes is on display with other artists' and craftsmen's work. By 2002, the Nelsons added a second hospitality building and lakeside seating. In 2004, sales soared to 4,000 gallons of wine annually.

"We've tried to create a relaxed, cozy atmosphere, a place where people can enjoy themselves," Dana says. "People buy wine by the glass or bottle along with imported cheese and meats, or munchies. Sometimes, they bring their own picnic and a pack of cards, or enjoy our hot dog roasts by the lake or live entertainment on the weekends."

Viking Vineyards & Winery's wines have won several medals: both a Silver and a Bronze for the Nordic Myst, Bronze Medals for the Chambourcin and Valhalla, and a Silver for the Vidal Blanc Ice Wine.

Viking Vineyards and Winery

Directions Take I-76 to exit 31 (State Route 43 and Kent exit). Proceed south on State Route 43 for 2 miles. Turn right on Old Forge Road for less than 2 miles to the winery on the left.

Hours January–March, Tuesday–Thursday 5–9 p.m., Friday and Saturday 12–11 p.m.; April–December, Tuesday–Thursday 1–9 p.m.; Friday and Saturday 12–11 p.m.

Tours Informal, pending availability

Tastings All wines available for sampling, price depends on price of wine

Gifts Gift shop features wine-related items, many hand-painted and hand-crafted

Picnics Encouraged during good weather on beautiful deck by lake

Highlights at Winery Cozy, friendly, relaxed atmosphere; small-batch, award-winning wines

Events Summer bonfires/hot dog roasts; themed dinners during the winter

Restaurant Light menu

Prices $8.49–$26.99

Brand Names Viking Vineyards

Type of Production Small-batch, limited production

Method of Harvesting Hand-harvested

Pressing and Winemaking Small bladder press used to do whole-berry press for ice wine, or crushed-berry press for other wines

Aging and cooperage All wines are fermented in stainless steel, some with oak staves

Vineyards Founded 1999

County Portage

Appellation American

Acreage 1.5

Climate Typical Midwestern with no lake-effect moderation

Soil Sandy loam where the grapes are planted

Varieties Vidal Blanc, Traminette, Lemberger

Wines Vidal Blanc, Riesling, Chardonnay, Pinot Gris, Cabernet Sauvignon, Chambourcin, Marechal Foch, various blends

Best Red Valhalla

Best White Nordic Myst

Other Best Wine Salmon Run

Quote "Typically, the wines may be characterized as palate-friendly and lighter than other wines on the market—especially the reds." —Jeff Nelson

Nearby Places to Visit Kent Museum of Fashion; Aurora Premium Outlets

*Vidal Blanc grapes glistening
on the vine at Viking Vineyard*

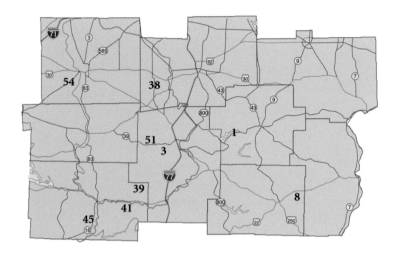

Appalachian Country Tour

Vineyards at dawn at The Ohio State University/Ohio Agricultural Research and Development Center

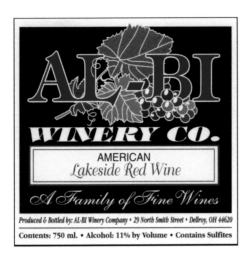

AMERICAN
Lakeside Red Wine

A Family of Fine Wines

Produced & Bottled by: AL-BI Winery Company • 29 North Smith Street • Dellroy, OH 44620

Contents: 750 ml. • Alcohol: 11% by Volume • Contains Sulfites

Al-Bi Winery

29 North Smith Street
Dellroy, OH 44620
Tel: (330)735-1061
Web site: www.ohiowines.org
Owners/Winemakers Alan Rummell
and Bill Burrow
Founded 2003

The Al-Bi Winery, founded in 2003, is located in Dellroy in Carroll County, eight miles west of Carrollton, the county seat, on the eastern shore of beautiful Atwood Lake. This quaint hamlet of 350, a dry town until the spring of 2004, represents a modern-day version of life in the agricultural heartland, which began in the early 1800s.

Partner Alan Rummell, an owner of a metal-fabricating shop, had an inclination for business. Partner Bill Burrow, a sales-man for a steel company, had a love for home winemaking. While in the steel industry, they crossed paths and their interests merged.

"I made wine for fifteen years as a hobbyist," says Burrow, a Mineral City native. "I bought kits that used either grape concentrate or fresh juice to make wine." In time, Rummell learned of Burrow's winemaking, which aroused his curiosity in mastering this fine art. "One day, we decided we wanted to do something," Burrow says.

So, the gentlemen of Carroll County created a catchy name for their new wine venture. Rummell took the "Al" from his first name and hyphenated it with the "Bi" from Burrow's first name to get Al-Bi. "It had an Italian-sounding name that complemented our new Italian winemaking equipment," Burrows says.

Next, the partners searched for a historic building in tree-lined Dellroy that they converted into a working winery. They were challenged by an archaic county ordinance restricting where wine could be produced and sold on the same premises.

"We purchased a simple wood-frame building on the main thoroughfare that had previously housed other businesses," Burrows says. "We renovated the building ourselves, giving it a rustic look by showcasing some of the natural wood. We designed a rough-sawed poplar tasting bar and a place to display the Al-Bi Winery wines, a focal point in the main room with tables and chairs for twelve."

Al-Bi Winery contracts its berries from Washington and its cherries from Michigan. Its grape juice originates from Ohio's Virant Family Vineyards and Chalet Debonné Vineyards as well as from Pennsylvania's Presque Isle Wine Cellars. "We produce 1,600 gallons of wine, roughly 4,000 bottles annually," Burrow says. A small artisan winery, it emphasizes specialty hand-crafted berry and fruit wines and two styles of dandelion wines. "Five of our Al-Bi wines are dry, and the rest of our wines are varying degrees of sweet."

The fresh berries and cherries, along with the grape juices, are shipped by refrigerated truck to Dellroy, where they are off-loaded into Italian stainless steel tanks and American polymer barrels. The berry and cherry wines undergo a classic crushing and destemming before pressing and fermentation. Pending the nature and style of the wines to be made, they are held in barrel for various lengths of time. The wine is properly balanced, then filtered and fined several times before it is hand-bottled, corked, and labeled. Viniferas and more complex wines are aged up to one year in barrel, with additional bottle age.

Al-Bi Winery features twenty wines in its collection. The Atwood Secret, a blended red wine, and the Atwood Mist, a blended white wine, are among the most popular in the collection.

"Our customers come from all walks of life—from local construction workers to the woman, eighty-five, who buys cherry wines every two weeks. They are devoted customers who have heard about us by word-of-mouth or through friends," says Burrow, who recently hosted a private tasting for a delegation of future Russian entrepreneurs. "People enjoy coming here!" In addition, the winery wholesales to retail establishments in the region, from Canton to Apple Creek. "We want to make a wine that tastes good and sells. We strive to be friendly and gracious to our customers," he says.

Al-Bi Winery

Directions Take I-77 to U.S. Route 30 east toward East Liverpool/Canton. Merge onto State Route 43 toward Waynesburg. Turn right on State Route 183/West Libson Street and left onto West Street, which becomes Silver Street, which becomes Morges Street, which becomes Bark Road NW. Turn left on State Route 542 to the winery on Smith Street.

Hours Monday–Friday 5–8 p.m.; Saturday 10 a.m.–8 p.m.

Tours Self-guided

Tastings Daily when open

Gifts Wine

Picnics Small gazebo in the town of Dellroy

Highlights at Winery Friendly, down-home nature of place and character of owners; rustic but relaxing step back in time

Events Ohio Wine Producers Wine Trail

Prices $8–$13; 10 percent case discount

Brand Names Al-Bi Winery

Type of Production Small artisan fruit and berry wines

Aging and Cooperage Predominately stainless steel and polymer

County Carroll

Appellation American

Varieties Chardonnay, Merlot, Concord, Delaware, Vidal Blanc, Niagara, Elderberry, Strawberry, Blackberry, Black Cherry, Red Cherry, Plum

Wines Chardonnay, Merlot, Concord, Delaware, Vidal Blanc, Atwood Mist, Atwood Secret, Atwood Rose, Roadhouse Red, Niagara, Elderberry, Strawberry, Blackberry, Black Cherry, Red Cherry, Plum, Golden Brown Dandelion Wine, Dandy-Dandy Dandelion Wine

Best Red Wine Atwood Secret

Best White Wine Atwood Mist

Best Other Wine Dandelion Wines

Quote "We want to make a wine that tastes good and sells. We strive to be friendly and gracious to our customers." —Bill Burrow

Nearby Places to Visit Atwood Queen Cruise Boat; Algonquin Mill Complex

Breitenbach Wine Cellars

5934 Old Route 39 NW
Dover, OH 44622
Tel: (330)343-3603
Fax: (330)343-8290
E-mail: amishwine@tusco.net
Web site: www.breitenbachwine.com
Owner Cynthia Bixler
Winemaker Dalton Bixler
Founded 1981

The road west on State Route 39 through Ohio's historic Amish Country passes through steep, rolling hills and wide, gracious valleys to Breitenbach Wine Cellars in Dover. The purple and peach Rhine castle, with its twin towers and gold finials, rises out of the valley as a tribute to the many generations of Swiss Germans who have worked these beautiful farmlands. The winery was named Breitenbach, which means broad or wide stream in German, for the waterway that crosses the 120-acre property.

Founders Cynthia and Dalton "Duke" Bixler, German descendants from Sugarcreek and Bolivar, respectively, were among the first pioneers in the region to cultivate the culinary arts. The Bixlers began with a retail establishment in 1980 featuring Swiss cheese, quality meats, and fresh produce. Today, they share this legacy with their daughters, marketing and retail manager Anita Davis and winemaker and wholesale manager Jennifer Kohler.

Breitenbach evolved out of the Bixlers' creativity and talents. Duke was the designer; he loved to do integrated marketing, sales, and public relations. Cynthia was the planner; she thought out each step of the business. "My father did some line drawings that illustrated what he envisioned the place might look like," Davis says. "My mother gave his ideas style, adding the stained glass and antiques." The retail environment was conceived to flow from one venue to the next. Each part of the operation, from the market, gift shop, and tasting room to the picnic facilities and café, belongs to the whole concept.

"At the onset, our customers were an older Germanic population. Now we see younger professionals with small children," Davis says. "We used to sell 90 percent of our wine at the winery. We now manage our

The culinary arts are an age-old tradition at Breitenbach

crusher-destemmer and transferred to the two bladder presses, which on average process thirty to forty tons of wine grapes per day.

The rich color is extracted on the skins during the primary fermentation of the red wine grapes—Cabernet Sauvignon, Merlot, Syrah, and Pinot Noir. The taste and the flavor are achieved during the secondary malolactic fermentation. All the white wine grapes—the Chardonnay, Rieslings, Gewürztraminer, Vidal Blanc, and Seyval Blanc—are cold-fermented in temperature-controlled, jacketed fermenters. Once the fermentation is complete, the wines are racked off the lees, then held in stainless steel tanks or oak aging barrels in the cellar.

"Our wines average nine months to two years in barrel before they are balanced, then bottled, labeled, sealed, and stored," Davis says. "We started at 1,500 gallons annually and have now grown to 120,000 gallons annually."

One of Ohio's largest producers, Breitenbach Wine Cellars has achieved notoriety for its Gold Medal winner and

own distribution with drivers and a fleet of trucks—60 percent is sold at the winery, and 40 percent is sold at wholesale to the trade."

The winemaking began simply enough in the cellar below Der Marktplatz, German for "marketplace." In 1985, Duke Bixler converted the threshing barn, which had housed the girls' riding and show horses, into a modern wine-production center. As winemaker, he outfitted it with new state-of-the-art equipment and implemented the latest research and technology. This included stainless steel fermentors, American, French, and Hungarian oak aging barrels, an automated bottling line, and a wine lab.

The wine grapes are purchased from top Lake Erie growers. Once the grapes are transported to Dover, they are dumped into the best red, Roadhouse Red, a semi-sweet blend of Concord, Niagara, and Baco Noir; its best white, Frost Fire, a blend of Niagara, Delaware, and Vidal Blanc; and its Culinary Institute Gold Medal winner and other best wine, Festival, a blend of California Cabernet Sauvignon and Zinfandel with New York Pinot Noir.

"My father takes pride in having pioneered some fifteen natural fruit and berry wines," Davis says. "The elderberries and the strawberries are grown by Amish farmers, the raspberries and the apples originate from Geneva growers, and the plums and the peaches come from Michigan growers. Our dry red Breitenbach vitis vinifera wines are also very popular."

Breitenbach Wine Cellars

Directions Take I-77 to the Dover/Sugarbush exit. Proceed 5 miles west on State Route 39 to the winery.

Hours Monday–Saturday 9 a.m.–6 p.m.

Tours By appointment; call for scheduled tours

Tastings Daily when open

Gifts Full range of gifts

Picnics Encouraged

Highlights at Winery Friendly atmosphere; beautiful surroundings; purple barn; award-winning wines

Events Annual Dandelion May-Fest; National Dandelion Cook-off

Prices $8.50–37.98

Brand Names Breitenbach

Type of Production Vitis vinifera, French hybrids, vitis labrusca, fruit and berry wines

Pressing and Winemaking Bladder press with traditional winemaking practices

Aging and Cooperage Hungarian and French oak barrels

County Tuscarawas

Appellation American

Varieties 35 total

Wines Chardonnay, Johannisberg Riesling, Gewürztraminer, Vidal Blanc, Seyval Blanc, Cabernet Sauvignon, Merlot, Syrah, Pinot Noir, Old Dusty Miller, First Crush, Millennium, Charming Nancy, Silver Seyval, Roadhouse Red, Frost Fire, Festival, Solera Cream Sherry, Tawny Port, Jacks Apple Amish Wine, Amish Country Wine, fruit and berry wines (including Dandelion wine)

Best Red Roadhouse Red

Best White Frost Fire

Other Best Wine Festival

Nearby Places to Visit Amish Country; Roscoe and Zoar villages

Coffee Cake Winery

48018 Giacobbi Road
Hopedale, OH 43976
Tel: (740)937-2572
Fax: (740)937-2053
E-mail: ccwinery@cohio.net
Owners Frank and Janet Kuchan
Winemaker Frank Kuchan
Founded 2001

Coffee Cake Winery, ensconced in the forests of the Appalachians in Hopedale, sits in a peaceful clearing sixteen miles from the Ohio River Valley in southeastern Ohio. Proprietors Frank and Janet Kuchan, educators from nearby Steubenville and Dillonvale, descended from Croatian ancestors who migrated to this isolated territory in the 1800s. Frank's grandfather was a recognized chef at the Fort-Steubenville Hotel, which had a reputation for offering the best accommodations on the toll road between Pittsburgh and Columbus. Proud of this culinary heritage, Frank, a biologist, and Janet, a science teacher, found themselves in the wine industry well over a century later. They honored their forbearers by translating their German surname, Kuchan, into English; the resulting word refers to a type of coffee cake, and named their winery accordingly.

In 1969, the Kuchans purchased a farm on eighty-five acres in Harrison County, where they raised their children, Telicia, Verner, and Julianne. "The place was an absolute disaster," says Frank, who is also a naturalist. "The land was ruined, as no reclamation laws existed in Ohio during the fifties. We were determined to provide our children a country environment."

The Kuchans embarked on a multitude of improvements that characterized the country atmosphere of their home and winery establishment. Their farm provided them a lifetime of unexpected adventures. At first, they industriously maintained a herd of cattle, flocks of chickens, rabbits, and huge gardens. Some evenings, Janet observed Frank with a glass of wine in hand as he surveyed his empty fields. "I saw him look at the wine, then look back across the fields. Then he looked at the wine, and I knew he envisioned a field planted with wine grapes," she says.

In 1991, the Kuchans cultivated the clay soil on their farm and planted a test vineyard. The varietals were De Chaunac, Millot, Foch, Biagio, Baco Noir, Chancellor, Seyval Blanc, Vignoles, Vidal Blanc, Traminette, Aurora, and Cabernet Franc. "We made more wine than we could ever sell," Frank says. Additional grapes were planted in 1994, some two hundred vines in 1996, and one hundred vines each year thereafter. Today there are more than two thousand vines. Coffee Cake Vineyards made its first profit by selling its wine grapes to a vintner friend and to other regional wineries. Their friend encouraged them to start their own winery, and in 2001, the Kuchans opened Coffee Cake Winery and featured their first estate-grown wines.

Today, the gravel driveway leads to a landscaped parking area and a wood-shingled tasting room and gift shop. A sheltered terrace for outdoor wine and food events captures views of the gently sloping vineyards and farm buildings. Steps lead up to a porch and the family residence, a huge log cabin with winemaking and aging cellars. "We are located out where the fast lane ends," says Janet. Her friendly dogs wag their tails as they escort guests around the property.

Each September, the Kuchans invite three groups of thirty friends to their annual vintage celebration. "People harvest grapes over three days for four hours, then we fire up the grill, relax, and invite our guests to stay for as long as they wish. In appreciation, we give them a gift of wine from our private cellar," Frank says.

Volunteers haul the lug boxes from the vineyards to the crusher-destemmer under the house, where a ton of grapes per day is pressed in an Italian hydraulic basket press. The red and white wines are fermented in 50-gallon plastic drums; the wines remain there until completion of the first settling. All the new wines are racked and pumped over, then clarified in stainless steel tanks. "If the Romans had stainless steel," Frank says, "the oak barrel would never have been invented." The wine is held indefinitely in 15-gallon units, mounted on wheels, and bottled as needed.

Coffee Cake Winery produces 2,000 gallons of wine a year—predominately French hybrids and two vitis viniferas, Chardonnay and Cabernet Franc. The wines vary from dry to semi-dry and semi-sweet to sweet. "We promote quality Ohio grapes paired with good Ohio food. People often make judgments based on what they are told. At Coffee Cake Winery, we are different. We feature the best wine grapes grown from our wine estate," Frank says. "What we get from other farms is fruit for our apple and strawberry wines."

Coffee Cake Winery

Directions From U.S. 22 east, take Hopedale exit 151 east in a northerly direction, followed by a quick left onto dirt Giacobbi Road to the winery.

Hours April–October, Monday–Thursday 11 a.m.–6 p.m., Friday–Saturday 11 a.m.–9 p.m., closed Sunday; November–December, Monday–Saturday 11 a.m.–6 p.m.; January–March, by appointment

Tours Informal

Tasting Daily when open

Picnics Yes

Highlights at Winery Good wine and lots of fun; relaxed atmosphere; lovely setting; friendly people interested in wine

Events Monthly "Sophisticated Cowboy Parties" featuring Coffee Cake wines with bison burgers and all the trimmings

Prices $9–$13; 10 percent case discount

Brand Names Coffee Cake Winery

Type of Production French hybrids and vitis vinifera

Method of Harvesting By hand

Pressing Traditional methods

Aging and Cooperage Stainless steel

Vineyards Founded 1991

County Harrison

Appellation American

Acreage 3

Climate Cold winters and hot, humid summers

Soil Clay

Varieties De Chaunac, Leon Millot, Foch, Biagio, Baco Noir, Chancellor, Seyval Blanc, Vignoles, Vidal Blanc, Traminette, Aurora, Cabernet Franc

Wines Cabernet Sauvignon, Black Knight, Nightfall, Midnight Ruby, Frosted Blush, Chardonnay, Crystal Glow, Autumn Gold, Satin, Red Satin, Ohio Amber, Strawberry

Best Red Black Knight

Best White Crystal Glow

Other Best Wine Autumn Gold

Quote "If the Romans would have had stainless steel, the oak barrel never would have been invented." —Frank Kuchan

Nearby Places to Visit Clark Gable and Coal museums in Cadiz; Wheeling Downs

Perennial Vineyards

11877 Poorman Street
Navarre, OH 44662
Tel: (330)832-3677
Fax: (330)832-3677
E-mail: info@perennialvineyards.com
Web site: www.ohiowines.org

Owner Damon Leeman

Winemaker Damon Leeman; assistant
winemaker: Nick Novak

Founded 2002

The founding of Perennial Vineyards, located in a white 1848 bank barn in the rolling hills of Navarre, marked the advent of viticulture to an Ohio region long steeped in dairy farms, cheese houses, and croplands. Owners Damon Leeman, a native of

Massillon, and his cousin Nick Novak, a native of Brewster, merged their resources in 1999 to start a winery in a community ready for change.

In 1999, Leeman purchased an attractive forty-acre Stark County farm at a lofty elevation for Ohio—960 feet. It featured classic architecture dating from the Civil War. An elegant two-story red-brick colonial house dominated the striking tree-lined property, along with a red-shingled dairy barn and a lofting shed. Leeman, a graduate in fermentation sciences, preceded Novak, a graduate in animal sciences, at Ohio State University. Good luck brought them together.

"We discovered that we shared a common interest in wine and both approached it as a hobby," Novak says. "When we started this venture, we didn't have any expectations about anything. Our winery concept was to be different, and the winery has literally taken off!"

Initially, Perennial Vineyards was established along Poorman Road as a four-acre plot of grapes in a depression protected by trees. "The vineyards were tiled, with a limestone underpan and a clay overlay of topsoil, with a standard, bilateral trellising system," Novak says. The vineyard was expanded to eleven acres to include Vidal Blanc, Cayuga, Chancellor, Riesling, Concord, Niagara, Delaware, Vignoles, and Chambourcin. Chardonnay, Cabernet, and Syrah are purchased from Ryan Leeman, Damon's brother and the winemaker at the

Van Ruten Winery in Lodi, California.

Leeman and Novak tossed around a number of ideas on how best to introduce their Perennial Vineyards wines. They decided to convert the barn and lofting shed into a winery. "We did all the work ourselves," Novak says.

They built an entrance with an oval glass-and-oak door, accentuated with urns and antiques. They gutted the lofting shed, reused the walnut beams, and laid concrete and urethane floors. Hans Leeman, Damon's Swiss grandfather, painted European landscapes above the walnut tasting bar. They hung a wine painting above the fireplace at the far end of the room. And they furnished the tasting room, which has a window into the wine-production center, with rich mahogany tables, chairs, lamps, and oriental rugs.

A ramp leads to a larger room, which features a quarried-river-stone wall (part of the foundation of the bank barn) and reused walls. It is designed for crowds who sit at Leeman's hand-hewn wooden tables and chairs to listen to an acoustic guitarist or a local band. "Our intent was to create a comfortable but relaxed place. We appeal to an after-dinner crowd, who like to socialize while pairing wine and food," Novak says. A grape arbor and sunset patio draw groups of people who enjoy the evening bonfires or informal barbeques.

During harvest, the grapes are hand-picked, then brought to the winery, where they are dumped in the crusher-destemmer. Traditional wine practices are followed using an automated, hydraulic wooden bladder basket press. The white and red wines are fermented in stainless steel, then aged and held in stainless steel or American oak and central European oak. "Lighter-style Beaujolais wines are aged for two months, while our reserves are aged from eight months to one year," Novak says.

Perennial Vineyards produces True North, a moderately dry Chardonnay and Vidal blend; Vino Rose, a blend of eight varietals; Eclipse, a dry Merlot, Zinfandel, and Chambourcin; a bone-dry Eclipse Reserve; and Sangria. Leeman and Novak, dedicated wine enthusiasts, are committed to educating the public on new tastes, styles, and discoveries. "Wine opens the secrets of the soul," Novak says.

Perennial Vineyards

Directions From Cleveland, take I-77 south to exit 172A toward Akron. Merge onto State Route 21 south and take exit 136 toward Massillon. Follow State Route 241 and exit at Oberlin Avenue. Turn right and take State Route 241/Finefrock Road SW. Turn left on 17th St. SW, which becomes Carmont Avenue SW. Turn right on Poorman Street SW to the winery. From Columbus, take I-71 north to exit 176, U.S. Route 30. Continue on U.S. 30 east toward Wooster. Take State Route 241 exit to State Route 93/Massillon. Turn right on State Route 241/Millersburg Road SW. Turn left on State Route 93/Manchester Avenue SW. Turn left on Poorman Street to winery.

Hours December–March, Thursday 5–10 p.m., Friday–Saturday 1–11 p.m.; April–November, Thursday-Saturday 1–11 p.m.

Tours By appointment

Gifts Wine and clothing

Picnics Encouraged

Highlights at Winery Unusual décor; friendly attitude; upbeat and fun-loving after-dinner crowd; good wine, food, and entertainment

Events Fourth of July and annual pig roast

Restaurant Light fare—appetizers, antipastos, bread, cheeses

Prices $10–$16; Reserves $25; 10 percent case discount

Brand Names Perennial Vineyards

Type of Production Traditional

Method of Harvesting By hand

Pressing and Winemaking Automated hydraulic, wooden, bladder, basket press

Aging and Cooperage Stainless steel and American and central European oak

Vineyards Founded 1999–2000

County Stark

Appellation Ohio

Acreage 11

Climate Cold winters and hot, humid summers

Soil Tiled, limestone, underpan, clay overlay

Varieties Vidal Blanc, Cayuga, Chancellor, Riesling, Concord, Niagara, Delaware, Vignoles, Chambourcin

Wines True North, Vino Rose, Cayuga White, Eclipse, Eclipse Reserve, Sangria

Best Red Eclipse

Best White True North

Other Best Wine Vino Rose

Quote "Wine opens the secrets of the soul." —Nick Novak

Nearby Places to Visit Akron Symphony; Cuyahoga Valley Scenic Railroad

Rainbow Hills Vineyards

26349 TR 251
Newcomerstown, OH 43832
Tel: (740)545-9305
Owner/Winemaker Leland C. Wyse
Founded 1989

As you wind your way off of U.S. Route 36 west onto State Route 751, the Coshocton viticultural district comes alive. By the time you reach Township Road 251, there is a feeling of possibly being lost, but the farms of Newcomerstown seem to say, *Keep going. The winery is just around the corner.*

The road into Rainbow Hills Vineyards is a path to a pot of gold, one of the prettiest places in Ohio. The one-lane road twists and turns past an open meadow with two brooks running through it, around contoured vineyards, and to the winery in the flat of the valley. Up ahead lies an artistic enclave—an enchanting rustic sandstone and wooden tree house, moving flower gardens, and a soaring fountain.

Years ago, after owners Leland and Joy Wyse had lived in Oregon and, later, Australia, where he was a biologist, they were jolted by an unexpected experience. "We were leaving Australia for good and were near the Outback, some sixty miles from the airport. Off in the distance, we saw a distinct rainbow; the next moment, we drove right through it," Leland says.

It wasn't until much later, when the Wyses returned to the United States, that they began to look for property in Ohio. "We discovered a deserted eighty-two-acre farm and named it Rainbow Hills Vineyards." Suddenly the meaning of their Australian rainbow experience began to bear fruit. The Wyses cleared the land. "It was like a jungle," Leland says. Next, they laid the foundation for their three-level, 3,000-square-foot mountain retreat. "We built every building, we laid every stone, and we planted every grape."

Steep stairs lead past a sandstone foundation, cut as blocks from a quarry on the property, to the tree house. An oak door on a viewing porch graces the exterior of the building, which is cantilevered off the mountain. Walkways and lookouts with sitting benches for tasting wine parallel the hillside and end at the patio, where barbeques and picnics are held. Splendid views take in Joy Wyse's four-hundred-plant perennial garden, which jumps with seasonal color. The woods are teaming with maple, sugar maple, beech, red oak, and white oak trees, which hang over swift streams with dancing waterfalls. There is wildlife everywhere.

The interior, designed for cozy groups, consists of slate floors, paned windows, and poplar and ash walls. A tasting bar serves homemade bread, cheeses, fruit, and, of course, the wines of Rainbow Hills Vineyards. The room ascends some eighteen feet, dominated by a fireplace made of river stone and surrounded by white walls mounted with the Wyses' favorite paintings. Artist Guy Manning's untitled picture of an Indian chief captivates the viewer with the reverence and strength of the subject. An 1831 log cabin on the premises has been newly renovated into a 2,000-square-foot, four-unit bed and breakfast.

The south-facing vineyards were planted in 1985, 1986, and 1987. They consist of four acres of three-wired, standard trellising planted in well-drained, shallow-acid limestone soils. Similar to the Ohio River Valley, the climate is suitable for growing Seyval Blanc, De Chaunac, Catawba, Niagara, Cabernet Franc, Riesling, and Chardonel. During the harvest, the wine grapes are hand-picked, then tumbled by a crusher and destemmer at the modern steel winery. ("The ancient barn fell into the creek, so we had to replace it," Leland says.) Next, the grapes are pressed in an oak stave, wooden basket press, then fermented in either stainless steel tanks or American oak barrels. The Chardonel, for example, is aged in American white oak. The red wines, on the other hand, are aged in stainless steel tanks and American oak barrels for up to four years. Afterward, the finished wines are clarified, then bottled, corked, foiled, and properly stored. Rainbow Hills Vineyards has high demand for its Cabernet Franc, its best red, Riesling, its best white, and Rainbow Rose, a delightful Catawba. Other choices go by poetic names like White Gold, Prism, Spectrum, Drumming Grouse, and Aires. "I believe that for the Ohio wineries to be well known, we must all be careful and keep the quality of winemaking high," Leland declares. "Quality wines, not mediocre ones, reflect on all of us."

Rainbow Hills Vineyards

Directions From I-77, exit onto U.S. Route 36 west toward Newscomerstown/Coschoton for 6 miles. Turn right on State Route 751 for 2 miles, then left, following signs to the winery.

Hours June–September Monday–Thursday 11 a.m.–6 p.m., Friday and Saturday 11 a.m.–9 p.m., closed Sunday

Tours Self-guided through vineyards and woods

Tastings Always available

Picnics Picnics are encouraged

Highlights at Winery Lovely, rolling hills of Coschocton County; delightful cheese and bread boards with favorite wines

Events Summer cookouts and barbeques featuring steak, chicken, salad, and dessert (reservations needed); winter wine tasting dinners on Fridays and Saturdays (reservations needed)

Restaurant Cookouts and wine tasting dinners

Prices $7.75–$13.00; Cookouts $24 per person; Wine tasting dinners $35 per person

Brand Names Rainbow Hills Vineyards

Method of Harvesting Hand-harvested

Pressing and Winemaking Basket press and traditional winemaking

Aging and Cooperage American oak

Vineyards Founded 1985, 1986, and 1987

County Coschocton

Appellation Ohio viticultural district

Acreage 4

Waterways Two streams run through property

Climate Central to Ohio River Valley

Soil Shallow acid, well-drained, limestone soils

Varieties Seyval Blanc, Catawba, Riesling, Cabernet Franc, De Chaunac, Niagara, Chardonnay

Wines Grensell Red, White Gold, Rainbow Rose, Prism, Spectrum, Drumming Grouse, Aries, Chardonel, Riesling, Cabernet Franc

Best Red Cabernet Franc

Best White Riesling

Other Best Wine Catawba

Quote "We must all be careful to keep the quality high." —Leland C. Wyse

Nearby Places to Visit Roscoe Village; The Longaberger Company

Raven Rouge
SEMI-SWEET RED TABLE WINE

Alcohol 13% by volume

Raven's Glenn Winery

56183 County Road 143
West Lafayette, OH 43845
Tel: (740)545-1000
Fax: (740)545-9162
E-mail: vino@ravensglenn.com
Web site: www.ravensglenn.com
Owners Robert and Renee Guilliams
Winemaker Tony Carlucci
Founded 1997

The Raven's Glenn Winery sits on the banks of the languid Tuscarawas River at the crossroads of U.S. Route 36 and Coshocton County Road 143 in West Lafayette. The modern winery was named for the raven, a twenty-five-inch-long black Corvid, the largest of the perching birds, common to the west, north, and, recently, the east.

The raven is noted for its vocalizations, intelligence, acrobatics, and love of soaring. For owners Robert and Renee Guilliams as well as their son Robert Beau,

grandson Roland Morgan, and Robert's brother Jeff Guilliams, the legendary bird is the symbol of a family that has launched its winery and is ready to soar.

For years, the Guilliamses owned and operated several long-term care facilities in the area. Each year, the family took a trip to California's Heavenly Valley Ski Resort in South Lake Tahoe. Afterward, they would escape to the Napa Valley, where they enjoyed touring the wineries. The Guilliamses were fascinated by the integrated lifestyle-work ethic and wine products. "I used my digital camera to record details that intrigued me," Robert says. "Certain elements caught my eye—architecture, design, interiors, equipment, cellars, barrels, tasting rooms, retail displays, doors, floors, windows, and gardens. We were inspired!"

In 1997, the Guilliamses purchased one hundred acres so that Robert could plant grapes and Renee could pasture her horses. In 2000, they sold their interests in the health care business and set out to execute their wine venture. Robert contacted a farmer friend about buying an additional seven acres of real estate—once corn and soy beans—by the river. "The location for the winery was ideally situated across from Unusual Junction, the third largest and highly trafficked bridal center in America. The benefits were huge!" he says.

A meandering drive leads to the red-roofed Raven's Glenn Winery, a gray

The dining room offers views of the Tuscarawas River

structure with white trim and a mission-style porch stacked with wine barrels. Robert, the wine ambassador, greets visitors with a short talk followed by an educational tour of their spectacular first-class facilities. The tour includes a look at the wine-production center with its crusher-destemmer and Scharfenberger and Wilmes presses; the fermentation room with its variable-capacity, stainless steel, temperature-controlled, jacketed fermentors; the high-tech lab; the wine cellars; the bottling room; and the case storage.

A path along the Tuscarawas River invites patrons to the Raven's Glenn Restaurant, where Beau Guilliams oversees the Italian open-air market eatery and the tasting bar. "We designed the place ourselves," Robert says. "We wanted a spacious building with two-by-six-foot wood-plank floors from an old mill and lots of floor-to-ceiling glass." The restaurant, designed for indoor and outdoor dining, has a river-rock fireplace with arched windows

and French doors that open to a patio with views of the river and the golf course.

A short drive through gorgeous hills and valleys bursting with flora and fauna heads up to the one-hundred-acre Sonnet Hills Stables and Vineyards and the Guilliamses' hilltop colonial residence. A friend excavated a winding road through the steep valley, which hides a natural tributary shrouded by trees. "The north side of the hill was created for the horses, the stable, and the pasture of Renee Guilliams, marketing and public relations manager. The south side of the hill, roughly ten acres, was contoured for our vineyard, which crests at 987 feet," Robert says.

Jeff Guilliams, a health care social service-coordinator and part-time musician in addition to being vineyard manager, had the challenge of preparing the heavy clay soil, eight to twelve feet in depth, chisel-ripping the ground before planting the vineyards. The varietals featured are De Chaunac, Vidal Blanc, Traminette, Gewürztraminer, Niagara, Chardonel, Frontenac, Leon Millot, and St. Croix.

Tony Carlucci, a noted wine consultant, worked with the Guilliamses to design a collection of wines based on their location and diverse customers. Raven's Glenn Winery's $12–$14 black and red premium label graces its Chardonnay, Cabernet Sauvignon, Merlot, and Red Zinfandel; there is also a $16 Chantilly Lace, a 10 percent residual sugar Muscat Canelli dessert wine. The $10 premium table wine label includes Vidal Blanc, a semi-sweet white wine; Sweet Harmony, a semi-sweet Concord; and Sweet Sonnet, a blended Niagara. Raspberry, blackberry, and apple, at $10–$14, are offered for a change of pace. "Wine should be fun: just keep it simple!" Robert says.

Raven's Glenn Winery

Directions Eight miles west of I-77 on U.S. Route 36 at the intersection of Coshocton County Road 143. Or from Coshocton take U.S. 36 east 9 miles to County Road 143.

Hours Tasting room and retail sales: Monday–Thursday 10 a.m.–7 p.m., Friday–Saturday 10 a.m.–9 p.m.

Restaurant Open for lunch Monday–Saturday 11 a.m.–4 p.m., Friday–Saturday 10 a.m.–9 p.m., closed Sunday

Tours Guided tours by appointment

Tastings Daily when open

Gifts Wine, food, and related gifts

Highlights at Winery Modern, new Ohio Winery; sip wine on shaded decks overlooking Tuscarawas River; indoor and outdoor Italian dining and tasting

Events Posted on Web site

Restaurant Raven's Glenn Restaurant serves Italian cuisine

Prices $8–$18; 10 percent case discount

Brand Name Raven's Glenn Winery

Type of Production Vitis vinifera, French hybrids, vitis labrusca, fruit wines

Method of Harvesting Hand-harvest-ing and single row machine-harvester

Pressing and Winemaking Wilmes and Scharfenberger, Membrane Press, traditional winemaking

Aging and Cooperage Stainless steel, temperature-controlled, jacketed fermentors and French and American oak barrels

Vineyards Founded 1997

County Coshocton

Appellation Ohio

Acreage 10

Waterway Tuscarawas River

Climate Hot, humid Ohio weather

Soil Heavy clay

Varieties De Chaunac, Vidal Blanc, Traminete, Niagara, Chardonel, Frontenac, Leon Millot, St. Croix

Wines Chardonnay, Cabernet, Merlot, Red Zinfandel, Chantilly Lace, Vidal Blanc, Sweet Sonnet, Sweet Harmony, Blackberry, Red Raspberry, Apple

Best Red Wine Red Zinfandel

Best White Wine Vidal Blanc

Other Best Wine Chantilly Lace, dessert wine

SHAWNEE SPRINGS

WINERY

OHIO CONCORD
MIDNIGHT MIST

Slightly Sweet Red Table Wine
NET CONTENTS 750 ML
Alcohol 11% by Volume

PRODUCED AND BOTTLED BY:
SHAWNEE SPRINGS WINERY
20093 C.R. 6 • COSHOCTON, OHIO 43812

Shawnee Springs Winery

20093 County Road 6
Coshocton, OH 43812
Tel: (740)623-0744
Fax: (740)622-5477
E-mail: rphall@smurfit.com
Web site: www.ohiowines.org
Owners Randy and Susan Hall
Winemaker Randy Hall
Founded 1997

Shawnee Springs Winery, nestled into the deeply wooded foothills of the Appalachians in Coshocton, is situated near the confluence of the Tuscarawas and Walhonding rivers, where they merge to become the Muskingum River in southeastern Ohio.

Susan and Randy Hall, natives of Coshocton, chose to name their winery for the Shawnee Nation, which hunted in the hills on their land above the Tuscarawas River Valley. Shawnee comes from the Algonquin word shawun, meaning southerner, a reference to their original home in the Ohio Valley. The Shawnee considered Coshocton, which means "union of the waters," and the Delaware nation that headquartered there their grandfathers and the source of all Algonquin tribes.

Aside from the occasional glass of holiday wine that the Halls shared with Randy's Italian grandparents, the couple did not know much about wine until one day in the early nineties they visited Rainbow Hills Vineyards in Newcomerstown and found themselves thinking, "Why not start a winery on our ninety-five acres of mountain property?"

Randy and his twin sons, Jess and Benjamin, cleared two-and-a-half acres of prime land by hand. Shawnee Springs' vineyards, in Ohio's Appalachian hill country, were planted in dense clay soils to cold-weather-resistant varieties: Catawba, Niagara, and Concord. "We needed hardy varieties that could adapt to the late Midwestern frosts," Randy says.

At harvest, family members (including Randy's eighty-year-old mother) and friends harvest the grapes into lug boxes. Tons of grapes per day are processed in a stainless steel destemmer and pressed in an

Randy and Susan Hall during harvest days

oak stave, wooden-basket press with a water bladder. The white grapes are pressed and fermented the same day, then pumped downstairs in the main house and cold-stabilized at 55 degrees Fahrenheit in 80-gallon stainless steel, jacketed fermentors with variable floating heads. The red grapes are fermented on the skin to extract character, then pumped outside and held in stainless steel tanks until they are clarified and aged. All the wines are filtered and fined before additional bottle age.

"We deal in small lots of hand-crafted wines," says Randy. "We try to be consistent. Fruit varies depending on the quality of a particular vintage. I strive for balanced prunings and a more vigorous vine."

At Shawnee Springs Winery, the Halls extend a unique brand of hospitality in common with the wisdom of Tecumseh of the Shawnee Nation, who once said, "Seek to make your life long, and its purpose in the service of your people." Guests can spend leisurely time in the red barn, which resembles an Appalachian mountain hideaway, or the outdoor shelter, suitable for picnics and barbeques. The interior has a tasting bar and gifts at one end and comfortable tables and chairs and a large fireplace at the other. Paintings of Indians, landscapes, and wildlife decorate the walls. "It is both peaceful and rustic here," Randy says.

As head of sales and marketing, Susan has built a stellar reputation for hospitality to her guests and visitors, who come from one hundred miles in any direction of the winery. "People come in all sorts of vehicles—including twelve members of the Model T Old Car Club, who chugged up the dirt road in unison at twenty miles per hour," Randy says. "People tell us they like the friendly and congenial atmosphere and the taste of pure, homemade wines. There are no vitis vinifera or French hybrid wines."

Shawnee Springs Winery produces 1,000 gallons of wine per year, named for reflective times of the day or night—Midnight Mist, Sundown, Sunny Day, Red Dawn.

"It is not how you start, but how you finish that is remembered by others," Susan says. "You will remember the journey."

Shawnee Springs Winery

Directions From I-77, take exit 65 onto U.S. Route 36 west to Newcomerstown/ Coshocton. Stay on State Route 16/State Route 83. Turn right on County Road 6 to the winery.
Hours Tuesday–Saturday, 11 a.m.–6 p.m.
Tours Self-guided vineyard tours
Tasting Daily when open
Gifts Wine-related
Picnics Covered and open decks with grills, light snacks, and wine
Highlights at Winery Peaceful, rustic setting; American wines
Events Friday steak and chicken dinners June–August 4–8 p.m.
Prices $7–$9; 10 percent case discount
Brand Names Shawnee Springs Winery
Type of Production: Vitis labrusca
Method of Harvesting: Hand-harvested
Pressing and Winemaking Oak stave-wooden-basket press with water bladder
Aging and Cooperage Stainless steel tanks
Vineyards Founded 1992
County Coshocton
Appellation Ohio
Acreage 2.5
Waterway Shawnee Springs
Climate Temperate
Soil Clay
Varieties Concord, Niagara, Catawba, Fruit
Wines Midnight Mist, Sundown, Sunny Day, Red Dawn, Apple, Elderberry
Best Red Midnight Mist
Best White Sunny Day
Other Best Wine Red Dawn
Nearby Places to Visit Roscoe Village; Longaberger Company

Swiss Heritage
Winery

BACK TO THE 40'S
RED WINE

12% ALC./VOL.   750ML

Swiss Heritage Winery

6011 Old Route 39 NW
Dover, Ohio 44622
Tel: (330)343-4108
Fax: (330)343-1092
E-mail: broadrun@tusco.net
Web site: www.swissheritagewines.com
Owner Nancy Schindler
Winemaker Chad Schindler
Founded 2002

The Swiss Heritage Winery is cradled in the centuries-old Broad Run Valley. In 2002, entrepreneurs Nancy Schindler and her late husband, Hans, established the winery on the site of the famous Broad Run Cheese House on Old Route 39 in Dover. "Our goal was to marry wine and cheese," Nancy says.

Broad Run Valley has a strong historic connection to several generations of the Schindler family. In 1933, Amish farmers had built a structure from river stone and formed a successful cheese cooperative. As a young girl in the thirties, Margie Fankhauser, Nancy's mother, used to walk from Sugarcreek past the Broad Run Cheese House to Dover. "Hans was the cheesemaker there during the seventies and bought milk (used in making cheese) from the same Amish farmers," Nancy says. "They were facing hard times due to a declining market."

Subsequently, the Schindlers, who loved the restoration process, purchased the Broad Run Cheese House in 1978. They hired a skilled architect, who replaced the eight-by-twelve-foot retail market with a fancy Swiss Chalet. Over the next twenty years, the Schindlers added retail space and new merchandise five times.

The Swiss Chalet, situated at a bend in the road, was enhanced with two towers topped with weather vanes and highlighted by windows with awnings and dormers with edelweiss shutters. Flags and banners dance in the wind. Bright flowers and green shrubs highlight the landscaped grounds, decorated with urns, vases, pedestals, and fountains.

"We sell Victorian merchandise and nostalgia," says Nancy, who has created a niche market and following. She gestures to the juxtaposition of Swiss clothing, lamps, curtains, heritage lace, artwork, china, and accessories with Swiss Heritage wines, cheeses, and meats. "Customers are pleasantly surprised!"

The Schindlers realized they had the location and equipment to start a 4,000-

gallon Tuscarawas County winery. Their uncharted approach to winemaking involved relying on their own ideas and their talent for pursuing the unusual.

"We continued with the Victorian theme," Nancy says. "We gave a Canadian design firm ideas for the logo, old photographs of our mother, aunt and uncle, and dog, Dewey. We also showcased Hans as a winemaker and cheesemaker, then Chad Schindler, our son. We took a fresh approach."

Swiss Heritage Winery sources high-quality frozen crushed fruit and berries from Ohio and Chardonnay juice from New York. The wine grapes are fermented in stainless steel, temperature-controlled, jacketed fermentors and held in a mixture of stainless aging tanks. The wines are racked and pumped through a coarse filter. They are then fined and filtered several times before the wine is clarified and ready for bottling.

"Our customers characterize our Swiss Heritage wines as mellow with good feedback after tasting them," Nancy says. "Our market niche definitely prefers sweet wines, and we also produce a few dry ones as well."

Swiss Heritage Winery

Directions Take I-77 to exit 83. Go west on State Route 39 for 4 miles toward Sugarcreek. Turn right on County Road 139 to Old State Route 39 to the winery.

Hours 9 a.m.–6 p.m. daily

Tours Broad Run Cheese House morning tours for $1.50

Tastings Daily when open

Gifts Victorian nostalgia—heritage lace, lamps, china, wine, and accessories

Highlights at Winery Swiss cheeses and Swiss heritage fine wines; eclectic shopping; gourmet Ohio wine and cheese gift boxes; picturesque old farms in beautiful Amish countryside

Events Ohio Swiss Festival (September); Christmas on the Square at Sugarcreek

Deli Broad Run Cheese House—Swiss cheeses, domestic meats, and Swiss Heritage wines

Prices $6.95–$11.95; 10 percent case discount; cheeses and meats for $2.99–$5.00

Brand Name Swiss Heritage Winery

Type of Production Vitis labrusca, vitis vinifera, fruit and berry wine

Winemaking Original and practical

Aging and Cooperage Stainless steel tanks and other cooperage

Appellation American

Best Red Cranberry

Best White Victorian Lace

Other Best Wine Peach

Nearby Places to Visit Amish Country; Swiss Village of Sugarcreek

Troutman Vineyards

4243 Columbus Road
Wooster, OH 44691
Tel: (330)263-4345
Fax: (330)263-5337
E-mail: info@troutmanvineyards.com
Web site: www.troutmanvineyards.com
Owners Deanna and Andy Troutman
Winemaker Andy Troutman
Founded 1998

The Troutman Vineyards, nestled on a crest on Columbus Road in leafy Wooster, exemplifies the small-farm winery movement in Ohio.

In the late nineteenth century, many land grant universities, such as Ohio University, had moved away from agricultural and mechanical arts. So, the U.S. Congress passed the Hatch Act of 1887. It provided funds for states to establish an agricultural experiment station under separate federal funding. Wayne County, Ohio, won the bid for an agricultural experiment station, and Wooster's reputation as a plant repository and tech laboratory became known worldwide.

In the 1990s, future devoted founders of Troutman Vineyards, Deanna and Andy Troutman, met at Ohio State University and discovered their mutual fascination with agriculture and farm products. At the time, Deanna was on the fast-track to becoming a marketing executive and Andy was a Lonz Winery Fellow in produce and floriculture. He graduated in 1996 with a BS in agriculture with a specialty in horticulture and microbiology.

Wooster, with its charming homes and century-old farms, arboretums and gardens, and theater and arts, was well known to the Troutmans. In 1997, while plying the country roads on the outskirts of town, they saw a rustic farm that was up for sale. Struck by its potential as a site for a wine venture, they quickly merged their talents and resources to purchase the property from its owner, Russell Stauffer.

In essence, Troutman Vineyards rekindled the spirit of the farm and its sense of place. "We reignited the land's natural *terroir*," Andy says. First, the Troutmans renovated the lovely old farmhouse with a new walkway, flower garden, and trellis. Next, they turned the old chicken coop into a winery and outfitted it with stainless steel equipment and oak barrels.

In 1998, the Troutmans launched Wooster's first and only high-quality artisan winery. The red wooden barn and surrounding pasture are home to their horses, cows, goats, sheep, and dog. "We encourage people—families with children—to experience life on a small farm winery with animals, especially our famous pigs!" he says.

The superiority of the Wayne County agricultural legacy, which looms large in the eyes of Ohio growers, motivated the Troutmans to reach for the stars. But their stars came with names like Cabernet Franc, Vidal Blanc, Chardonnay, and Chambourcin. In the late nineties, they prepared and tiled six acres of trellised vines, planted in gravelly loam and silty loam, in a true continental climate. What was the result? "Beyond our expectations!" Troutman says. "The fruit in Wooster has a character all its own."

After three years of good weather, the Troutmans hand-harvested their first crop of grapes into lug boxes in 2000. The wine grapes were placed in a destemmer-crusher, then pressed in a membrane-basket press. The wine was pumped into stainless steel tanks, racked, pumped over, and lightly filtered. All the wines are held in stainless steel for six to eight months with the exception of two wines: The Chardonnay is held in French oak puncheons and the Cabernet Franc is aged for six to eight months in half American oak and half Hungarian oak cooperage.

"Our first Troutman Vineyards wines were introduced in 2001," Andy says. The winery produces a variety of still wines. They include a dry but fruity Cabernet Franc with smooth tannins and a long finish; an inky but light and earthy Red Menagerie made from Chambourcin; a toasty, medium-flavored Chardonnay; a nearly dry German blend of Cayuga White and Seyval Blanc called White Menagerie; an aromatic, peachy-apricot German-style Farmer's White; and a sweet Farmer's Red, a swilling wine. Troutman also produces a mineral but earthy Chambourcin Ice Wine.

"All our wines are estate-grown from the earth," Andy says. "We spend a lot of personal time crafting these fine artisan wines for our customers."

Troutman Vineyards

Directions Located southwest of Wooster on State Route 3, 4.5 miles south of where U.S. Route 30/State Route 3 split on the west side of Wooster.

Hours Adjusted seasonally; please call or visit Web site

Tours Self-guided tours; group tours by appointment ($3 per person includes tasting)

Tastings Daily when open

Gifts Wine accessories, clothing, and gift baskets

Highlights at Winery Small vineyard estate winery; farm animals

Prices $12

Brand Name Troutman Winery and Vineyards

Type of Production Classic

Method of Harvesting By hand

Pressing and Winemaking Membrane press and basket press

Aging and Cooperage Half American oak and half Hungarian oak; six to eight months in barrel

Vineyards Founded 1998

County Wayne

Appellation American

Acreage 6

Climate Continental

Soil Gravel loam and silt loam

Varieties Vidal, Chardonnay, Cabernet Franc, Chambourcin

Wines Cabernet Franc, Red Menagerie (Chambourcin), Chardonnay, White Menagerie (Seyval Blanc) Farmer's White (Vidal Blanc), Chambourcin Ice Wine, Farmer's Red

Best Red Cabernet Franc

Best White Vidal

Other Best Wine Ice Wine

Quote "Cabernet Franc has great potential here." —Andy Troutman

Nearby places to Visit Pine Tree Barn; Mohican Country

Mountains to the Plains Tour

Flint Ridge Vineyards

HOPEWELL RED
RED TABLE WINE
OHIO

Flint Ridge Vineyard & Winery

3970 Pert Hill Road
Hopewell, OH 43746
Tel: (740)787-2116
Fax: (740)787-9810
E-mail: info@flintridgevineyard.com
Web site: www.flintridgevineyard.com
Owners Carl and Diane Jahnes
Winemaker Diane Jahnes
Founded 2003

Flint Ridge Vineyard and Winery, artistically designed and hand-crafted to hug the contours of the Appalachian Mountains in Hopewell, is situated near a huge rock dubbed the Black Hand, which extends out into the Licking River Gorge. This peace rock defined an unspoken boundary of cooperation among ancient and often warring civilizations—Iroquois, Shawnee, French, British, and Americans—who journeyed from near and far to reach these valued lands. Their common interest, which lay five miles to the south, was the "purest flint in the western hemisphere," traded all over North America.

In 1978, Carl and Diane Jahnes, founders of Flint Ridge (with their farm partners), discovered large pieces of different-colored flint in the soils of their newly purchased eighty-acre wooded hillside property. This flint that could break a plow blade was a yet-to-be-realized gift of nature. Wild grapevines naturally covered these lands, which had also been used to grow crops and raise cattle. In this rustic setting, the Jahneses approached their lives as artisans and created products by hand.

The Jahneses were inspired by Wendell Berry, a conservationist and the author of *Gift of Good Land*, who championed the idea of sustainable agriculture. Berry based his thinking on the idea that one should be a steward of the land, keenly aware of all who will follow on the land. In keeping, the Jahneses apply methods of agriculture that are ethically, environmentally, and economically sound.

"Life should be whole," says Carl, a renaissance man and architect. "We nurture people, community, environment, and meaningful work to maintain a healthy ethic."

So, the Jahneses and their friends began to experiment. They raised cows, grew Christmas trees, and planted vegetable gardens and an assortment of blueberries, blackberries, strawberries, and currants. "Nothing we grew was totally disease-resistant," says Diane, a physical therapist for children with disabilities. Carl, Diane, and their children, Ben, Jeff, and Megan, built an Adirondack-style house and a cozy winery by hand with landscaped terraces, floral gardens, and an il fornaio.

During a visit to Monet's home in Giverny, France, Mike Seiler, a partner and artist, noticed the French grew grapes in a topography and latitude similar to Hopewell. Seiler suggested the Jahneses grow wine grapes. David Ferree and David Scurlock, agricultural researchers at the Ohio Agricultural Research and Development Center in Wooster, were asked to evaluate the property as a potential site to grow grapes.

Confirmed to be appropriate, Flint Ridge was cultivated on the northwest edge of a south-facing slope. "The hill starts at an altitude of 1,010 feet to an altitude of 900 feet, and the air drains to the Dillon Reservoir," Carl says. "Our soils consist of gravel, clay loams, pottery grade clay, four to six feet deep, over a shale foundation. The weather comes from the northwest and the Gulf of Mexico."

As artisan producers, the Jahneses hand-craft a wine product expressive of their family spirit and the spirit of this beautiful place. It is a quiet joy for them to look through the mist of morning across the trellised vines of fourteen different grape varieties. Red-tailed hawks soar above the vineyard protecting the fruit that goes into Flint Ridge's 90 percent estate-grown wines. "I am trying to discover which grapes grow easily on our land, and to achieve the best quality wine from our grapes," says Diane, who as the winemaker collaborates with their son, Ben. "Through careful selection of varietals, cultivation, leaf and cluster-thinning, and land management, we attempt to keep spraying at a minimum."

Flint Ridge wines are fresh, dry, usually blended, very earthy wines typical of these flinty lands. "Our plan is to stay a 2,500-gallon artisan producer, improving the overall quality and making drier-style wines while also offering a few in the sweet to semi-sweet range," Diane says.

Flint Ridge Vineyard & Winery

Directions From I-70, get off at U.S. Route 40. Turn right on U.S. 40, then go right and West on Dillon Falls Road (note convenience store with red roof). Turn right and go 100 yards uphill on Jersey Ridge Road, which winds around and intersects Pinecrest Drive at a T. Go left on Pinecrest Drive for 5 miles. Go right onto Pleasant Valley Road, past a church, over Poverty Run. Take a left on Pert Hill Road to the winery.

Hours Saturday 11 a.m.–6 p.m.; other days by appointment

Tours Self-guided

Tastings Daily when open

Gifts Wine- and food-related

Picnics Welcome

Highlights at Winery Small Ohio winery producing drier wines than others; hand-built Adirondack house, winery, and landscaping inspired by Wendell Berry's model for sustainable live-work community ethic

Events Fall harvest and luncheon for helpful friends and volunteers; small group tasting events

Restaurant Light fare—fresh bread and cheeses

Prices $6–$12; 10 percent case discount

Brand Names Flint Ridge Vineyard

Type of Production Hand-crafted wines

Method of Harvesting: By hand

Pressing and Winemaking: Bladder and basket presses

Aging and Cooperage Stainless steel tanks

Vineyards Founded 1995

County Muskingum

Appellation Ohio

Acreage 6

Waterways Poverty Run and Dillon Lake

Climate Breezes blow over the hill and keep vines dry and ventilated on humid days

Soil Clay loam glacial spoil 4–6 feet deep over shale base, peppered with flint

Varieties De Chaunac, Steuben, Delaware, Cayuga White, Niagara, Marechal Foch, Ventura, Bianca, Chambourcin, Traminette, Vidal Blanc, Chardonnay, Cabernet Sauvignon, Cabernet Franc

Wines Marechal Foch, Traminette, New World White, Cayuga White, Adena White, Red Tail, Hopewell Red

Best Red Hopewell Red

Best White Adena White

Other Best Wine Marechal Foch

Quote "Our goal is to craft distinctive wines which express our spirit and the spirit of the place." —Diane Jahnes

Nearby Places to Visit Hartstone Pottery; Fioriware Art Pottery

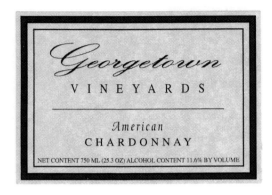

Georgetown Vineyards

62920 Georgetown Road

Cambridge, OH 43725

Tel: (740)435-3222 or (866)435-3222

Fax: (740)439-5995

E-mail: info@georgetownvineyards.com

Web site: www.georgetownvineyards.com

Owner/Winemaker John Nicolozakes

Founded 1999

Georgetown Vineyards is located in the foothills of the Appalachian Mountains in southeastern Ohio's Guernsey County. A steep drive leads past hillside vineyards to a yellow farmhouse, an arched pavilion, a hospitality center, and a period winery. This hilltop paradise, which overlooks historic Cambridge, stands on land that President Thomas Jefferson granted to Zacheus Biggs and Acheus Beatty in 1801. Georgetown Vineyards was established there as a joint venture of its founders, Kay and John Nicolozakes, in 1999.

John Nicolozakes's maternal and pater-

nal grandparents hailed from the isle of Crete in Greece. Between 1905 and 1912, one branch of his family immigrated to Ohio, and the other one settled in California. The Greek custom of sharing wine and food among friends in an unhurried environment was a deeply held family tradition. During a creative sojourn in the nineties, John had the good fortune to revive these practices in his own family when he ventured into winemaking.

"I produced my first wine from Cabernet Sauvignon concentrate; I also tried Ohio and Pennsylvania purveyors. I was most encouraged, however, by wine I made from fresh juice from Sonoma. I made more batches and bought oak barrels," John says. He was hooked by his discovery.

Between 1989 and 1990, Nicolozakes constructed an eighteenth-century colonial house with an American oak aging room and a wine cellar for his private collection. "This was the heart of our wine production," he says. He made the leap from amateur to professional in 1996 when he applied for a basic wine permit. In 1998, Georgetown Vineyards released its first premium wines—Chardonnay, Niagara, and Concord.

As demand grew, John joined forces with Sam, his son, who manages the newly designed retail sales and tasting room. French doors open into a beautiful room with track lighting, white walls, and a green-and-white tiled floor. Sam holds court behind the wine-tasting bar as the resident expert on the winery's newest releases. A black potbellied stove spews warmth in the dead of winter. The gift shop is a treasure trove for the curious, offering fine wines, glasses, corkscrews, baskets, mugs, cards, china, and accessories. "We sell Ohio foodstuffs, like jams, jellies, pastas, balsamic vinegar, and an imported Nicolozakes Olive Oil from Greece," he says.

Kay Nicolozakes, founder of Vineyards Catering, and her daughter Emma, bookkeeper for the vineyards, design variations on Greek menus for small groups on the weekends. A favorite consists of Greek meatballs, feta cheese, dolmades (grape leaves with rice, onions, and minced beef), bread, olive oil, and Georgetown Vineyards wines.

By 2000, John had constructed an outdoor pavilion for parties up to fifty guests and a handsome winery for his annual 1,000-gallon-production. The fifteen-acre, three-wire trellis vineyards are planted in sandy clay soils. The temperate southern Ohio climate bodes well for the Fredonia and Concord planted in the north vineyard and the west vineyard. The bulk of the fresh juice—Chardonnay, Chardonel, French Colombard, Sauvignon, Merlot, Pinot Noir, White Zinfandel, apple, blackberry, and cherry—is shipped to the winery in refrigerated trucks from Ohio growers.

"I buy fresh juice, then ferment it into wine in stainless steel tanks in the winery or the barrel cellar," John says. "I rotate the wines, then cold-stabilize them in temperature-controlled, jacketed, stainless steel tanks, then transfer them back into stainless steel vessels. Here they are aged for three to six months until they are clarified, then properly bottled. The red wines are fermented on the skins, then pumped over and racked several times, then held in stainless steel or American oak before they are bottled."

Georgetown Vineyards produces one-third dry wine and two-thirds sweet wine. Its typical customer starts with sweet wines, then graduates to dry ones. "Although our dry wines are of higher quality, there is less of it," John says. "Many people go winery to winery doing comparative wine tastings, and their taste buds are geared to a sweeter taste." To satisfy this market, Georgetown Vineyards produces Concord, its best red wine, Niagara, its best sweet white wine, and a dry Chardonnay and a sweet Blackberry, both other favorites.

"It's my philosophy to try to eliminate wine snobbery as much as possible," he says. "I don't believe that certain wines should go with certain foods, but rather people should enjoy what they like."

Georgetown Vineyards

Directions From I-70, take the Cambridge/Byesville exit (State Route 209). Go north and take the first left (before Bob Evans Restaurant) on Georgetown Road. Continue to the first stop sign. Turn right and go up the hill. As you descend, Georgetown Vineyards is located on the right.

Hours Tuesday–Saturday 11 a.m.–5 p.m.

Tours By appointment

Tastings Daily when open

Gifts Array of products and gifts

Picnics Two tables with scenic view and outdoor grills

Highlights at Winery Good wines, great view, homey atmosphere

Events Friday night steak cookouts; Fourth of July picnic and fireworks

Restaurant Greek cuisine; Vineyards Catering provides catered meals for small groups

Prices $8; 10 percent case discount

Brand Name Georgetown Vineyards

Type of Production Vitis vinifera, French hybrids, vitis labrusca

Method of Harvesting By hand

Pressing and Winemaking Bladder basket press with standard fermentation and winemaking practices

Aging and Cooperage American oak barrels

Vineyards Founded 1999

County Guernsey

Appellation: American or Ohio

Acreage 15

Climate Temperate

Soil Sandy clay

Varieties Fredonia and Concord

Wines American Chardonnay, Ohio Chardonel, American French Colombard American Sauvignon Blanc, Lake Erie Niagara, American Merlot, American Pinot Noir, Lake Erie Concord, White Zinfandel, Ohio Apple Wine, American Cherry Wine, Blackberry Wine

Best Red Concord

Best White Niagara

Other Best Wine Chardonnay

Quote "It is my philosophy to eliminate wine snobbery." —John Nicolozakes

Nearby Places to Visit Mosser Glass; The Living Word Outdoor Drama

Ravenhurst Champagne Cellars

34477 Shertzer Road
Mt. Victory, OH 43340
Tel: (937)354-5151
Fax: (937)354-5152
E-mail: raven_ink@hotmail.com
Owners Chuck Harris and Nina Busch
Winemaker Chuck Harris
Founded 1997

Ravenhurst Champagne Cellars, the only Buckeye State establishment with emphasis on the production of classic methode champenoise champagne with still wine as a byproduct, lies on the outskirts of Mount Victory, a charming, rural 1800s village in central Ohio. "We are the only one who uses free-run juice for the champagne and press for the still wine. Everyone else uses the whole grape for either process. And this accounts for our wines, with bubbles or not," say entrepreneurs Nina Busch and Chuck Harris, natives of Van Wert, Ohio, who established their wine venture in 1997 after starting an artisanal accessories business.

"I met a woman who wanted to drink more champagne than I could afford, so I needed to learn to make good champagne," jokes Chuck, an Ohio State University graduate in history. "Fortunately, Nina was a graduate in chemistry, also from Ohio State University." Both are organic gardeners and accomplished cooks, so having their own wine on the table when they entertained was merely an extension of that lifestyle.

In 1980, the couple relocated to their cedar-sided farmhouse to grow grapes at this unique spot, just east of the 1,549-foot-high Campbell Hill in Bellefontaine, the highest point in Ohio. "The storms come out of the West, and as they hit Campbell Hill, they progress north and south, then reconfigure near Marion," Chuck says. "Our vineyard is like a pebble in a stream. We miss the fall storms, but get rain the rest of the year. Between August 1 and October 1, the place is as dry as Death Valley."

Ravenhurst Champagne Cellars, which owns three Union County vineyards, benefits from the warmer climate, good air, and proper drainage. Dave Kohli, vineyard manager, oversees the two-acre estate vineyard, predominately Cabernet Sauvignon with some Pinot Noir, Chardonnay, and Chambourcin; the four-acre Clayborn Vineyard, mainly Pinot Noir, Chardonnay, and Cabernet Sauvignon; and the four-acre Chalamar Vineyard, which has

Cabernet Sauvignon, Cabernet Franc, Pinot Noir, Vidal Blanc, and Seyval. "We are vineyard driven," Chuck says. "We find what our *terroir* gives, and we maximize that aspect of the place."

A pink magnolia brightens the doorway to the cedar-sided winery, trimmed in white paint. It opens into a bright white California-style tasting room, featuring Columbus artist Brooke Hunter-Lombardi's Sunrise Over Ravenhurst and accentuated by vaulted ceilings and natural skylights. The room has hand-hewn crossbeams and a board and batten (stained with Pinot Noir) tasting bar, held together by hand-crafted pegs and pins. "During a storm, our century-old red oak tree was downed. Once the tree was milled, it took four years before it was dry enough so we could work with it," recalls Chuck, who with Kohli did all the winery construction.

"The winery is like a kitchen. High-quality produce coming in is the only way to have high-quality produce coming out," Chuck says. He teams up with Nina to make champagne and still wine in their stainless steel production center and their American and French oak aging cellars. He points to the gold, bronze, and silver medals they have won in more than fifty-four wine competitions from coast to coast, including prestigious events in Los Angeles, San Diego, Riverside, and by the American Wine Society.

The Ravenhurst Champagnes are all hybrid, with the exception of the Grand Cuvee. La Terre Riche Grand Cuvee consists of a blend of three vintages of Chardonnay and two Pinot Noir vintages. Cellared for five years, the champagne is approximately seven years old. Grand Rouge Champagne is produced by bleeding the juice off the skins of Chambourcin grapes to achieve the color of garnet. With aromas of mandarin orange, this Grand Rouge exudes delightful flavors of cherry and strawberry.

Frequently an Ohio Gold Medal winner, the Busch-Harris barrel-fermented Chardonnay Reserve is aged on the lees to produce a silky, papaya-mango-flavored premium wine. The garnet red Cabernet Sauvignon Reserve, with a berry nose and taste and soft tannins, is ready to consume. And the richly blended Cabernet Sauvignon called "Velvet Hammer," an unfiltered wine of some magnitude, is produced from exceptional lots, with additional French oak barrel aging.

Open one weekend a month on Fridays and Saturdays, Ravenhurst Champagne Cellars bills itself as a tempting destination for wine lovers with the most discriminating of palates.

"Winemaking, like life, is a constant source of miracles," Chuck says. Truly, Ravenhurst is one of them.

Ravenhurst Champagne Cellars

Directions From Cleveland, take I-71 south to State Route 30 west, Mansfield exit, to State Route 309 west to Kenton. Take State Route 31 south through Mt. Victory, 3 miles south to Yoakum Road. Turn east (left) to first stop sign. Back up 50 feet to the winery.
From Columbus, take State Route 33 northwest toward Marysville to State Route 31-State Route 4 exit. Take State Route 31 north toward Kenton, approximately 15 miles, through Byhalia. Turn on the second road to the east, then right on Yoakum Road to the last stop sign. Back up 50 feet to the winery.

Hours Open one weekend per month, Friday 12–7 p.m., Saturday 12–6 p.m.

Tours No organized tour

Tastings When open

Gifts Wine-related items

Highlights at Winery Lovely central Ohio farm country; wide-open spaces; one-of-a-kind destination champagne cellars

Wines $9–$34; 10 percent case discount

Brand Names Busch-Harris and Ravenhurst Champagne Cellars

Type of Production Methode champenoise champagne and still wine

Method of Harvesting By hand

Pressing and Winemaking Italian bladder and hydraulic press

Aging and Cooperage American and French oak cooperage

Vineyards Founded 1980

County Union

Appellation Ohio

Acreage 10

Waterway Headwaters of Scioto River

Climate Located on the leeward side of Campbell Hill in Bellefontaine, the highest point in Ohio, different from most of central Ohio

Soil Clay

Varieties Chardonnay, Pinot Noir, Cabernet Sauvignon, Cabernet Franc, Chambourcin, Vidal Blanc, Seyval

Best Red Velvet Hammer

Best White Chardonnay Reserve

Other Best Wine Le Corbeau

Quote "Winemaking, like life, is a constant source of miracles." —Chuck Harris

Nearby Places to Visit Mount Victory for antiques; Piatt Castles

Shamrock Vineyard

111 Rengert Road
Waldo, OH 43356
Tel: (740)726-2883
Fax: (740)726-2000
E-mail: shamrockmail@aol.com
Web site: www.shamrockvineyard.com
Owners Tom and Mary Quilter
Winemaker Chuck Harris
Founded 1997

The long, perpendicular north-central Ohio county roads bisect the flat soybean and grain fields of Morrow County until they reach Shamrock Vineyard in Waldo. A one-lane dirt road curves through gracious vineyards to an 1800s wine atelier, barns, and a summer swing shrouded by elegant pines and leafy maples. Sages Tom and Mary Quilter, proprietors, were the first and only growers in the district to pioneer hardy

European-American varietals in 1971. The Quilters attribute their appreciation of wine to Tom's chiropractor father, a gregarious wine aficionado who often invited Sandusky vintners to the Quilter home to compare Ohio Grape Belt wines in the 1930s. These vivid memories stayed with Quilter through medical school and his time serving in the U.S. Navy through 1954. Thereafter, Quilter accepted a urology assignment in Marion and a teaching appointment at Ohio State University. "We grew beautiful roses in our garden," the Quilters say, "but in time, we had an urge to plant French and American hybrids—possibly even vinifera, though difficult due to the extreme cold."

The Quilters joined Dr. Richard Miller, a friend in internal medicine, to scout sites for vineyards. "There is no right climate around here for anything," Miller said. "Growing grapes is worthless!" He withdrew from the wine project. Undaunted, the Quilters persevered. "We had so much desire that we purchased 150 grapevines, but naturally we had no place to plant them," Tom says.

So what did the Quilters do next, and how did they resolve their grape dilemma? The Quilters' daughters had a nanny, Winnie Baker. She and her husband, Albert Baker, both semi-retired, owned an old German farmhouse and eighty acres of land near Waldo. The Quilters purchased the farm and planted an eight-acre test vineyard in clay soils. "Our purpose was to see if it would

Tom and Mary Quilter

grow grapes in a climate not perfectly suited for the cause. Over time, we learned that some grapes did well," Tom says.

The Quilters consulted the wine experts for the best advice. An early influence was the Ohio Agricultural Research and Development Center in Wooster. Journalist Philip Wagner from Boordy Vineyard, who pioneered East Coast wines from French hybrid varieties, recommended Seyval Blanc. "He just didn't know how cold it was here," Tom says. A fourth-generation grape grower from western New York, Chris Stamp of Lakewood Vineyards suggested Seyval Blanc, Cabernet Franc, and Cabernet Sauvignon after a mild winter.

What the Quilters discovered was how to grow other vines and not cater to any one specific vine. "We dabbled, testing some forty-five varieties," Tom says. "We gave up any previous notion of what a specific fruit might taste like in Waldo. Some dry red wine might taste very differently. In the same way, we learned that different yeasts, for example, Epernay, produced different whites."

After decades of experimenting, Shamrock Vineyard settled on Seyval, Delaware, Vidal, Niagara, Horizon, Marechal Foch, Chambourcin, Cabernet Franc, and Chancellor. At harvest, grapes are picked by hand and brought to the grape-processing barn, where they are put in the crusher-destemmer. Then, the grapes are separated and cleaned to utilize the best grapes, free from rot and spoilage. "We produce classic, old-style, hand-crafted, premium wines," Tom says. Their wine cellar lies beneath the farmhouse. "We cold-ferment our white wine in small stainless tanks. Our red wines are fermented on the skins, also in small stainless steel tanks, but they are aged for two years in American or French oak barrels."

Shamrock Vineyard produces Seyval, Seyval D, Delaware, Shamrock Rose, Vidal, Royal Gold, Buckeye Red, Windfall White, Marechal Foch Rose, Waldeau Red (a derivation of Waldo), and Chancellor Noir. "Wine is an evolution," the Quilters, now well into their eighth decade, say. "We willingly try new things. When consumers demanded sweet wine, we changed in a heartbeat!"

Shamrock Vineyard

Directions From Cleveland, take I-71 south to exit 151. Turn right (west) on State Route 95 for 1.7 miles. Turn left (south) on County Road 20 for 4 miles. Turn right (west) on County Road 25 for 13.3 miles to entrance on right. From Columbus, take U.S. Route 23 north and exit at Waldo. Turn right (north) onto State Route 98, then right (east) on Waldo-Fulton Road. Turn left (north) on Gearhiser Road, then right (east) on Rengert Road to entrance on left.

Hours January–March, Monday–Saturday 1–5 p.m.; April–December, 1–6 p.m. daily

Tours By request

Tastings Daily when open

Gifts Wine-related

Picnics Lovely shade trees, picnic tables, and grills

Highlights at Winery Shade trees with sunset views; nineteenth-century farm winery and estate; outdoor picnic area and swing; wine appreciation, tasting in small community

Events Three Summer Twilight Dinners at Vineyard

Prices $6.99–$13.99; 10 percent case discount

Brand Name Shamrock Vineyard

Type of Production Classic, old-style

Method of Harvesting By hand

Pressing and Winemaking Wooden basket press

Aging and Cooperage Italian stainless steel and French and American oak

Vineyards Founded 1971

County Morrow

Appellation Heartland

Acreage 8

Waterway "The Crik," part of Olentangy Watershed

Climate Central Ohio—brutally cold winters; late spring frost; unforgiving, hot, humid summers

Soil Three types of clay

Varieties Seyval, Delaware, Vidal Blanc, Edelweiss, Niagara, Horizon, Marechal Foch, Chambourcin, Cabernet Franc, Chancellor

Wines Seyval D, Seyval, Delaware, Shamrock Rose, Vidal, Royal Gold, Buckeye Red, Windfall White, Marechal Foch Rose, Waldeau Red, Chancellor Noir

Best Red Buckeye Red

Best White Vidal Blanc

Other Best Wine Chancellor

Nearby Places to Visit Ohio Wesleyan University; Sunbury (a farm town)

Slate Run Vineyard

1900 Winchester-Southern Road
Canal Winchester, OH 43110
Tel: (614)834-8577
Fax: (614)834-5751
E-mail: keithp001@msn.com
Web site: www.slaterunwine.com
Owner/ Winemaker Keith Pritchard
Founded 1997

Slate Run Vineyard, defined by the rural-suburban farms in Canal Winchester, is named after the waterway Slate Run, which is part of the greater Olentangy River and Walnut Creek Watershed just outside of Columbus. During the growing season, the nearby reclaimed Slate Run Wetlands, water-logged areas covered by water or land, are abundant in wildlife—owls, frogs, ducks, and herons—that depends on the native grasses, flowers, and trees for sustenance.

Keith and Leslie Pritchard, natives of the Buckeye State, had the good fortune to sharpen their goals in mid-life. They searched for an outdoor environment that better embraced their family ethic and their children's lives. The Pritchards settled in Fairfield County, a region new to viticulture, and in 1997 opened Slate Run Vineyard. Keith Pritchard was born and raised on a livestock farm near Bucyrus, where he experienced the rigors of caring for animals as a child. His talents rested with the art of nurturing plants. "I enjoyed my fruit trees and tomato garden," he says.

During the seventies, Keith got hooked on the growing American passion and fervor for wine. While at Ohio State University, where he graduated with a BS in business administration with emphasis on production operations management, Keith also worked for a carryout in Columbus. "I attended trade tastings and developed a taste for wine," he says.

Keith's post-college career included distribution and package management, wine store management, and inside and outside sales. A wine hobbyist, he joined the American Wine Society and the Amateur Winemaker's Guild. Meanwhile, Leslie Pritchard pursued an upwardly mobile fast track as a human resources executive. The couple lived happily in a Reynoldsburg townhouse, where Keith crafted wine and Leslie critiqued it.

During the eighties, Keith's interest in wine grew in stages. In 1983 and 1984, he apprenticed for Tom and Mary Quilter at Shamrock Vineyard in Waldo. There he harvested grapes and pruned vines. "I actually collaborated with and learned to grow vinifera grapes from Dr. Robert Pugliese at Darby Creek Vineyards near Plain City from 1985 to 1992," he says.

That same year, the Pritchards purchased one acre of land and moved with their young children to a home in the countryside. They removed the trees and ploughed the earth to plant Vidal Blanc, Cayuga, Chancellor, Chambourcin, Cabernet Sauvignon, and Cabernet Franc. In 1988, the Pritchards acquired six additional acres, which they finished in vines. "Our plan was to sell grapes to amateurs and acquaintances, whom we befriended through societies and guilds. We had no intention whatsoever of becoming a winery. Amateurs interested in science, we experimented with a lot of varieties," Keith says. But it was Leslie who urged Keith to obtain his wine permit. "She mentioned it

A selection of Slate Run wines

A.J. Zanyk

once. I guess that was all it took," he says.

The now four-acre Slate Run vineyards consist of a three-wire, multiple-trunk trellis system featuring fifty-eight varieties of vitis vinifera, vitis labrusca, French, German, Hungarian, and American Hybrid, planted in silt loams. "We make small batches of thirteen blended grape wines, one fruit wine, and an apple wine," Keith says. Their primary emphasis is on classic, elegant, complex wines that age well, and they plan to upgrade the volume of semi-dry and sweet wines. Their secondary emphasis is to upgrade the quality but selectively reduce the volume of dry wines.

Friends voluntarily harvest the wine grapes, which are transferred into a destemmer-crusher, then put into a Wilmes bladder press. The white wines are cold-fermented in the fifty-degree-range for better balance and proper aging. The red wines, which are aged in part oak barrels and part stainless steel (with oak chips), are skillfully blended before bottling.

Slate Run Vineyard produces a vinous apple wine, a mild to sweet labrusca series, a hybrid German-style series, and its premium European vitis vinifera and high-quality hybrid series, which includes Premblage, Premcru, Prembourg, Premblanc, Premcess, and Finale, a 13 percent residual sugar late harvest Vignoles. "We like our red wines, and some white wines, well aged to taste like wine, not fruit," Keith says.

Slate Run Vineyard

Directions From downtown Columbus, take I-70 east to U.S. Route 33 toward Lancaster to State Route 674. Drive 6.5 miles south to winery.

Hours Monday–Saturday 1–7 p.m.

Tours Casual tours by request

Tastings During business hours and by appointment

Gifts Wine- and grape-related items

Picnics Picnic tables and gas grills available

Highlights at Winery Quality proprietary wines from 58 varieties of estate-grown grapes; unique, stylized wines made from blended grapes

Events Holiday Open House first Saturday in December

Prices $6.99–$17.99

Brand Names Slate Run Vineyard

Type of Production Small batches of 13 blended grape wines and one apple wine

Method of Harvesting: Hand-harvested by friends and volunteers

Pressing and Winemaking Wilmes bladder press

Aging and Cooperage Variable capacity, stainless tanks, and small barrels

Vineyards Founded 1985

County Fairfield

Appellation Ohio

Acreage 4

Waterway None on premises; nearest creek is Slate Run

Climate Cold winters; warm to hot, humid summers

Soil Celina and Miami series of silt loams

Varieties 58 varieties of labrusca, French, German, Hungarian, and American hybrids; vitis vinifera varieties

Wines Apple Wine, Winsome, Rosily, Rurban Red, Slate Gem, Slate Blanc, Slate Rouge, Slate Garnet, Premcess, Premblanc, Premblage, Premcru, Prembourg, Finale

Best Red: Premblage

Best White: Premblanc

Other Best Wine Finale

Quote "Don't make wimpy white wines—like oak as spice, not a dominant flavor. Make wines in a classic, elegant style for complexity, not for fruit bombs. Make wines that age very well and do not fall apart in a couple of years." —Keith Pritchard

Nearby Places to Visit Slate Run Metro Park & Living Historical Farm; Barber Museum and Mid-Ohio Doll Museum

Terra Rosa
Rose Table Wine
ALCOHOL 12% BY VOLUME

Terra Cotta Vineyards

2285 Rix Mills Road

New Concord, OH 43762

Tel: (740)872-3791

Fax: (740)872-3376

E-mail: terra@clover.net

Web site: www.terracottavineyards.com

Owners Donna and Paul Roberts

Winemaker Paul Roberts

Founded 1996

The hills and valleys along Rix Mills Road in New Concord take the traveler past quaint cattle farms where black Herefords reign as kings of the mountain and freshly mown hayfields become a canvas for art. Visitors who experience Terra Cotta Vineyards' striking panoramic views say they are overcome with awe. "It is where lasting memories begin," proprietors Paul and Donna Roberts say.

During the mid-eighties, the Robertses began to realize their dream to start a winery. "We visited many Ohio wineries," says Donna, a business manager for a Zanesville hospital, "and for three years we looked everywhere for acreage." In 1995, after an exhaustive search, the Robertses purchased fifty-three acres of land overlooking a lovely valley. "The site was ideal for wine grapes, with good air drainage and wind flow," says Paul, a talented welder.

Over time, the Robertses and their daughters, Alysia and Misty, saw the ideas for their wine venture take shape. They creatively drew on New Concord's rich history, its people, its land, its crafts, and their personal experience with these elements. "These lands were originally strip mines," says Donna. The Robertses rejuvenated their property by replacing hayfields with vineyards—and derived the name, Terra Cotta Vineyards, from the red clay soils that penetrated their property to a depth of forty feet. The name also is meant to honor the region's reputation as a center for ceramics and Alysia's interest in making pottery.

Terra Cotta Vineyards was built with the help of family and friends and is character-ized by rustic architecture and a windswept landscape. The grounds include the Robertses' spacious residence, a two-story wooden winery with a peaked roof and lovely porches, a covered shelter for picnics and cookouts, and various farm buildings.

The interior of the winery, a great

gathering hall with poplar tables and chairs, has a cathedral ceiling, peach walls, wide poplar-plank floors, and paned windows. A center fan keeps the room cool. The gift shop features signature Terra Cotta Vineyards pottery vases and wine coolers designed by the Alpine Pottery in Crooksville, Alysia's painted glassware, and other artisanal crafts. A customer-relations coordinator, Misty conducts wine tastings and organizes wine and food events or special celebrations. The Robertses host wine tours by appointment and deliver personalized service and informative discussions.

The two-acre Terra Cotta Vineyards is planted along Rix Mills Road on a flat hilltop and down a steep hillside in red clay. The hardy, winter-resistant vines are planted to Chambourcin, Vidal Blanc, Seyval Blanc, Steuben, De Chaunac, Baco Noir, and Catawba. "The climate is typical Ohio

The view from Terra Cotta Vineyards

with hot and humid summers and no breeze. The sunsets are beautiful, but the thunderstorms are horrible," Paul says. After five years, the Robertses' biggest challenge is how to quell the influx of deer in Muskingum County, which has one of the highest populations in the state.

At harvest, the wine grapes are hand-picked and put in a crusher-destemmer, then pressed in a bladder-basket press and fermented in stainless steel tanks. The wines are pumped over and racked, then filtered and fined. They are aged in stainless steel tanks for one year with additional time in bottle.

Paul attended the Ohio State University wine short course for many years and obtained practical experience by observing the winemaking process at Willow Hill Vineyards in Johnstown. "Our goal is to produce good wines, and it is our belief that blending is an art," he says. "The emphasis was sanitation and chemistry—pH, acids, and residual sugars."

The wines at Terra Cotta Vineyards are French hybrids and American natives. The wine list is evenly divided between dry and sweet wines. "We are living the dream we have had for fifteen years of owning a winery and making quality Ohio wines," Donna says.

Terra Cotta Vineyards

Directions From I-70, take exit 169 and turn onto State Route 83 toward Cumberland. Take a right onto Sunflower Drive. Turn right onto Pleasant Hill Road, then left onto Rix Mills Road to the winery.

Hours January–February, Friday 4:30–7 p.m., Saturday 11 a.m.–6 p.m.; March–December, Tuesday–Thursday 5–8 p.m., Friday 3–8 p.m., Saturday 11 a.m.–8:30 p.m. Please call ahead to confirm hours.

Tours By appointment

Tastings Daily when open

Gifts Wine-related items, hand-painted gifts, custom-designed Alpine pottery

Picnics Outside shelter, porches, and side patio

Highlights at Winery Gorgeous view of Muskingum Valley; 53 acres of rolling countryside; informative wine discussions with owners and staff

Events Cookouts May–October; Valentine's Day event, special wine and food events

Restaurant Wine and cheese available for purchase; cookouts

Prices $6.50–$9.95; 10 percent case discount

Brand Names Terra Cotta Vineyards

Type of Production Traditional

Method of Harvesting By hand

Pressing and Winemaking Bladder press

Aging and Cooperage Stainless steel tanks and oak barrels

Vineyards Founded 1995

County Muskingum

Appellation Ohio

Acreage 2

Waterway Muskingum River

Climate Hot, humid, no breeze

Soil Clay

Varieties Vidal Blanc, Seyval Blanc, Chambourcin, Steuben, De Chaunac, Baco Noir, Catawba

Wines Seyval Blanc, Chambourcin, Terra Red, Vidal Blanc, Terra Rosa, Concord, Terra White

Best Red Chambourcin

Best White Terra White (sweet)

Nearby Places to Visit John and Annie Glenn Museum; Ohio Pottery

Ohio River Valley Tour

Vines at the Kinkead Ridge Estate Winery

Harmony Hill Vineyards

2534 Swings Corner Point Isabel Road
Bethel, OH 45106
Tel: (513)734-3548
Fax: (775)402-7424
E-mail: wine@hhwines.com
Web site: HHWines.com
Owners Bill Skvarla and Pat Hornak
Winemaker Bill Skvarla
Founded 2003

Just off of Swings Corner Point Isabel Road in Bethel lies Harmony Hill Vineyards, one of Ohio's smallest and newest wine estates. Established in 2003 by healers Bill Skvarla and Pat Hornak, it was lovingly named for the sacredness of the place and their harmonious approach to maintaining it. The couple has long shared a reverence for their natural environment, a passion for the protection of its flora and fauna, and a generous attitude toward learning. Their mere presence on this land gives sustenance to their most recent endeavor in grape growing and winemaking.

Natives of Pittsburgh, Pennsylvania, Bill graduated in nursing from the College of Mount St. Joseph, and Pat graduated in nursing-anesthesiology from St. Francis Hospital. Both institutions encouraged open inquiry and free thinking with respect for all humanity. In 1977, Bill and Pat began their married life in a small Cincinnati apartment. Before long, they purchased a larger Withamsville Cape Cod. "We bought a golden retriever named Amber, then a second one, dubbed CJ," Bill says. "In the winters, we ran the dogs without their leashes at the East Fork State Park, and eventually, we were asked to leave. So, we began to seriously shop for property."

By 1989, the Skvarlas had found a lovely seventy-acre Clermont County farm with a farmhouse and a horse barn in the Ohio River Valley. They planted medicinal herbs and raised two horses, two miniature donkeys, five dogs (usually strays, drop-offs, or rescues), and two cats. Their even-paced country life thirty miles east of Cincinnati balanced Bill's schedule as an emergency-room nurse at Bethesda Hospital and Pat's work as a nurse-anesthetist at Christ Hospital.

In 1996, Bill began experimenting as a home winemaker. "The reason we went into the wine business was my success in winning medals as an amateur winemaker," Bill says. "In 2002, I won a bronze medal for my Riesling at the Indiana International Wine Competition. Then, in 2003, I won a second bronze medal for my Chambourcin." As they planned for their retirement, they diversified into grape production and out of medicinal herbs—in part because of their success with home winemaking, and in part because of the possibility of future government regulation, which might push small herb farms out of business).

By 2000, Bill and Pat, with the help of an experienced grape grower, identified a three-and-a-half-acre site with glacial soils located in the hot and humid modified continental climate of southern Ohio. "We found a prime spot for a Cabernet Sauvignon and Cabernet Franc vineyard and an experimental French-American hybrid plot in search of our signature white wine—grapes like Riesling, Traminette, Vidal Blanc, and Seyval Blanc," Bill says. "Originally, our plan was to only sell red wine grapes. We were driven by the high market value of Cabernet Sauvignon and its positive health benefits, espoused by doctors we knew in the medical community. Our quest for an off-dry white was driven by local flavor."

The word-of-mouth reputation of Harmony Hill Vineyards is built on the authenticity of its hand-crafted artisan wines. A large, white 1,700-square-foot horse barn was transformed into a handsome winery, accentuated by white flowers and green trees. Open by appointment or invitation only, guests are encouraged to experience Harmony Hill, tasting wine in the café, visiting the vineyard gazebo, walking the trails, or taking in the gardens, herbs, or animals. With a maximum 1,500-case capacity, this boutique winery currently produces around 200 cases annually.

"My wife handles the marketing, and I personally attend to the details," Bill says. "We hand-harvest our grapes and oversee the wine production. We use fermentation bins and send three-fourths of the red grapes through the primary fermentation. The grapes are then racked-off and put in a basket wine press. We squeeze the grapes once and never want to overdo the tannin. We specialize in small batches of premium wine."

Among Harmony Hill Vineyards' most popular wines is Prelude, a Blush Nouveau with a blend of Marechal Foch and Cabernet Franc that has a cherry taste and light finish. Also popular is a Germanic-style Concerto, made from 100 percent Vidal Blanc at 1.8 percent residual sugar and noted for its taste of apple and pear. Harmony Hill also makes an Estate Peach, a promising dessert wine. "Our goal is not to be Ohio's largest winery but to select only the finest grapes to produce our premium-estate Cabernets in limited quantities," Bill says.

Harmony Hill Vineyards

Directions Take I-275 to State Route 125 east to Bethel. Turn right at the first light onto State Route 232, then take the first left onto Swings Corner Point Isabel Road to the winery.

Hours By appointment

Tours Tours of vineyard, gazebo, café, walking trails, scenic gardens, medicinal herb garden, and miniature donkeys

Tastings By appointment

Highlights at Winery Harvests only the finest grapes to make premium, estate-bottled Cabernets; lovely seventy-acre working farm

Prices $6.95–$7.95; 10 percent case discount

Brand Names Harmony Hill Vineyards

Type of Production Bordeaux-style wines

Method of Harvesting By hand

Pressing and Winemaking Basket press and refrigerated stainless steel tanks

Aging and Cooperage Stainless steel and American oak

Vineyards Founded 2000

County Clermont

Appellation Ohio River Valley

Acreage 3 (on a 70-acre farm)

Waterway 1 ⅓-acre lake

Climate Modified continental

Soil Glacial

Varieties Cabernet Franc, Cabernet Sauvignon, Traminette, Vidal Blanc, Seyval Blanc

Wines Prelude, Concerto, Estate Peach

Best Red Prelude

Best White Concerto

Other Best Wine Estate Peach, specialty dessert wine

Quote "Our goal is not to be Ohio's largest winery but to select only the finest grapes to produce our premium estate-bottled Cabernets in limited quantities." —Bill Skvarla

Nearby Places to Visit Historic River Villages; birthplace of Ulysses S. Grant

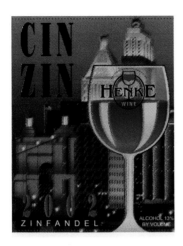

Henke Winery

3077 Harrison Avenue
Cincinnati, OH 45211
Tel: (513)662-9463
Fax: (513)662-9444
E-mail: info@henkewine.com
Web site: www.henkewine.com
Owners Joe and Joan Henke
Winemaker Joe Henke
Founded 1996

The present-day Henke Winery is ideally located in a white 1880s two-story residence on Harrison Avenue, the old east-west corridor between Cincinnati and Indianapolis, in Westwood, a neighborhood of stately homes, wrought-iron gates, and green lawns. Partners Joe and Joan Henke, native Ohioians, established their urban winery and restaurant as a home away from home for friends and neighbors.

Joe's wine odyssey, one of learning by doing, began with his first batch of sweet rose in 1973, expanded after he won a commendation in his first amateur wine competition in 1989, and moved into the noble varietals in the nineties. "Joan and my band of followers supported me," he says. The Henkes launched Henke Winery in 1996 in an old-fashioned nineteenth-century confectionery and ice cream parlor in Cincinnati's Winton Place. By 2001, they had outgrown this first location and moved to Westwood.

"We wanted to bring friends to a place with atmosphere, where they could socialize with their family and friends," says Joan, who fills the role of general manager. The response was substantial. Upon arriving in this old German, tree-lined neighborhood, surrounded by ethnic eateries, antique stores, and ski shops, one quickly realizes that this urban wine experience is unlike a trip to any country winery.

Thus, Henke Winery's success unfolded. Today, a trellised vineyard of varietals—Pinot Noir, Pinot Gris, Seyval, Chardonnay, and Cabernet Franc—borders the parking lot. "Customers participate in our adopt-a-vine program and learn about them," says Joe, a retired programmer.

The foyer into the main house is decorated with ancient bottles, historic wine labels, ribbons, and medals. "Each artifact tells a piece of our wine story," Joe says.

The European-style, windowed meeting room is tastefully decorated with a mahogany bar filled with glassware and Henke wine bottles, a faux marble tasting bar, softly draped chairs and glass tables, and artwork by featured artists in the Grapevine Gallery. "Guests meet the owners at our personalized wine tastings. We pour each individual wine in antique glassware and spend time pairing our wine with food, prepared by our chef," says Joan, who oversees the kitchen. "People literally stay all evening," Joe says. "And we welcome this practice."

Henke's logo, a bird of paradise resting on a dogwood above a glass of claret, is a reproduction of an original ebony glass etching featured at the winery's first location. Over the logo is a quote: "From the heart and the vine," which explains their winemaking philosophy. Below the logo are concepts representative of the Henke Winery's European style of winemaking: passion, quality, and pride.

The 1,600-gallon, boutique Henke Winery has grape contracts with wine-growers in Ohio, New York, and California. It exemplifies a uniquely urban winery that is able to create French-style wines without owning a vineyard and that treats guests to a gourmet restaurant that caters to groups of up to 125 in period dining rooms.

Joe explains his small-bin technique: "The dry white wines are barrel-fermented, then aged on the lees to give the wines body and structure. The sweet white wines are fermented cold-style to retain the fruit flavors. The red wines, however, undergo a longer maceration to expose the grape's tannins and flavors, often cellared in American and French oak, with additional time in bottle."

Henke Winery focuses solely on vitis vinifera and French hybrid wines, and has its highest sales at the winery and within Ohio. The label of Cin Zin, its first slightly sweet Zinfandel from Lodi, California, depicts the Cincinnati skyline. The label of its coveted Cabernet Sauvignon Reserve features a taxicab with a reserve sign against the Cincinnati hills. The next time you are on the wine road, head for Henke Winery in Westwood for fine wine and good food. Cheers!

Henke Winery

Directions From I-75, take the Harrison Avenue exit. Proceed 4 miles west on Harrison Avenue to the winery on the left. From I-74, take the North Bend exit. Proceed south on North Bend, then east on Harrison Avenue to the winery.

Hours Monday–Thursday 5–9 p.m.; Friday 3–11 p.m.; Saturday 11 a.m.–11 p.m.; closed Sunday

Tour By appointment

Gifts Wine-related

Highlights at Winery Urban winery with a *Cheers* type of atmosphere; informative tasting or casual dining

Events Amateur Home Winemaker's Contest; cork-sculpting competition; Grapevine Gallery featuring local artists monthly

Restaurant American cuisine—cheese board, garlic bread, shrimp cocktails, soup and salad, pizzas, honey mustard chicken breast, and filet mignon. Chef specials and vegetarian entrees are available.

Prices Wines vary from $7.50–$24.00; 10 percent case discount

Brand Names: Henke Winery

Type of Production European-style vitis vinifera and French hybrid

Pressing and Winemaking Traditional

County Hamilton

Appellation Ohio River Valley

Varieties Chardonnay, Seyval, Vidal Blanc, Riesling, Cabernet Sauvignon, Cabernet Franc, Cabernet Sauvignon, Zinfandel, Merlot

Wines Chardonnay, Seyval, Vidal Blanc, Riesling, Cellar Blush, Vin de Rouge, Cabernet Sauvignon, Cabernet Franc, Red Zinfandel, Merlot, Vendange a Trois, Sparkling Chardonnay

Best Red Cabernet Sauvignon

Best White Seyval

Best Other Wine Chardonnay

Quote "Our wines have passion, quality, and pride." —Joseph Henke

Nearby Places to visit Cincinnati Art Museum; Paramount's Kings Island

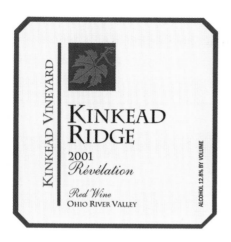

Kinkead Ridge Estate Winery

904 Hamburg Street
Ripley, OH 45167
Tel: (937)392-6077
Fax: (775)416-9184
E-mail: NBentley@KinkeadRidge.com
Web site: www.KinkeadRidge.com
Owners Ron Barrett and Nancy Bentley
Founded 1999

The road to Ripley, a fifty-five-acre National Historic District on the Ohio River Scenic Byway, heads over hills and through valleys along the Appalachian Trail. It was in this southernmost viticultural district in 1823 that Nicholas Longworth, "the father of American wine," successfully planted the first Catawba vines and made the state's first sparkling wine. Just east of Ripley in the Ohio River Valley Appellation of Origin stands Kinkead Ridge Estate Winery, where in 1999 Ron Barrett and Nancy Bentley came to prove that world-class red wines could be grown on these unglaciated limestone soils.

Descended from a Columbus farming family, Ron was an electrical engineer before he was employed by Knudsen Erath Winery in Oregon. In 1987, he purchased the forty-acre Chehalem Valley Vineyards, which he planted to Pinot Noir, Riesling, and Chardonnay and later sold to Pacific Northwest vintners. In Portland, he met his partner, Nancy, who had careers in graphic design and technical support before becoming a Cordon Bleu chef. They settled permanently in the picturesque Ohio River Valley, where they purchased the 129-acre William Kinkead Jr. farm and a Gothic Revival farmhouse built in 1880.

"Our goal is to make high-quality wines exclusively from vinifera," Ron says. The five-acre Kinkead Ridge Estate Vineyard is planted on a ridge rising more than four hundred feet above the nearby Ohio River in bluegrass country. It was named for the Kinkead family from Scotland that settled the road in the 1790s. Once the bottom of a prehistoric inland sea, this district consists of ancient limestone soils that are unmodified by glaciation. Nearly thirty inches deep to broken limestone, the well-drained soils are rich in clay. In this warm and humid but forever-changing climate, the growing season turns drier and cooler at harvest time. It is ideal for most Rhone and Bordeaux varieties during late September, but the winters can be cold and hard on vitis vinifera.

The primary varieties planted are Syrah, Cabernet Sauvignon, Cabernet Franc, Petit Verdot, Viognier, Roussanne, Riesling, Sauvignon Blanc, and experimental Sangiovese and Nebbiolo. The vines are cane pruned and vertically shoot positioned at a density of fifteen shoots per meter. The practices of leaf pulling and crop thinning selectively maximize the overall potential for high-quality wine grapes. Additionally, the vines are spaced seven-and-a-half feet apart to minimize their vigor and maximize their fruit intensity. "Harvest parameters vary, but in general, fruit will be harvested with high sugars and low acids at full maturity and optimum flavors," Nancy says.

Typically, the grapes are left to hang until fully mature without excessive concern for brix, acid, and pH levels. The grapes are then harvested by hand and transported to the Kinkead Ridge Estate Winery, a small, yellow, wood-and-stone artisan house near the 126-acre estate. "Our focus is to make select premium wines in very limited quantities," says Ron. "We have complete control of our estate from hand-grafting our own vines to making our hand-crafted, estate-grown wines."

Ron and Nancy are deeply committed to revitalizing this historic grape-growing district. The couple advocates for limited production of fine vitis vinifera wines. The white wines are cool-fermented to preserve any volatile components. The fruit from the vineyard defines the wines, and little or no oak is used. Red wines are made in small lots, a time-consuming and labor-intensive practice. The combination of cold maceration and hot fermentation produces robust wines with intense fruit and chewy tannins that are aged in both French and American oak.

These dedicated wine enthusiasts say their motto is encompassed in a quote from Goethe: "Whatever you can do or dream you can, begin it." They have experienced a profound response

The farmhouse at Kinkead Ridge

Courtesy of Nancy Bentley/Kinkead Ridge Estate Winery

to their vintages from the Ohio River Valley. Their wines include Syrah, Cabernet Franc, Sauvignon Blanc, a Cabernet Sauvignon blend named Revelation, and Riesling. "We pick the fruit ripe, and people cannot believe these wines are from Ohio," Nancy says. Try them and see for yourself!

Kinkead Ridge Estate Winery

Directions Take I-275 to U.S. Route 52 east toward New Richmond. Continue east about 50 miles to Ripley. The winery is three blocks east of downtown.

Hours Holiday weekends; tastings and retail sales by appointment

Tours Educational

Tastings Group tastings by appointment or holiday weekends

Gifts Glasses with logo

Picnics Picnic area along Ohio River in Ripley

Highlights at Winery Production of world-class vinifera; dedication to revitalizing the historic grape-growing area with new growers and vintners; working with Kentucky to improve the Ohio River Valley Appellation of Origin

Events River Village Christmas the second weekend of December

Prices $10.95–$19.95; 10 percent case discount

Brand Names Kinkead Ridge and Kinkead Cellars

Type of Production Hand-grafted vines to hand-crafted premium, estate-grown wines

Method of Harvesting By hand

Pressing and Winemaking Bladder press, with limited production of vinifera wines

Aging and Cooperage French and premium American oak

Vineyards Founded 1999

County Brown

Appellation Ohio River Valley

Acreage 5

Waterways Proximity to Eagle Creek, which drains to the Ohio River

Climate Modified continental

Soil Unglaciated limestone

Varieties Syrah, Cabernet Sauvignon, Cabernet Franc, Petit Verdot, Viognier, Roussanne, Riesling, Sauvignon Blanc, experimental plantings of Nebbiolo and Sangiovese

Wines Syrah, Cabernet Franc, Sauvignon Blanc, Revelation (a Cabernet Sauvignon, Rousanne/Viognier blend), Sauvignon Blanc, Viognier, Rousanne, Cabernet Sauvignon, Riesling

Nearby Places to Visit Rankin and Parker houses; Ripley antique shops

REIÉM

Champagne

PREMIUM AMERICAN SPARKLING WINE
CHARMAT BULK PROCESS
♦ NATURALLY FERMENTED ♦
ALCOHOL 12% BY VOLUME

EXTRA DRY

PRODUCED AND BOTTLED BY
CHATEAU REIEM CO., CINCINNATI, OHIO

Meier's Wine Cellars

6955 Plainfield Road
Cincinnati, OH 45236
Tel: (513)891-2900 or (800)346-2941
Fax: (513)891-6370
E-mail: info@meierswinecellars.com
Web site: www.meierswinecellars.com
Owner Paramount Distillers, Inc.
Winemaker Bob Distler
Founded 1865

In 1856, the visionary John Michael Meier, founder of Cincinnati's Meier's Wine Cellars, the oldest and largest winery in Ohio, journeyed from Bavaria's vineyards by train, across the Atlantic by schooner, and over the Appalachian Mountains by horse-cart to Reading, a German settlement near Cincinnati, in search of a better life. Meier and Kunigunde Seidenbaden, his new spouse, established a 164-acre homestead with a farm, livestock, and vineyard in Kenwood on the Cincinnati-Zanesville Pike.

Meier longed for aspects of his European homeland, especially the fine wines and plentiful bounty. Rhine wine-growers shipped him healthy German rootstock, but when he planted it, it died from the severe winter temperatures and the humid summer molds. Meier's son John Conrad Meier, the vineyard manager for his father's vast holdings, contacted aristocratic lawyer Nicholas Longworth, one of the wealthiest winegrowers in America. Longworth had had legendary success growing Catawba, a native American grape, in Cincinnati, and the Meiers wished to share in his good fortune. So, they replaced their German varietals with six hundred acres of Catawba. This decision defined wine-growing and winemaking at Meier's Wine Cellars for the next 140 years.

As Cincinnati prospered in the late 1800s, so did Meier's Wine Cellars. In 1895, John Conrad's sister (whose name is lost) tasted some unfermented wine and unintentionally discovered that Catawba grapes make excellent fresh grape juice. Thus, the John C. Meier Grape Juice Company was born.

In 1900, John C. Meier sold the Kenwood property and purchased five acres of Silverton land along the Baltimore & Ohio Railroad line. A Spanish stucco winery was built—and it remains Meier's

Wine Cellars' present location today. The winery features a wood-and-stone great room with tile floors, hand-hewn beams, a stone fireplace, and an elongated tasting bar. The bookcase, by far one of the most interesting historic features, displays Meier's wines, labels, medals, awards, and photos. The outdoor terrace, with hanging flower baskets, leads to what was once a posh 1920s garden with pedestals and statuary, now used for entertaining. John C. Meier's portrait hangs over the fireplace in the gift shop, which sells books, baskets, gadgets, glasses, and wine. The winery also features a five-acre wine-production center and an aging cellar equipped with stainless steel and oak.

During Prohibition, Meier's Wine Cellars survived by making grape juice. By 1941, the winery had expanded its reach and purchased vineyards on the tiny Isle of St. George, the northernmost of the Erie Islands northwest of Sandusky.

The island's century-old winegrowing legacy in glacial limestone soils, with a growing season six weeks longer than the mainland, produced Catawba, Delaware, Concord, Niagara, and other grapes. Meier's also imported grapes from winegrowers throughout Ohio, New York, Michigan, and California.

In 1976, Robert Gottesman, the owner of Paramount Distillers in Cleveland, acquired Meier's Wine Cellars along with two hundred acres of vineyard on North Bass Island in western Lake Erie.

Paramount also owned Firelands Winery, Lonz Winery, and Mon Ami Restaurant and Historic Winery. A founding member of the Ohio Wine Producers Association, Gottesman contributed to the rebirth of the Ohio wine industry and preservation of the Erie Islands. After his death in 2003, Paramount Distillers sold all its wine and vineyard holdings to John Kronburg, an Ohio and Florida real estate developer, with the exception of the Meier's Wine Cellars.

Today, Meier's purchases the bulk of its processed wine from Firelands Winery in Sandusky, fermenting 2.8 million gallons of wine annually. In 1995, Bob Distler, who had been champagne maker at Weibel Champagne Cellars, then

winemaker at Taylor's Great Western, was hired as one of several winemakers at Meier's Wine Cellars. "People have been drinking Meier's wines all their life," he says. "Our goal is to deliver them the best glass of wine. Thirty-year Pink Catawba customers expect a consistent product."

Meier's Wine Cellars

Directions From I-71, take exit 12, Montgomery Road. Head west on Montgomery Road and turn right on Plainfield Road to the winery.

Hours Monday–Thursday 10 a.m.–6 p.m.; Friday–Saturday 9 a.m.–6 p.m.

Tours Video presentation in lieu of tours

Tastings Daily when open; group reservations must be made in advance. ($2 per person includes tastings of three wines and one sparkling juice.)

Gifts Wine accessories, books, glassware, wines, jewelry, and clothing

Picnics Outdoor patio

Highlights at Winery One of Ohio's oldest and largest wineries

Events Summer event and Christmas event

Prices $4–14; 10 percent case discount

Brand Names Meier's Wine Cellars and J. C. Meier Sparkling Non-Alcoholic Juice

Type of Production Still wine and bulk-process champagne and sparkling juice

Aging and Cooperage Stainless steel tanks and American oak

Appellation American

Varieties 42 types

Wines Sauternes, Haut Sauterne, Bianco, White Catawba, Walleye White, White Zinfandel, Lakeside Niagara, American Merlot, Burgundy, Rubio, Lakeside Vines Rubio, Concord, Red Seedling, Spiced Wine, Black Berry, Sangria, Captain's Table Blush, Rosato, Pink Catawba, Lakeside Vines Rosato

Champagnes Reiem Brut, Reiem White, Reiem Pink, Reiem Spumante, Il de Fleur

Sparkling Wines Meier's Raspberry, Meier's Cranberry, Meier's Wildberry, Meier's Peach, Meier's Spumante

Best Red Merlot

Best White Haut Sauterne

Other Best Wine No. 44 Sherry and No. 44 Port

Quote "We make a wine product our loyal customers will always enjoy." —Robert Distler

Nearby Places to Visit Paramount's Kings Island; Newport Aquarium

A varietal white table wine produced from the Vidal 256
grape to create a bright, fresh-tasting wine with a dry finish.

ALCOHOL CONTENT 12% BY VOLUME

Moyer Vineyards, Winery & Restaurant

3859 U.S. Route 52

P.O. Box 235

Manchester, OH 45144

Tel: (937)549-2957

Fax: (937)549-4795

Owner Robert and Cindy Gilbertson; Jim and Wanda Bowman; Les and Kay Grooms; Tom Hamrick; Ben and Carol White; and Brett and Sherry Spencer

Winemaker Jim Bowman

Founded 1972

The green Appalachian foothills rise from the earth as you travel over rushing water-ways and through cypress-lined byways along the banks of the Ohio River Valley toward Manchester, home of Moyer Vineyards, Winery & Restaurant.

Decades ago, one of Manchester's high-lights was The River-By, a once-fashionable 1926 restaurant and dance hall on the Ohio River reached by motor coach or steamboat. The River-By pulled in droves of people with its nickelodeon music, square dancing, and prohibited bootleg beer. In 1935, Ezzard Charles, called the "Cincinnati Flash," who would become a world heavyweight boxing champion, fought a boxing match on the site. But the dramatic 1937 Ohio River flood buried the place in six feet of mud, leaving silty streets and twisted flood debris. By the late forties, this landmark building had been renamed The Top Hat, a private gambling club; through the late sixties, the place reinvented itself several times.

In 1972, Texas wine enthusiasts Ken and Mary Moyer refurbished the site of The River-By and established Moyer Winery and Vineyards, one of a handful of producing vineyards located along the fertile banks of the Ohio River. In addition to renovating the building, they added a lovely deck and landscaped the grounds. Soon Moyer Vineyards, Winery & Restaurant was showcasing Ohio River Valley wines and foods. Among its most loyal customers were Jim and Wanda Bowman, Terry and Peggy Ayres, Les and Kay Grooms, Ben and Carol White, Brett and Sherry Spenser, Tom Hamrick, and Robert and Cindy Gilbertson. "When the Moyers put the place on the market in 1998, we decided to purchase it as a group in 1999," says Jim Bowman, proprietor and winemaker.

These friends redesigned Moyer Vineyards, Winery & Restaurant with style. They started by landscaping the gazebo and flower gardens with color. The exterior received a new roof, burgundy board-and-batten siding, and an enlarged deck with moveable windows. "The views of the Ohio River became the focus," Bowman says. They brightened the interior, installed new floors, and accented the room with purple fabrics and fresh flowers to add flair. The kitchen was newly equipped, and the menu recalibrated to account for Midwestern tastes. Appetizers, salads, sandwiches, pastas, beef, seafood entrées, and deep-fried dishes were perfected to accompany the new Moyer wines. The new owners even booked a piano player and singer to entertain on the weekends.

The historic, thirty-year-old metal-post-and-wire trellised vineyards, interspersed with red roses, are located in sandy Adams County's riverside soils and planted to Vidal Blanc, Chambourcin, De Chaunac, Chardonnay, and Cabernet Sauvignon. The Ohio River Valley Appellation at this locale has a hot and humid growing season cooled by summer river breezes. "Our goal is to make fine wine and make a success of this place," says Bowman, who is assisted in the vineyards and the cellar by Jeffrey Riggs and Jonathan Bowman.

Below the restaurant lies the friends- and family-oriented winery. The winemakers do pressing, crushing, and fermenting in stainless steel; bottling, corking, and labeling are done by hand. "Down here in the cellar, there is always something going on," Bowman says. "I like wine and food, but I especially like the people. The reason I am doing this is for my enjoyment—from creating fine wine to making the place look good. As a 1,200-case producer, we make small batches of hand-crafted wine with a capacity of 2,500 to 3, 000 cases annually."

Moyer Winery produces Merlot, Cabernet Sauvignon, Chambourcin, River Valley Red, Country Home Red, Chardonnay, Vidal Blanc, and River Valley White along with rose wines and fruit wines—raspberry, strawberry peach, a Brut Champagne, and a semi-sweet champagne. "Our market, five to one, prefers a sweet wine to a dry one," Bowman says. "Our major sales are at the winery and the remainder at stores in Manchester, Ripley, Aberdeen, Portsmouth, and Georgetown."

Moyer Vineyards, Winery & Restaurant

Directions From Columbus, take I-71 south toward U.S. Route 62 south to U.S. Route 52 at Ripley. Then turn left and proceed 15 miles to the Moyer Winery on the right in Manchester. From Cincinnati, take I-275 south to U.S. Route 52. Follow U.S. 52 for 70 miles along the Ohio River to the Moyer Winery in Manchester.

Hours Monday–Thursday 11:30 a.m.–9 p.m.; Friday–Saturday 11:30 a.m.–10 p.m.; closed Sundays

Tours Guided tours

Tastings Daily when open

Highlights at Winery Fine food and award-winning wines; beautiful Ohio River Valley

Events Vintage Car Festival; Riverboat Day

Restaurant American Cuisine

Prices $7.00–$12.75; 10 percent case discount

Brand Name Moyer Winery

Type of Production Hand-crafted wines

Method of Harvesting By hand

Pressing and Winemaking Basket press

Aging and Cooperage Stainless steel

Vineyards Founded 1972

County Adams

Appellation Ohio River Valley

Acreage 8

Waterway Ohio River

Climate Four seasons

Soil Sandy

Varieties Vidal Blanc, Chambourcin, De Chaunac, Chardonnay, Cabernet Sauvignon

Wines Cabernet Sauvignon, Merlot, Chambourcin, Moyer River Valley Red, Moyer Country Home Red, Chardonnay, Moyer River Valley White, Zinfandel, Blush, Moyer River Valley Rose, Moyer Raspberry Wine, Strawberry Wine, Champagne Brut, Semi-Sweet Champagne

Best Red Moyer Chambourcin

Best White Moyer River Valley White

Other Best Wine Moyer Country Home Red

Nearby Places to Visit Unity Woods; Serpent Mound

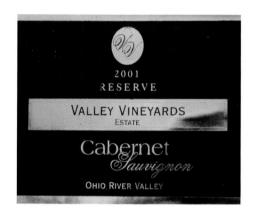

Valley Vineyards

2276 East U.S. 22

Morrow, OH 45152

Tel: (513)899-2485

Fax: (513)899-9022

E-mail: info@valley-vineyards.com

Web site: www.valley-vineyards.com

Owners Kenneth G. Schuchter and
Kenneth J. Schuchter II

Winemaker Greg Pollman

Founded 1970

There is an unassuming sense of longevity about Valley Vineyards in Morrow. A handsome Tudor winery and weathered residence sit in the flat of a wide agricultural valley located along the well-traveled U.S. Route 22, opposite sixty acres of undulating hillside vineyards thriving in the Ohio River Valley Appellation of Origin.

When Lawrence and Evelyn Schuchter, Bavarian immigrants, arrived in Morrow at the turn of the nineteenth century, they were struck by the promise these verdant farmlands held. They successfully cultivated fruits and vegetables for farm markets. But it was Lawrence's son, Kenneth G. Schuchter, and his spouse, Margaret, who decided to take a risk and plant wine grapes in the 1960s. "The Schuchters planted twenty-seven varieties of wine grapes, some vitis vinifera—Cabernet Sauvignon, Cabernet Franc, Chardonnay, and Riesling—French hybrids, and three American varieties," says Gail Haines, currently sales manager at Valley Vineyards.

The Schuchter wine legacy was defined by the character of its good-natured and hard-working founders. Patriarch Kenneth G. Schuchter, an energetic, hands-on man, loved the outdoors. "My grandfather admits being the happiest riding his tractor and tending his vines," says his grandson, Kenneth J. Schuchter II. The matriarch Evelyn, who was very much a people-person, thrived on her lifestyle choices. "My grandmother was content cooking in the kitchen or pruning the vineyards," Kenneth J. says. The Schuchters shaped the culture of Valley Vineyards winery: They emphasized family, they welcomed their friends and neighbors, and they celebrated life with German food and estate-grown wines. This has influenced the modern-day Schuchters and their loyal employees to take a unified approach to their work.

What began as a small family farm

mushroomed into a top Ohio restaurant and twenty-thousand-case wine estate. The Schuchters hired contractor Everett Done to replicate a Bavarian wine castle on the Rhine, Germany's famed winegrowing district. A two-story stucco winery with a peaked roof, dormer windows, and a brick foundation was built and framed by trees and decorative landscaping. A large wooden doorway opens into a spacious tasting room at the center of activity. One wing houses a great dining hall in the tradition of a European wine garden, complete with beamed ceilings, brick fireplace, artifacts, and wine murals. Another wing houses a high-ceilinged dining hall, the Cabernet Room, that is used for private parties. The specialty chef, Anna Sharik, caters to patrons who favor her chicken schnitzel, die deutsche platte, hunter schnitzel, German sausages, and sauerbraten. On the lighter side, she also serves salads, burgers, and pizzas.

Kenneth J. Schuchter, of the third-generation and the vineyard manager, and his wife, Dodie, restaurant manager, are now the proprietors. His son, Kenneth J. Schuchter II, says his father worked with Cabernet Sauvignon, Cabernet Franc, Chardonnay, Seyval, Vidal Blanc, De Chaunac, Niagara, and Catawba, all planted in clay loam in a typically continental climate. "My father gives the viniferas extra care, protecting them from winter freezes by utilizing a grape hoe, which ploughs the dirt over the graft. This step ensures a good crop, with yields varying from three-and-a-half to eight tons per acre, pending the specific variety," he says.

A 7,200-square-foot stainless steel wine-production center and an American- and French-oak aging cellar lies under the restaurant. Greg Pollman, the present-day winemaker, has pursued quality through experimentation with his winemaking. "Our newest achievements are bigger and better," he says. As examples, he cites the winery's growing volume of Traminette, its launch of the appellation's first Ice Wine, and its production of its first Cabernet Sauvignon Reserve. The increasing interest in the wines from Valley Vineyards rests in their dry, fruity Chardonnay; dry, oak-aged Seyval; rich, medium Vidal Blanc; and delightful Syrah. Still, another segment of customers supports the purchase of their medium to sweet wines. The winery has carved out its role as a frequent recipient of commendations and medals, and remains a serious contender in the Ohio River Valley wine saga.

Valley Vineyards

Directions Take I-71 to exit 28 (State Route 4). Turn south on Route 48 to U.S. Route 22 and U.S. Route 3. Turn left and east for 3 miles to the winery.

Hours Monday–Thursday 10:30 a.m.–8 p.m.; Friday–Saturday 8 a.m.–11 p.m.; Sunday 1–8 p.m.

Tours Self-guided, educational, and historic

Tasting Daily when open

Gifts Gift baskets, VV glasses, T-shirts, and personalized wine bottles

Highlights at Winery Beautiful Ohio River Valley and hillside vineyards; Tudor architecture of winery; historic oak aging cellars

Events Valley Vineyards Wine Festival every September; Valley Vineyards grill-your-own-steak dinners Fridays and Saturdays

Prices $7–$40; 10 percent case discount; steak dinners $45 per person

Packages/Specials Gift baskets, gift boxes, personalized labels

Brand Names Valley Vineyards Winery

Type of Production American hybrids, vitis vinifera, French-American hybrids

Method of Harvesting By hand

Pressing and Winemaking Traditional

Aging and Cooperage French and American oak barrels, stainless steel tanks

Vineyards Founded 1970

County Warren

Appellation Ohio River Valley

Acreage 60

Waterway Ohio River

Climate Continental

Soil Clay loam, Glacial till

Varieties 20 varieties

Wines Cabernet Sauvignon, Cabernet Franc, Hillside Red, De Chaunac, Seyval, Chardonnay, Blue Eye, Vidal Blanc, Valley Blush, Niagara, Concord, Pink Catawba, Honey Mead, Ice Wine, Champagne, Blanc de Blanc Champagne

Best Red Cabernet Sauvignon

Best White Chardonnay

Other Best Wine Vidal

Quote "The art of winemaking has been a tradition in southern Ohio for nearly two centuries." —Schuchter Family

Nearby Places to Visit Paramount's Kings Island; Fort Ancient State Memorial

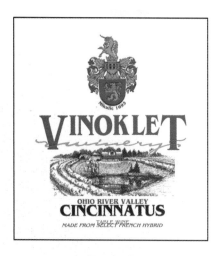

Vinoklet Winery

11069 Colerain Avenue
Cincinnati, OH 45252
Tel: (513)385-9309
Fax: (513)385-9379
E-mail: vinokletwinery@fuse.net
Web site: www.vinokletwines.com
Owner/Winemaker Kreso Mikulic
Founded 1980

The thirty-acre Vinoklet Winery sits high on a hillside overlooking gently rolling vineyards, cypress-lined ponds, and perennial gardens with spectacular vistas of Cincinnati and the Ohio River Valley. This beloved wine country estate, Vinoklet, which means "little house in the vineyard" in Croatian, reflects the artistry of its founder, Kreso Mikulic, who brought a "little bit of heaven" to this remote corner of Hamilton County.

"My father taught me to make wine," says Mikulic, a native of Mimici, a Croatian village of sixteen families and sixteen wineries. He is also the winemaker, and you'll often find him jauntily dressed in a red beret, glasses, a faded shirt, and worn jeans. "If one family didn't make wine in my hometown, everyone would have thought that something was wrong."

At thirty, Kreso departed Europe for the United States, where he pursued his dreams and lived his philosophy—"start and never quit." He reached prominence as an engineer for Reuland Electric, where he built the B-1 bomber fuel pump. As an aerospace engineer at Wilco Corporation, he designed commercial applications and high-speed motors.

"My father had his own winery in Croatia, and he made classical wine. I did what I loved," Mikulic says. "I had land and thought, what could I do?" He hired ten bulldozers to clear seventeen acres for a south-facing hillside vineyard. "Foot by foot, we pulled out every root, then graded and shaped the land, adding topsoil to the rocky acidic clay underpan."

First he planted 150 plants, and none sprouted. Next, he planted two hundred vines, and they died. "I was persistent," he remembers. "Something was wrong with the soil and the climate." Then, he ordered five hundred plants from the Finger Lakes, and every one came up. "I made wine just for friends," he says. Mikulic planted one thousand vines, then two thousand vines, and finally six thousand vines before adding winery buildings in 1986 and outfitting them with the latest winemaking equipment.

"Wine helps in this life; it adds to one's health and happiness," Mikulic says. "I wanted to create a winery with ambiance, reflective of the goodness in life."

Along Colerain Road stands a charming tan farmhouse with red shutters, framed by trees and accentuated with boxes of red, purple, blue, and yellow flowers and a patio with a café table and chairs. Mikulic's cozy home is a step back in time. A European-appointed Vinoklet Bed and Breakfast, located on adjacent property, is richly decorated in textured fabrics, mahogany furniture, oil paintings, and oriental rugs.

A quarter-mile away, a grape arbor leads into a courtyard, where there is a brick winery and restaurant with elegant lanterns, wrought-iron furniture, an ivy-covered flowing fountain, and a gazebo with breathtaking vineyard views. A renovated 25,000-gallon redwood wine barrel suitable for small year-round parties has a fireplace and air conditioning.

Vinoklet provides customers an elegant dining experience in its fresh-air gazebo, solarium, or main dining room, featuring green and red tablecloths, red chairs, woodcuts, and a fourteenth-century Italian mural. Mikulic loves to invite his guests to taste Vinoklet wines with steak, fish, chops, or chicken, which they grill themselves in the high-tech grill room, served with a fancy buffet and serenades by strolling violinists.

"People like Vinoklet wines. They are light, easy to drink, and not too tart or too soft," he says. With the completion of a new 50,000-case winery, Mikulic has renewed his commitment to traditional winemaking. The grapes are harvested by hand, then destemmed and crushed in a Vaslin press. The whites are cold-fermented in stainless steel with time in stainless steel and bottle for "clarity and flavor." The reds are fermented in stainless steel and/or oak with additional aging in barrel and bottle.

"People who drink wine are the ultimate judge," Mikulic says. "The best wine is the one which pleases the consumer the most. Wine is a very personal experience."

Courtesy of Vinoklet Winery

Vinoklet Winery

Directions Take I-275 to exit 33 (Colerain Avenue) north to Old Colerain Avenue. Turn left for 1.25 miles to Vinoklet on the left.

Hours Tuesday–Thursday 12–8 p.m.; Friday–Saturday 12–11 p.m.; Sunday 1–7 p.m.

Tours By appointment for small groups

Tastings Daily when open

Gifts Glasses, shirts, wine, and accessories

Highlights at Winery Our you-grill-to-perfection dinners and buffet; banquet room for parties and special events; bed and breakfast; strolling violinist and bonfire on weekends

Events September Art and Wine Festival with 66 artisans and 12,000 guests; outdoor wedding ceremonies, receptions for 160; Sunday pig roasts June–September for the family

Restaurant Patrons grill their choice of steak, fish, chicken, or pork with Vinoklet wines

Prices $11–$12 for retail wine; $28 includes dinner, wine tasting, entree, buffet, dessert, coffee/tea

Brand Names Vinoklet Wines: Cincinnatus, Tears of Joy, Sunset Blush, Dreamers, In Vino Veritas, La Dolce Vita

Type of Production Traditional

Method of Harvesting Hand-harvested

Pressing and Winemaking Traditional

Aging and Cooperage Stainless steel and oak

Vineyards Founded 1980

County Hamilton

Appellation Ohio

Acreage 17

Waterways Three lakes, some surrounded by cypress trees

Climate Hot, humid spring and summer; fair to cold winter

Soil Rocky, acidic clay with excellent drainage

Varieties Catawba, Chambourcin, Niagara, Vidal Blanc, Concord

Wines Cincinnatus, (comparable to Merlot), Tears of Joy (comparable to Chardonnay), Sunset Blush (comparable to White Zinfandel) Dreamer (comparable to Chablis), In Vino Veritas (comparable to sweet Riesling), La Dolce Vita (comparable to Port)

Best Red La Dolce Vita

Best White Tears of Joy

Other Best Wine In Vino Veritas

Quote "Wine helps in this life; it adds to one's health and happiness." —Kreso Mikulic

Nearby Places to Visit Cincinnati Zoo; Cincinnati Art Museum

AMERICAN RED WINE
Darke Red
Alcohol 11.8% by Volume
Produced and Bottled by
The Winery at Versailles
6572 St Rt 47 E, Versailles, OH 45380

www.wineryatversailles.com

The Winery at Versailles

6572 State Route 47
Versailles, OH 45380
Tel: (937)526-3232
E-mail: mikewav@bright.net;
    carolwav@bright.net
Web site: www.wineryatversailles.com
Owners Carol and Mike Williams
Winemaker Mike Williams
Founded 2002

The road weaves its way through beautiful open stretches of Ohio farm country before it reaches The Winery at Versailles. The only winery in Darke County, it was established in 2002 by Pennsylvanians Mike and Carol Williams, who relocated to this elegant Midwestern hamlet to be near their children.

The Williamses met in Switzerland in 1972 while Carol was on tour and Mike was studying business at the University of Augsburg/Munich. It was Mike's mechanic who first turned him onto the idea of winemaking. "My mechanic, a failed master wine taster, was unsuccessful in identifying over 85 percent of Germany's three thousand vineyards by flavor," Mike says. However, he successfully advised Mike to buy a pricey German Trockenbeerenauslese, a rich, nectarous wine with concentrated sugar and flavor made from overripe, nearly dry grapes left on the vine and harvested at maturity.

For an impressionable young man from St. Mary's, Pennsylvania, the town that produces the all-natural Straubs Beer, it was the perfect incentive. From there, Mike began to read voraciously about centuries-old German wineries and breweries, and his love of wine unfolded.

In 1974, the Williamses married in Wisconsin and went to Germany while Mike completed a tour in the Signal Corps. They returned to the United States in 1978. Mike pursued several endeavors: He raised quail, worked with the handicapped, and managed factories. For relaxation, he made wine at home for his seven siblings, who were among his best and worst critics. "As the wine got better, my reputation improved," he says. "By the early 1990s, I was making more and more wine."

In 1994, the Williamses established the Winery at Wilcox in the Allegheny National Forest. Under the Presidential Proclamation of 1923, a 513,000-acre forest of hardwoods, since replaced by black cherry and maple, was created in the heart of the oil and gas region. Subsequently, many of these lands were reclaimed and planted to grapes. "We produced 1,000 gallons of eight varieties, and by 1996 expanded to 25,000 gallons, or thirty wines," Mike says.

In 2000, the Williamses relocated to Versailles, a gentrified farm community recognized for eggs, shipping, and medical equipment. They purchased a historic twelve-acre farm (which had a grand old manor house where Annie Oakley—Darke County's own Phoebe Moses, who shot the ashes off Kaiser Wilhelm's cigarette—spent her summers), an 1850s tobacco barn, and land for winegrowing. The Williamses, their children, Jamie and Lisa, and Mike's brother, Dave, ran the Wilcox and Versailles operations.

Four miles west of town stands the Winery at Versailles, a renovated grey barn trimmed in white paint with an overhanging porch and rail fence. The bright main room is appointed with a wrought-iron chandelier, a right-angled tasting bar, and tables and chairs covered in rich, red-patterned fabrics. Merchandise available for purchase—winemaking equipment, gift baskets, gourmet foods, myriad wine accessories, and fashionable clothing—is displayed everywhere.

With two of ten acres in Versailles under development, Mike has gambled on the Darke County clay soils, the moderate yet humid climate, and the absence of severe cold and partnered with local farmers to plant Cayuga, Chancellor, Traminette, and Chambourcin.

Until Versailles's Vineyards bear fruit, Mike sources grapes from growers in Northwestern Ohio and Pennsylvania. destemmed and crushed. Within eight hours, the juice is shipped to Versailles, where it is fermented in stainless steel temperature fermentors. "I am a minimalist and do very little fiddling," Mike says.

The Winery at Versailles showcases some twenty-six fruit-forward wines. They are an American oak-aged Pinot Grigio, a barrel-fermented Chardonnay and a stainless steel-fermented Chardonnay, a fragrant Viognier, a classic Cabernet Sauvignon, a rich Cabernet Franc, and a medium-bodied Chambourcin aged in oak. The Williamses also produce semi-dry and semi-sweet wines, a collection of sweet sparkling fruit wines, and a delightful Old Forte Port.

The Winery at Versailles

Directions From I-75, head west on State Route 47 for 24.7 miles, then continue 4 miles west of Versailles.

Hours Monday–Thursday 10 a.m.– 6 p.m.; Friday–Saturday 10 a.m.–9 p.m.; closed Sundays

Tours Daily educational tours when open

Tasting Daily when open

Gifts Winemaking equipment, wine accessories, glassware, and clothing

Picnics Encouraged

Highlights at Winery Variety of unique and innovative wines; winemaker dinners and wine tastings; all levels wine education and winemaking classes; personalized labels

Events Annual Wine Fest

Restaurant Eclectic, catered dinners

Prices $7–$20; 10 percent case discount

Brand Names The Winery at Versailles

Type of Production Traditional

Method of Harvesting By hand and machine

Aging and Cooperage French and American oak

Vineyards Founded 2005

County Darke

Appellation Ohio and American

Acreage 2, to be developed into 10 within 10 years

Climate Moderate but humid with air drainage but no severe cold

Soil Deep clay with stone

Varieties Cayuga, Chancellor, Traminette, Chambourcin

Wines Pinot Grigio, Chardonnay, Viognier, Cabernet Sauvignon, Cabernet Franc, Chambourcin, Merlot, Brits Blush, Darke Red, Stillwater White, Gewürztraminer, Autumn Leaves, Buckeye Blush, Pinot Auxerois, Hunter Red, Celebration Sparkling Wine, Blueberry Sparkling Wine, Peach Mist Sparkling Wine, Shawnee Blush, Wedding White, Rodeo Red, Niagara, Rosatto Muscatto, Olde Fort Port, Port of Chardonnay, Schwartzbeeren

Best Red Port of Chambourcin

Best White Viognier

Other Best Wine Sparkling Blueberry Wine

Quote "We will serve the Lord" —Joshua 24:15

Nearby Places to Visit Inn at Versailles; Garst Museum in Greenville

Woodstone Creek Winery

3641 Newton Avenue

Cincinnati, OH 45207

Tel: (513)474-3521 (office)

(513)569-0300 (tasting room)

Fax: (513)474-9384

E-mail: mead@gbronline.com

Web site: www.woodstonecreek.com

Owner/Winemaker Donald R. Outterson

Founded 1999

The brick Woodstone Creek Winery, headquartered in a former stamping factory at the corner of Newton Avenue and Dana Avenue in Cincinnati's Evanston, has distinguished itself as the state's only winery with a distillery. Woodstone Creek has Ohio's only licensed pot still in operation, and is one of three distilleries in the state.

The idea to combine the winery and distillery ventures was a natural one for owner Donald Outterson. "I made beer and wine in 1979, after legislation permitted for home production," he says. He then spent time as an exchange student, which he says further defined his styles of making beer and wine. Once back in the United States, Outterson won the New York State Amateur Beer Championship in 1982. This led to an apprenticeship at the William S. Newman Brewing Company in Albany, New York, where he made English ales.

Outterson is a Certified Brewmaster who received his credentials from the Siebel Institute of Chicago in 1986. A member of the Master Brewers Association of America, he also partook in Alltech seminars in distillation. "This began my journey of running breweries," Outterson says. At James Page Brewing in Minneapolis, he formulated a wild rice-based European Lager that won accolades at the National Brew Festival.

As a consultant, Outterson did contract work for brewpubs in famous places, such as Telluride Lager Beer. These upscale designer brew products resulted in an Australian multinational chain of breweries hiring Outterson as their brewmaster through 1989.

While in Canberra City, Australia, Outterson acquired the U.S. importation rights for the Adelaide Malting Company floor malts, originally made by the historic Cooper's Brewery, Australia's last family-owned producer of beers, ales, and stouts. "I honed my malt-analysis skills as it pertained to varieties, species, and grains, with an inroad to distillation," he says. Outterson began to study the industrial application of distilled alcohol. Over the course of a decade, he progressed from brewmaster to winemaker to distiller. "I now had completed my training as a fermentation technologist."

Just as the brewpub fad was fading, Outterson's desire to make wine was blossoming. He took a job selling production equipment to wineries, distilleries, and brewpubs. His exposure to people in the wine business had a major impact on him, and he established many lasting business relationships. As was customary among many brewers, Outterson produced mead, the most ancient of fermented beverages made from honey, water, and yeast. Mead is regulated by the U.S. government and categorized as a wine. If he wanted to produce it commercially, he had to open a winery. When Outterson discovered that mead was little understood and difficult to market, he tried his hand at adding wine from grape varietals to his budding wine list, and Woodstone Creek Winery took form.

Today, Woodstone Creek Winery welcomes friends and neighbors to share in the culture of art and wine. Outterson's wife, Linda, a graphic designer and artist, designs their wine labels and paints oils—landscapes and florals—that are displayed with her handmade jewelry and crafts in the tasting room. Comparative wine tastings with commentary by the owners commence at the curved 1930s maple tasting bar with a paneled front and butcher-block top, accented by a solid mahogany rail. The shop retails varietals, blends, ports, sherries, brandies, honey wines, and accessories. The owners share the building with a home winemaking and brewing supply store.

"We produce small batches," Outterson says. He challenges himself by introducing new concepts and techniques in his winemaking, conducting his experiments in his efficient stainless steel production tanks and wine cellars. "I shop the world for the best quality … from the mountain to the valley … on our economy of scale."

Among the Woodstone Creek Winery products are a lightly-oaked California Central Valley dry Chardonnay; a semi-dry Finger Lakes Chardonnay called Diva; a dry Central Ohio Riesling; a California Central Coast Cabernet Sauvignon; a sweet, fruity Ohio called Lake Erie Niagara; a complex lemon-ginger herbal mead called Taliesin; a semi-dry Raspberry Honey Wine; a semi-sweet, balanced Central Ohio Vidal Blanc; ports; and other varieties. "Here we make dreams come true!" Outterson says.

Woodstone Creek Winery

Directions From I-71, take the Dana Avenue exit, then proceed west for two blocks to the winery.

Hours Saturday 1–5 p.m.; by appointment for groups of ten

Tours None

Tasting When open

Gifts Handmade jewelry, craft items, artwork

Highlights at Winery American-Ohio wines of different tastes, styles, varieties, blends; dessert wines produced as spirits in on-site pot still; specialty Ohio ports and port-style honey wines

Prices $9.00–$34.95; 10 percent case discount

Brand Names Woodstone Creek Winery

Type of Production Innovative

Method of Harvesting By hand

Pressing and Winemaking Traditional

Aging and Cooperage Stainless steel and American and French oak barrels

Appellation 70 percent American, 30 percent Ohio River Valley

Varieties Vidal Blanc, Chardonnay, Riesling, Cabernet Sauvignon, Merlot, Sauterne, Cabernet Franc, Niagara

Wines Vidal Blanc, Diva, Riesling, Chardonnay, Haut Sauterne, Mead Honey Wine, Raspberry Honey White, White Honey Wine, Honey Mist, Ginger Honey Wine, Royale, Rialto Red, Cabernet Sauvignon, Taliesin Dry, Metheglin Mead, Niagara, Ambiance Tawny Port, Laureate Tawny Port, Crowne Amber Spiced Honey Dessert Wine, Legacy Honey Port

Best Red Cabernet Sauvignon

Best White Vidal Blanc

Other Best Wine Diva

Quote "Give a person a bottle of wine and one can waste an afternoon. Teach a person to make wine and one can waste a lifetime."
—Donald R. Outterson

Nearby Places to Visit Xavier University; Krohn Conservatory

Phil Masturzo

NEW to the OHIO WINE COUNTRY

Myrddin Winery

3020 Scenic Avenue
Berlin Center, OH 44401
Tel: (330)654-9181
E-mail: ksa@neo.rr.com
Web site: www.myrddinwine.com
Hours: Opening late summer 2005

Myrddin Winery is located near the picturesque Lake Milton in Berlin Center. Chris Sperry, an architect, and his wife, Evelyn, started their new venture in 2005 and named it for Merlin, the late sixth-century prophetic wild man and wizard who conceived Arthur and then featured himself in the Arthurian legend. The Sperrys plan to offer their patrons a twenty-first-century outdoor Merlinesque adventure tasting wine in the deeply wooded forests of Mahoning County.

Myrddin originated as a small, handcrafted 3,000-gallon winery. As winemaker, Chris sources grapes from two coasts, then blends them to produce oak-aged Ohio premium wines. Myrddin Winery will include six wines under the Myrddin 1 and Myrddin 2 labels.

Quarry Hill Winery

8403 Mason Road
Berlin Heights, OH 44814
Tel: (419)588-2858
E-mail: macmclelland@aol.com
Web site: www.ohiowines.org
Hours: Monday–Saturday 10 a.m.–6 p.m.;
Sunday 10 a.m–6 p.m., wine sales after 1 p.m.

Quarry Hill Winery lies at the highest point in Berlin Heights in the rolling foothills of Erie County. Proprietor Mac McLelland, who garnered career experience as winemaker at John Christ Winery, founded this exciting venture in 2005. Named for its unique geographic properties, Quarry Hill Winery boasts spectacular panoramic views of beautiful Lake Erie. McLelland remodeled the former cider mill on the land and outfitted it for the production of fruit and grape wines.

Mac emphasizes that the location in proximity to Lake Erie, combined with the district's excellent soils and climate, is ideal for growing vineyards and fruit orchards. The establishment proudly features Ohio-made farm products and Quarry Hill premium wines at its on-site farmer's market.

Mastropiétro Winery

14558 Ellsworth Road
Berlin Center, OH 44401
Tel: (330)547-2151
E-mail: mastropietrowine@aol.com
Web site: www.mastropietrowinery.com
Hours: Tuesday–Thursday 5–9 p.m.;
Friday 5–11 p.m.; Saturday 1–11 p.m.

For three generations, Mastropiétro family members have created good wine for personal enjoyment in their private cellar. So it wasn't a surprise in the 1990s when principals Daniel and Marianne Mastropiétro and Daniel's sister Cathy purchased a farm and designed a vineyard that they planted to classic vitis vinifera and French-American hybrids. Their inspiration came from their grandfather Joseph and their father, Daniel, who both loved the art of winemaking and the camaraderie shared among the family.

In 2005, they opened the Tuscan-influenced Mastropiétro Winery, located beside a beautiful lake known for its sunsets in Berlin Center. The winery features an Italian tasting room with a huge stone fireplace, a banquet room, a gift shop, and a scenic patio. In the modern stainless steel production center, Daniel, the winemaker, makes Chardonnay, Riesling, Cabernet, Chambourcin, Dolce Rosso, Merlot, Zinfandel, and Valley Red. The family conducts personalized tours by appointment.

Tinroc Vineyards

521 Warwick Road
Hamilton, OH 45013
Tel: (513)887-9133
E-mail: tinroc@aol.com
Hours: Opening spring of 2006

The foundation for Tinroc Vineyards was established in 2002 by Jack and Brigitte Cornitt, wine collectors and business partners, in the southwestern Ohio town of Hamilton. The winery name is derived from their surname, Cornitt, sounded out backward. Located between Dayton and Cincinnati, this sixty-two-acre vineyard estate was planted incrementally to a total of 4,200 vines: Chardonnay, Sauvignon Blanc, Riesling, Cabernet, Cabernet Franc, Merlot, Pinot Noir, Gruderveltliner, Tempranillo, Grenache, and Viognier.

The Cornitts are modeling their Ohio business holdings—a winery, vineyard, and restaurant—after the prominent Napa Valley real estate developer Bill Harlan, who renovated Meadowood Resorts and created the high-end Harlan Estates and the well-known Merryvale. They plan to spare no expense in building this top-notch winery to produce high-quality wines.

Selected Bibliography

California Wineries of Sonoma and Mendocino, Patricia Latimer, St. Helena, California: Vintage Image, 1975.

Lake Erie, Harlan Hatcher, New York, New York: Bobbs-Merrill Company, 1945.

A History of Wine in America, Thomas Pinney, Berkeley and Los Angeles, California: University of California Press, 1989.

Salud! The Rise of Santa Barbara's Wine Industry, Victor W. Geraci, Reno and Las Vegas, Nevada: University of Nevada Press, 2004.

Conversation and interview with Judith Orkin Rosenthal, Cleveland, Ohio, July 6, 2004.

Conversation and interview with Sanford Silverman, Cleveland, Ohio, July 6, 2004.

Geneva Jewish Farmers, Reunions, Sanford Silverman, Cleveland, Ohio, 1990–1991.

Letter, Arnie Esterer, Markko Vineyard, Conneaut, Ohio, August, 4, 2004.

Wines of America, Leon D. Adams, 3rd edition, New York, New York: McGraw Hill, 1985.

Letter from Collection of the Shaker Historical Society, Nord Library, Shaker Heights, Ohio.

Vine Dressers Manual Vineyards & Winemaking, Charles Reemlin of Ohio. New York, New York: CM Saxton & Co., 1855, archives of the Western Reserve Historical Society, Cleveland, Ohio.

Letter from Nicholas Longworth to members of the Cincinnati Horticulture Society on the Cultivation of the Grape and Manufacture of Wine, 1846, archives of the Western Reserve Historical Society, Cleveland, Ohio.

Wines of the Midwest, Ruth Ellen Church. Athens, Ohio: Swallow Press Books, Ohio University Press, 1982.

Letter, Gary Heck, president Korbel Champagne Cellars, Guerneville, California, February 11, 2005.

Winegrowing Industry of the Lake Erie Island Region, Kyle J. Johannsen, Bowling Green University, Bowling Green, Ohio.

A History of the Kelleys Island Grape and Wine Industry, Kurt Boker, Kelleys Island Library, Kelleys Island, Ohio.

Conversation and interview with A. J. Hammer, former president of The Hammer Company, Cleveland, Ohio, December 2004.

Conversations and interviews with Jean Francis M. Latimer, Cleveland, Ohio, 2004 and 2005.

Letter Dr. James F. Gallander, professor emeritus, the Ohio State University, March 9. 2005.

Letter Dr. Garth A. Cahoon, professor emeritus, the Ohio State University, March 8, 2005.

Cleveland Heights, The Making of an Urban Suburb, Marian J. Morton, Charelston, S.C., Chicago, Portsmouth, N.H., San Francisco, California: Arcadia Publishing, 2002.

Acknowledgments

It is with appreciation that I thank the many people who have given so generously of their time and thought in assisting with this creative work.

With respect for those who shared their sight and insight over the years along the wine trail and made this book possible.

Leon D. Adams
Bouvier Beale Jr.
Darrell Corti
Jose Ignacio Domecq Jr.
Arnie Esterer
James Gruber
Louise Gund
Gladys Horiuchi
Geoff Kenway
John Kithas
Jean Miller Latimer
Phil Masturzo
Tom McCarthy
James Miller
Melissa Mytinger
Bonsal Seggerman
Sharon Till
Amy Wilson
Mary Wilson
Donniella Winchell

And my thanks to my colleagues at Emmis Books: Jack Heffron, editorial director, Stephen Sullivan, designer, and especially Jessica Yerega, editor.

About the Author

Patricia Latimer is founder of Patricia Latimer Associates, a public relations and strategic planning company located in San Francisco with a presence in Cleveland. Latimer also serves as the Director of the Sherry Institute of Spain and advocates for Spain and Sherry in the Western United States, representing the Asociacion de Criadores de Sherry, S.A. in Jerez de la Frontera, Spain.

She is the author of *California Wineries of Sonoma and Mendocino* (Vintage Image Publishers, St. Helena, California) in addition to being a one-time political writer and scriptwriter. Latimer has been published in more than one hundred national and regional magazines and newspapers, including *Connecticut, Colorado Magazine*, and the *San Francisco Chronicle*. She was a columnist on wine for the *Nob Hill Gazette, Bayviews*, and *Coast*, and was a columnist on women in business for the *San Francisco Examiner*. She began her career in New York as an editor for one of the Hearst Corporation magazines.

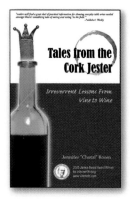

Tales from the Cork Jester
Irreverent Lessons of Wine and Vine
By Jennifer "Chotzi" Rosen
$14.95 Paperback   ISBN: 1-57860-256-4

James Beard Award-winning wine critic Jennifer Rosen offers memorable and hilarious essays on ordering, understanding, and appreciating wine. *Wine Enthusiast* called it "… consistently hilarious. A seamless blend of entertainment and instruction."

A Taste of the Murphin Ridge Inn
By Sherry McKenney
$20.00 Paperback   ISBN: 1-57860-155-X

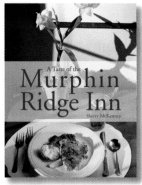

Lush, color photography accompanies more than 130 recipes from this acclaimed southern Ohio country inn, including the award-winning Onion Bisque, Buttermilk Fried Chicken with Rosemary-White Wine Gravy, and Amish Brown Sugar Pie.

Flavors of the Chokolate Morel
An Edible Education
By Dave Avalos and Pam Kennedy
$20.00 Paperback   ISBN: 1-57860-255-6

The chefs from Mason, Ohio's exquisite Chokolate Morel restaurant take readers on a culinary journey—complete with tantalizing color photos—that includes recipes for Sweet Potato Hash, Flourless Chokolate Cake, and dozens more.

Best Food in Town
The Restaurant Lover's Guide to Comfort Food in the Midwest
By Dawn Simonds
$14.99 Paperback   ISBN: 1-57860-146-0

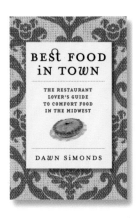

Perfect for road trips: *Best Food in Town* reveals more than 230 restaurants across Illinois, Indiana, Iowa, Kentucky, Michigan, Missouri, Ohio, and Wisconsin where home-cooking is still an art and taste reigns supreme.

To order, call: 1.800.343.4499 / www.emmisbooks.com
EMMIS BOOKS 1700 MADISON ROAD CINCINNATI, OHIO 45206